YOUR PROFESSIONALISM IS KILLING YOU

HOW TO BE A BETTER COMMUNICATOR

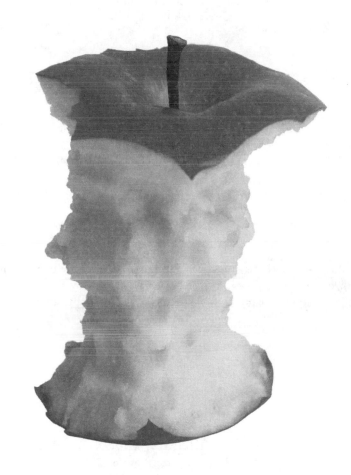

CHRISTINA HARBRIDGE

Allegory _{Inc.}

Allegory Inc.

Editing, Layout & Design by blake more
Printed in the USA by Bookmasters

Section divider artwork from Armature © 2008 by Steve Ollif
and is reprinted with permission from the artist
Flipbook illustrations on pages 187-253 © 2008 by Michael Christian

Allegory, Inc.
221 Main Street, Suite 920
San Francisco, CA 94105
www.allegorytraining.com

YOUR PROFESSIONALISM IS KILLING YOU

HOW TO BE A BETTER COMMUNICATOR

CHRISTINA HARBRIDGE

AUTHOR'S DELIGHT

Hi. You look nice today. I'm glad you picked up my book. What I say here will make the difference between you reading on or putting this book back on the shelf. This book is about communicating to be heard in life and business. We tend to get stifled in our communication when what we have to say is particularly important, so you can imagine why I am a little nervous now.

My name is Christina Harbridge. I am the founder of a company called Allegory, Inc. We are based in San Francisco, and, among other things, we teach corporate communication, conflict resolution, and professional development. Many of our clients have asked for this book, so finally, I am making good on my promise.

In case you are wondering, this is not a self-help book. It is a communication tool, a book with road-tested methods, examples and steps to bring your relationships— whether personal or professional—back on track. This means I talk a lot about listening and speaking. Don't worry; I explain these essential tools a thousand different ways in this book. Well, almost.

As you will see, I have the attention span of a spider monkey on too many bugs, attracted to shiny things, trapped in a disco ball factory with the sun shining through the skylights. I bounce back and forth between ideas. A lot.

I also repeat myself. I do this on purpose. Luckily, I only repeat the important things: The things I want you to know so well that you become a great communicator in your sleep as well as in your waking life.

The chapters in this book build upon each other. If you are reading this text to be better at public speaking, you will have to read it all to get the true impact. Though there are a few lists and shortcuts in this book, I don't really like them, so I avoid them as much as possible. Later on, you will read why that style of learning is destroying our culture.

Sitting on my mother's lap in Doraville, Georgia, my life was forever changed by what I thought was a car backfiring. I remember the entire room jumping at the sound, and my mother throwing up immediately after we heard it. The moment before that sound was the last time I ever truly saw my parents experience joy.

That sound was the gunshot that ended the life of my brother Sean. Our lives would never be the same again. It wasn't Sean's death that destroyed my family: It was our family's inability to communicate about it. Our inability to truly grieve.

My family could point to a single awful event and say "that is what blew us up." Most families, organization, associations, etc. do not have such an occurrence—they have many small conflicts that add up. The result is the same: Compromised relationships, reduced happiness, and emotional distance because of poor communication. This book will help you recognize the patterns in your communication and teach you methods to improve your relationships in business and in life.

Every human I have met has contributed to this book. I am an observer not a creator. You are part of this book. Thank you.

I have some words of gratitude for others besides you. I hope you keep reading. I want you to know about a few humans who make the big blue marble a better place.

Thank you to the rare and wonderful John Law for your encouragement on this book and for our amazing son.

Big thanks to Mark Levy: a writing god. If you ever want to write a book, contact him at www.levyinnovation.com. He didn't write this book, if he had, you would want to cut out the sentences and put them underneath a magnet on your fridge. He did coach me to write in ways I am forever grateful.

There are some humans who are blessed with more talent than the rest of us. Spend three minutes with Blake More, the editor of this book and you will know. Her ability to organize all my crazy thoughts and sentences make her a goddess among humans. Check her out at www.snakelyone.com. She helped me as a favor, she is a poet and her performance art will stay with you forever.

Chris Campbell, Courtney Knapp, Dhaya Lakshminarayanan, Marya Stark and Emily Maine—thank you for the countless hours of input and cheerleading. Michelle Maine thank you for the many hours of swapping stories and never getting tired of it. Deepest gratitude to Lorianne Swain for my care package and the best circus flip book anyone ever made. Betty, thank you for cutting your Dittos. And thank you Uncle Jim.

Thank you Michael Christian for creating the flipbook characters in this book, and thank you Steve Oliff for letting me include panels of your fabulously wise comic strip *Armature* as section introductions. Thank you Bill and Betsy Koefoed for fanning the tiny spark of confidence I had in public speaking so many years ago. Thank you David Matthias for having the courage to pull me from the brink—you were a teacher long before you received a credential.

I am blessed to have a sister-mom: Leta. Her wisdom and clarity are unparallel in the world: Without her I would not have survived. Leta gave me the gift of Tara, Raquel, Vanesa and Mico—now four adults—who change my perspective every time I am lucky enough to sit down with them. They give me so much hope in the new generation. So, in return, I gave Leta a man named Jay (Birdy), a fairly good surfer, my dear friend and a stellar human being.

When I was a kid my dad would grade my dives with either a thumbs up, thumbs down or thumbs sideways. I'd give anything to watch him read this book and give me the thumb. I love you dad and miss you terribly.

Most of all, thank you Sebastian James Law for teaching me what **real** truly is. You are a gift and I am honored to be your mom. ~Christina Harbridge

PREFACE

There are many stories in this book.

I first heard about storytelling from my father's best friend Tchaka Muhammed. When I was a teenager he told me he was a professional storyteller and taught me the power of the story. He could stop a room full of humans—toddlers and adults alike—and leave them mesmerized. I remember him simply sitting down and starting in the middle of a moment, with no one listening. He was a magnet, drawing all of us to him without asking. I didn't realize it until today, sitting in Ghirardelli Square tapping on these keys, just how much he influenced me.

There is a person I have not met who needs a paragraph in this book. He was truly a prophet. He died before I was born. Dale Carnegie. Read his books. Take the 12-week Human Relations class. It changed my life. He wrote his books in the early 1900's, and they still ring true today. He was also a brilliant storyteller.

I am blessed to have known and been raised by a man well ahead of his time. Please understand, this is not a daughter romanticizing her dad—he really was a change maker in this world. He could tell a story like no other. His life was so rich with experience.

I am a storyteller. Woven in the fabric of this book is yarn. All elements of the stories are true: Some have been amalgamated with others. Times, dates, places and names have been changed sometimes. I absolutely change some of the details in stories to protect people. These stories are written here the way I remember them—if you remember them differently you just proved my basic concept about perception. (Wink.) There is no reality—only our memories and the way we remember them. If you think I am talking about you in the story it is only you if it makes you feel happy. Truly.

It is the stories we do not want to tell that give the most meaning to others.

ONE MORE THING

I am struggling with using the word "you" in this book. You is often taken offensively in verbal communication. For example, "you need to arrive on time" sounds finger pointy and rude. "We need to arrive on time" sounds inclusive and increases listening.

"You need to communicate to be heard."

"We need to communicate to be heard."

Say these out loud. Can you hear the difference? In this book, I have been advised to use "you". So you must forgive me for my finger pointy use of YOU in this book. It hurts every time I write it. I had to get hypnotized to do it this way. Please understand that I do hear the difference. I too need to do everything I am writing in this book—I know.

Please, in <u>verbal</u> communication, avoid using the word YOU.

CONTENTS

CONFLICT RESOLUTION:

PUBLIC SPEAKING:

PART I

INTRODUCTION

CHAPTER 1:

STOP ACTING LIKE
A GREAT COMMUNICATOR

I have never met anyone who can't be a great communicator. The first step is to stop acting like a "great communicator." In other words, drop most of the rules communication teachers preach and lighten up.

For instance, "tricks" like smiling before talking, gesturing from the podium and using reflective language to "prove" you are listening are transparent and put the other person on alert. Great communication is difficult when the other person is on alert.

The secret sauce of great communication has one simple ingredient. You'll probably want to write it down to make sure you remember. I'll wait a moment while you get a pen.

While I'm waiting, let me tell you a little about the format of this book. This is not a self-help book. You are fabulous the way you are. Instead, this is a "be you" book that teaches you how to keep the hackles down. When the hackles are up (yours and/or theirs) the heels go down.

You might be wondering what I mean by hackles and heels. Think of it this way: When you are upset, the nerve endings in the back of your neck get stiff and prickly, in other words, hackly. The state of hackles causes alert. And what happens when you go into alert mode? Exactly. The body gets rigid and locks into defense position, i.e. heels go down. Listening is automatically reduced.

This is a hackle-control book providing examples, stories, exercises and information tools to improve your ability to be heard and remembered. It is designed to help you communicate. Sure, we all know the mechanics of communicating (just open your mouth and speak!), and this "skill" can be greatly improved by understanding the unconscious nuances you are communicating—only then can you make them conscious.

If you let it, this book will improve your communication techniques and hone your listening skills, which means other people are more likely to grasp what you are trying to say. In other words, this book will help you be heard.

This book is for:
- The Trembling Deer in the Headlights Presenters
- The Polished Professional Presenters like Tony Robbins
- The Great Negotiators who pay less than Blue Book for a car
- The Ordinary Folks who pay sticker price
- The Diplomats so great at conflict that they are called in when conflict is needed

- The Conflict Avoider who runs from difficult conversations so fast that they've broken their toe on the coffee table a couple of times
- Anyone who has a desire to be a great communicator

Are you paying attention to what I'm saying? Let me guess. Right now you are trying to focus on these words, while in the back of your mind you are guessing at my secret sauce ingredient for better communication. Or perhaps you have already looked ahead to satisfy your curiosity. Most humans are insatiably inquisitive and have an innate desire to figure out what is about to happen before it happens. This is one of the challenges for any communicator: How to keep the attention of the audience on the specific information you want them to hear and remember.

Are you still waiting for me to tell you the one ingredient that will make you a great communicator? Do you have your pen ready?

Yes, I am stalling. I am avoiding telling you because you might just say "Yeah, yeah, I know that already, Christina," and check it off your list as something you already know how to do. I do not want you to dump this book into the self-help category and forget how critical great communication is to your success—your happiness. So promise me you'll keep your mind and ears open, okay? Here goes…

Wait. There's one more thing I should mention to prepare you for the secret ingredient. It is simple—for people under the age of two.

Are you ready?

The one thing every person should do when delivering a speech, negotiating a conflict, having a tough conversation, dealing with a crisis or handling a media situation is:

Be the exact same person you are with your friends on a great day*.

That's it. That's the big secret. It sounds simple enough, and we all know being ourselves in front of strangers or in uncomfortable situations isn't as easy as it sounds.

Let me repeat.

Whether you are talking to one thousand people, having a conflict with your co-worker or trying to stay calm as a camera is being shoved into your face, be the exact same person you are with your closest friends.

*When not drinking.

CHAPTER 2:

THE ADVANTAGES
OF BEING YOU

There are really great actors in the world—most of whom are waiting tables in Los Angeles.

While there are the brilliant folks who get paid well to pretend to be someone else, most humans are lousy actors. Acting is the kiss of death for any communicator, because it can make us appear inauthentic or drab. Acting concerned and being concerned are not the same thing unless you are an Oscar winner. If we try to perform instead of just being ourselves, most people will be able to tell the difference.

Some communication trainers pimp the idea of putting on characters, following scripts and making hand gestures. They teach people how to be "professional" by instructing them to use specific language and follow codes of fashion.

Run like heck from this type of coaching.

This type of coaching and the resulting "professionalism" kills you and your message. It isn't really how—or who—you are. The part of you that is pretending is a black hole, sucking energy away from your authentic self, and thus your effectiveness. Yes, there once was a time when slick professionalism got you clients, and in today's relationship economy, people are repelled by professionalism. I'll revisit the idea of relationship economy a little later. For now, I'll say it again:

Run like hell from repackaging.

You must be the exact same person you are with your dearest friends. The you that you have always been. Integrate all the roles you play in your life: Child, sibling, parent, leader, spouse, professional, and employer. Bring all of these selves to the podium, boardroom or golf course.

Being you will infuse your speeches and conversations with a new creativity and vitality.

Being you will improve the relationships you want to improve and will also spill over into the others as well.

Be you. <u>Acting</u> warm and having a conversation is very different from <u>having</u> a warm conversation.

CHAPTER 3:

SELF-HELP GURUS
SCARE ME

There are no seven easy steps to success. Just like there isn't a formula guaranteed to make you a millionaire. Becoming successful and rich takes work. Yes, there are lucky people—those whose timing is perfect or who have financial backing from a rich uncle.

Most humans need to work at being successful, and, no matter how much we want it, no one can give us a sure-fire recipe for success. We all use different methods and ingredients. Some like spice, others like sweet. Some use blenders, others mix by hand. We all cook a little differently.

This book is not a self-help cookbook for communication. It is a trail guide from someone who has been to the lectern and back thousands of times all over the world. People frequently ask me where all my ideas come from, and I tell them "from my experience."

I do not know you. Your life is vastly different than mine. We might share some similarities, such as a need to share our thoughts with audiences. All you know about me is the part of me who spouts communication philosophy like it is easy. It isn't.

I saw the mistakes I made—horrid communication mistakes—because I avoided conflict like a hive of bees. My personal and professional relationships met fiery deaths. I learned some things, learned some more, and found that I love to learn and never want to stop. I went from being terrified of speaking in public, to being a complete ham. This didn't happen overnight. Later, I started teaching a confidence course, then realized we were teaching people to be fake. I changed myself yet again, and started teaching people differently, then noticed positive changes in my audiences. I started teaching with bright orange hair and a business suit and everything changed. You get the picture: This book is a life-long process of discovery, hard knocks, correction, and epiphany.

Communication is agonizing. Humans are always changing. You are always changing. You will try things that won't always work. You will spend hours trying to figure out how to recreate something successful, and it will crash.

Do it anyway.

This is not American Idol. You do not have one shot at success and glory. You have hundreds of them. Even if it takes you 99 attempts, each try gets you closer.

Here is an example of how we are probably different. I am a doodler. I have doodled since I was four. When I was a child I wanted to be an artist. I dreamed of drawing things to perfection, even though I never could. I worked hard at it. In ninth grade, my friend Diana could draw a bunny so well it looked like a photograph, while mine resembled an odd Picasso bunny-cat-rat-looking thing. I was embarrassed by my lack of talent.

Years later, I realized why I doodle. I think in pictures, and I think better when my hand is moving. It made me feel better about being a lousy artist. Now, I keep a box of colored pens on my desk. I doodle in all my meetings. At the office, we keep a binder of doodle notes, and it is a great way for our team to remember things about meetings—such as when I came up with the "moo" idea, or how blue the ocean looked when we strategized about an important speech in Berlin. Funny and odd things that jog the memory and bring us right back to the original meeting. It is great for remembering details, and my doodle binders have become a part of our Allegory culture.

I really like my doodles on the outside edges of this book's pages. I made flipbooks as a kid. Flipbooks reflect who I am, so I included a flipbook in this book, even though some people may end up rejecting the whole thing because flipbooks are too "unprofessional."

What did you do as a kid? Make booger balls? Okay, so maybe there's no market for booger balls. Though there is a place in your creative speaking style for that part of you that is unique. Bring it out. It is the "you" in guru. The you that likes to lick the bowl when no one is watching. The you that sings in the car or dances in your room alone. The you that comes up with interesting names for things. The you that…

That you.

Gurus know what works for them. Create what will work for you. You are your own personal guru.

CHAPTER 4:

WE ARE IN A NEW RELATIONSHIP ECONOMY

A study released in November 2002 indicated that each week 45 percent of Americans watched reality television. Certainly in 2008 that figure is well over 70 percent. [1]

What? Three out of four people who have a TV want to watch people being themselves?

This phenomenon doesn't stop with television. One million people watch YouTube.com every day. Many of the 65,000 videos uploaded are of ordinary people in unguarded moments doing plain ol' everyday stuff. People are drawn to this.

Guess what website gets 21 million individual visitors daily with this number increasing every day? MySpace.com, the online forum that exists solely for people to share information about themselves with anyone who cares to look.

What does all this data have to do with communication? With conflict communication? With crisis resolution? With public speaking? With handling the media?

Everything! Audiences want to know more about the individual than ever before. Seeing a professional face is not enough. We want to see behind the face. We want real.

Led by the Internet, we have entered the age of instantaneous information. This is a seismic cultural shift—all media is changing, and modes of human interaction are changing along with it. Perceived intimacy and insight has become a prerequisite in our desire to embrace each other, as well as our leaders and teams. We all want to see the real person.

Professionalism, perfection and shifting our personalities to get what we want is no longer effective. People are on the lookout for fake: We know it when we see it, and we hate it.

Another reason why step-by-step systems of communication no longer work. Folks do not like being manipulated. Communication is a long-term investment, not a get-rich scheme.

Communication is a long-term investment in relationships. Relationships matter now more than ever before, and in the communication economy one thing is true:

The human relationship is the true currency. Your Professionalism is Killing You™.

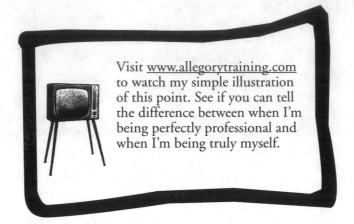

Visit www.allegorytraining.com to watch my simple illustration of this point. See if you can tell the difference between when I'm being perfectly professional and when I'm being truly myself.

CHAPTER 5:

WHAT DEBT COLLECTION TAUGHT ME ABOUT COMMUNICATION

How do I know all this great stuff? I get my knowledge first hand, directly from my life experiences. Much of what I know about communication I learned while working as a debt collector. Every exchange was rife with conflict. No one liked us, and the debtors avoided us and called us less-than-nice names. The government pursued us with legislative pick axes in addition to calling us names. Even our clients—individuals we were actually helping—hated us. They resented having to pay us commission on money they were rightfully owed and felt we should be able to collect 100 percent of their debts.

As I will describe in more detail later (see Felony Guy on page 222), I entered the collections business in my late teens and became a supervisor at a very young age—partly because I was willing to be aggressive and pushy like the people around me. I was a bit full of myself, and thanks to a potentially life-threatening situation, I looked inside and realized there was more to collections than bullying and shame.

My communication study had begun. From that moment on, I dedicated myself to changing the debt collection industry from the inside out. Eventually I started a collection firm without a single client, using only a telephone and a 286 IBM computer. I was committed to marrying public relations with debt collection.

I differentiated myself by explaining to potential clients that a nicer approach to debt collecting yielded better long-term results. Even if it meant a slight loss of revenue, the negative connotations were gone, which had to be good, right? At the time, I didn't realize how true that was—a nicer approach yielded two to three times better financial returns. Who knew?

In my new, nicer approach, I had to figure out how to leave a message that would make people want to call my back. I had to learn to write letters that got folks talking. I had to discover how to avoid the popular retort, "The check is in the mail," only to receive air in my mailbox. In short time, I realized the number one goal of a collection call was not to collect money.

That's right: The number one goal of our collection calls was not to collect money; it was to create enough rapport so the person felt comfortable enough to tell the truth.

That was it. Our job became a means to close the communication gap and turn it into revenue—revenue that was both social and financial.

Over time, I created a communication protocol that established enough rapport in a two-minute telephone call to be invited to a debtor's wedding. I knew we were on to something big.

I got involved in several organizations meant to build confidence and teach people and started noticing some things that bothered me. We were told to "act as if" and to practice specific techniques to get what we want. It started feeling a bit manipulative to me, and I lost some effectiveness by trying to be something I wasn't. I was told to be professional and different from who I really was. I taught people to do the same. I watched the wonderful weirdness of humans melt away so they were more "effective."

Before long, I started noticing the experts around me had the ability to turn "it" on and off. I saw how magic could be used for good and bad. I also perceived that once folks use a system, it stops being effective. I also noticed organizations (including mine) rife with relationship-destroying lack of conflict. There was a lot of indirect communication and very little direct and real communication.

Oscar Wilde said, "True friends stab you in the front." I started to realize professionalism and sugar were reducing effectiveness and relationships. I was not a great communicator.

Then I made a three-week commitment that changed everything. Everything. And the basic foundation for this whole book came to me in the first three days of that commitment. Yes, you heard me correctly—three days!

(The three-day-commitment story will come later. I promise. I know—thanks to my years of communication experience—if I go on about one thing too long, you will lose interest.)

I stayed in the collection industry for more than twenty years. Collections were my communication petri dish. Rest assured, the information in this book has been thoroughly road tested. If you consistently practice what I share, you will become a great communicator.

All communication is stronger when the main goal is to improve rapport.

People listen more closely when they have rapport with you. All communication is stronger when the main goal is to improve rapport.

CHAPTER 6:

PEOPLE WILL DO THE OPPOSITE OF WHAT IS GOOD FOR THEM

Here's a very important lesson I learned in the collection industry:

People will do the opposite of what is good for them if they do not like you or feel manipulated by you.

When we feel we have power over someone, we believe we can push that person into our way of thinking. As Abraham Lincoln said: Force is all-conquering; its victories are short-lived.

This is also true in communication. Look at most marriages. Spouses will speak to each other in ways they would never dream of talking to another person.

Often in our communication we ignore subtle human signs of compliance. Willing a person to act and that person wanting to act are two entirely different things.

To change a mind we must first be heard. To win an argument we must first be heard. To change the world, we must first be heard. Add your sentence here: To _____

_____, we must first be heard. Whatever you are trying to do, if you are in it for the long term, you must be heard to be remembered.

Nothing in this book promotes manipulation or phony, insincere attempts to communicate. I will show you why manipulation is never a good idea. Trust me, even if it doesn't happen right away, you will always end up losing in the end.

Use these powers for good.

Great communicators don't manipulate to be heard.

CHAPTER 7:

IF YOU AGREE WITH EVERYTHING IN THIS BOOK, ONE OF US HAS A PROBLEM

If you agree with everything I have to say, *one of us has a problem*.

- Either you are drinking the proverbial Kool-Aid and buying into everything without critical thought...

OR

- I am not risking saying what I really think for fear of offending you.

Being offended is good. If the title of my book offends you, I am glad. If you think my talky style of writing is odd, so be it.

Great communication includes raised eyebrows and the risk of being weird or even offensive. It is time for humans to dump their perfection at the junkyard. Greatness in communication involves risk. No risk, no gain.

Conflict builds and maintains relationships. Conflict is not a dirty word, though as an empathetic person, I used to be afraid of it. I wanted people to like me. I still do, though now I realize some people actually like me more for simply being myself.

The truth is not everyone will like us, respect us or enjoy our style of speaking. *Vive la différence!* If people like us for something we are not, the universal forces will work to uncover our unsavory things. We all have them. It is law.

I am not politically correct. The same people who protested the Vietnam War voted us into the Iraq War. Not saying what we really think, at the risk of offending someone, is killing our country. Consensus is not always a good thing.

We like people who say what they think. Michael Moore sent out an e-mail to folks with the thought I am about to paraphrase: Think of Michael Moore and the Dixie Chicks. Michael Moore's rogue ideas broke box office records, and the Dixie Chicks won five Grammy Awards after speaking disparagingly about the President of the United States. Being weird and outspoken is good for you.

Sure, it's tough to be outspoken. I am terrified of it. Hence my creation of a collection industry positive boot camp and my desire to write this book. I am forcing myself to do what I know works. I am also terrified of being sued for it.

Many people miss being great communicators because of conflict avoidance. This book will help fix that.

During a speech an audience member announced that he disagreed with my philosophy that people should be themselves no matter how weird. He yelled out that he would never do business with a person with "princess" on their business card (my business card says "Princess" under my name) or fire-engine red hair (I have fire-engine red hair). The audience was silent. A couple of people yelled out, "I would!" Lovely lads wanting to save me from his disdain. I put up my hands to silence everyone. I walked toward him and simply said, "I just saved us a lot of time, didn't I? You and I are not meant for each other. We are both better off working with someone more suited to our unique tastes."

The audience applauded. I stopped them. Listen. Wait. There is nothing wrong with what just happened. Conflict. Honesty. It is all good. I am serious. We are not for everybody. Falseness only prolongs poor matches.

Later, during the conference, that same audience member cornered me. He confessed that he realized he was an asshole and thanked me for pointing it out. He wondered how much he had lost in his life by judging people so incorrectly.

Similarly transformative "conflicts" have happened to me many times. I am unsure if his assessment of his reality is true or not. I'm still me. Same as before.

Healthy disagreement is a necessary part of great communication.

PART II

FOUNDATION

CHAPTER 8:

COMMUNICATION TECHNIQUES ONLY WORK IF NO ONE REALIZES YOU'RE USING THEM

In 1946, a self-taught engineer employed by the Raytheon Corporation experienced something very weird in the laboratory. The candy bar in his pocket melted. Well, this doesn't sound so weird unless you realize Dr. Percy Spencer was testing a new vacuum tube called the "Magnetron."[2] After many more tests, Dr. Spencer invented a device that would drive a new multimillion-dollar industry and, in the process, revolutionize cooking. That invention was the microwave oven.

It can be argued, that while this invention did not improve the quality of food in our world, it did have an immense impact on our food delivery systems. The cultural impact of the microwave oven is far-reaching and extends beyond the kitchen. Unwittingly, Dr. Spencer set the 'microwave' culture in motion—bringing on a worldwide movement which encourages people to demand instant results in everything.

You may never get instant gratification from your commitment to great communication. Your boss may still be a selfish, pushy jerk and your spouse may still chew with his or her mouth open. It will still be worth it though.

Communication is an organic, long-term investment in relationships, and relationships are complex.

Type "communication" into the amazon.com search engine and enjoy sorting through the search yield of 45,291 books. Each writer makes a valiant attempt to improve the reader's experience with various communication techniques. The retail fad at the moment is the microwave plan for communication: Simple steps and techniques to get what we want—fast!

Do these five things, say this specific phrase, respond in this way, and you will get what you want: Such an approach is impossible. Communication is a dynamic, individualized medium; step-by-step processes usually become overused and transparent. When we use a predetermined, set "process" to communicate, people often feel manipulated. No one likes to feel they are being worked. Communication formulas can work for a short period of time, and soon end up doing more harm than good.

The keys for communication greatness are sincerity and integrity. You know the joke: The key to life is sincerity—once you can fake that you have it made. Some books actually suggest this practice.

Great communication is spawned from hard work, integrity, and being true to oneself. A good communicator is a person who practices the fine art of verbal give-and-take. There is no microwave meal for good communication.

Great communicators are self-disciplined. They consistently practice communication techniques and principles.

Have the self-discipline to be a great communicator.

EXERCISE:

KARL ROVE IS DESTROYING
THE COMMUNICATION BUSINESS

People like Karl Rove, taking cues from Orwell, Huxley and General Alexander Haig have made communicating through use of a mechanical step by step system the rage. To truly have impact in today's society, we don't need to work a system; we need to change our behavior.

The moment a person figures out we are using a system it no longer works. They label us as a scammer, and our relationship with that person is forever damaged.

Grab a glass of water and a dash of pepper. Sprinkle pepper into the glass. The pepper should float on the surface of the water. Now dab a little bit of liquid dishwashing detergent on the end of your forefinger. Look into the glass of water. Dip your soaped finger in the center of the pepper. Watch what happens. It will happen quickly so pay close attention as you do this.

The pepper is people. See how they ran from you? The soap is insincerity and tricks. Tricks in communication do not work in the long-run.

Tricks impact relationship. They do not work when everyone knows about them. Using tricks will harm relationships.

The moment you dip into insincerity to achieve a communication result, people will run from you. Just like the pepper. You will never be able to get them back. They may feign that they are back. They really aren't.

I remind CEO's all the time of the common phrase "People don't leave organizations, people leave people." People have left the companies they work for, long ago, they are just still on the payroll. Tricks make them leave.

I know I've said this. It needs repeating.

Communication tricks become obvious and will not work for long. Avoid false, transparent, step-by-step methods.

 **EXAMPLE:**

TEMPLATES AREN'T GOOD
FOR ANYBODY

John worked for a lobbying firm in Washington D.C. He knew the skills he garnered working on the Hill were not easily translatable to the outside world; things worked in strange ways in the Rayburn building. Even so, his firm had been losing some traction with relationships of late, so after encouragement by a fellow lobbyist, he took a communications class. His first meeting at the House Committee on Energy and Commerce was his chance to use the steps he had learned in order to get the "yes" he needed from the Chairman's legislative aide.

As the aide, Carrie White, walked up to greet him, he hastily folded his seminar notes and placed them in his pocket. He looked her in the eye and let her know they were going to have a great meeting. As they sat down John asked, "If there were a way to take care of your constituents, you'd want to know about it wouldn't you?" During the meeting, he took pride in his ability to charm the aide, ask leading questions, use cushions, and ask long directed questions meant to leave the person with only two options, "Say yes or look like a bad person."

When met with any resistance, he used his new verbal formula to cushion the exchange back to his desire. He left the meeting feeling like he nailed it: He was sure he got the YES.

As Carrie White watched him exit, she turned to the receptionist and said, "Looks like someone attended the 'Get Them to Say Yes' seminar at the Omni last week." She quickly typed a memo to the chairman, omitting John's issue entirely. John not only lost his debate, he also lost some political capital by trying to manipulate his ally.

Most of us have experienced a salesperson trying to cinch the deal. Sales techniques anchored in an insincere desire to benefit the buyer only work the first time around, if at all.

Be real.

CHAPTER 9:

PEOPLE DON'T WANT PERFECT, THEY WANT TRANSPARENCY

My first draft of this book had every chapter starting with the letter B. It seemed like a cute way of making the case for imperfection. The B's opening every chapter would subliminally remind the reader to stop trying to get the A. Unfortunately (or fortunately), my creative idea soon seemed too gimmicky, like a trick, which is exactly what a great communicator avoids.

Perfection stifles great communication. Humans do not trust perfection. Perfect people make us uncomfortable. People who are comfortable with Bs are far more effective in today's communication economy.

Enron caused some of this.

What does an energy company have to do with communication? Tons. This organization was the golden child of the last decade of the 20th century. According to Wikipedia, Enron employed roughly 21,000 people and was one of the world's leading electricity, natural gas, pulp and paper, and communications companies, with claimed revenues of $111 billion in 2000.

Fortune Magazine named Enron "America's Most Innovative Company" for six consecutive years. Then, at the end of 2001, the company achieved infamy when the world discovered that Enron's reported financial condition was sustained mostly by institutionalized, systematic, and creative accounting fraud. Enron has since become a popular symbol of willful corporate fraud and corruption.[3]

We used to like perfection. Our culture loved the talking heads and polished speakers who showed us the utopian ideal of being human. Audiences do not trust appearances anymore; audiences do not respond as well to perfection.

Television caused some of this too

The film, *Goodnight and Good Luck,* helped me to realize that our current communication backlash can be attributed to the prevaricating communication style of the 50's. Made in 2005, *Good Night and Good Luck* is an Academy Award-nominated film that portrays the conflict between veteran radio and television journalist Edward R. Murrow and the anti-communist U.S. Senator Joseph McCarthy—focusing specifically on the Senator's actions toward the Senate Permanent Subcommittee on Investigations. As this movie portrays, the 1950's television presented a flawless America to the American people. The glowing incandescent box revealed nothing about American culture that was distasteful or real.

Clearly we are in a backlash. The old media style has morphed into today's surreally unpleasant commercial infotainment industry. In the past, the television gave us a polished utopian view of society, not the truth. What we see now appears almost exclusively based in bad taste, corruption, fear and greed. Contemporary reality TV shows, with their prime directive of product placement, are littering the airwaves with an onslaught of unparalleled mediocrity.

Obviously, both views are false. We know it is fake and designed to sell us (mostly) junk. Perhaps this is the reason for reality TV—all the lies are making our desire to see the unvarnished truth stronger than ever. Turn on the television today and witness the reaction to perfection. As Coca-Cola used to say "it's the real thing" that American's want more than anything. Now, reality TV isn't real either as the writers script and fabricate—ugh!

Last week, I attended a conference. During the afternoon presentations, I watched a speaker-to-be walk into the room, bully the help, act like a complete butthead, then brighten the room by leaving it. As soon as he was introduced to speak, a light suddenly switched and he became bigger than life, a positive and glowing personality. The audience hated him.

Why? Perhaps if I'd polled audience members as they left the room, they could not pinpoint exactly what caused them to get the ick from him. I know what it was: It was his overstressed and insincere professionalism. Polished professionalism is no longer a litmus test for success in our culture. In fact, the more professional we are, the more distant and plastic we appear.

Americans do not like plastic. We may put up with it. We may even be impressed by it. We won't rally behind it. We trust people who reveal who they are and maintain their authenticity at all times.

Your professionalism is killing you. By switching personas and trying to appear perfect, you can't share what you are REALLY great at in communication.

Visit www.allegorytraining.com to watch my simple illustration of this point.

CHAPTER 10:

SPEAK LIKE YOU
ARE ALIVE TODAY

Remember the TV show *Little House on the Prairie?* Yes, the one with Laura Ingalls. What did her school class room look like? Can you picture it?

- Desks in rows.
- Blackboard in front.
- Teachers desk to the left of the blackboard.

Imagine back to when you were in 3rd grade. What did your classroom look like? Really. Stop reading for a second and imagine it.

- Desks in rows.
- Blackboard in front.
- Teacher's desk to the right or left of the blackboard.
- Posters on the walls.

Ringing any bells?

Have you visited a classroom lately? If not, I'll bet you can guess how it's set up:
- Desks in rows.
- Blackboard in front.
- Teachers desk to the right of the blackboard.
- Posters on the walls.

Our communication world changed dramatically since the 1800's. Still, our schoolrooms are pretty much exactly the same. No wonder scores are decreasing and kids are having a hard time paying attention. Yes, our school system needs to pay teachers more. Yes, our government needs to invest more in schools than in war.

AND

Part of our failure may be that we are communicating in an old fashioned way, thus negatively impacting our kids' ability to listen. We are not communicating to be heard, and our kids are paying for our lack of great communication.

Kids today text each other. They understand computers better than us. They instant message constantly. They live, eat, sleep video games. Their attention span is about 7.5 seconds. Why haven't we updated our teaching to reflect their rapidly changing world?

The same is true in corporations, in the PTA, in Congress, at home—everywhere. We must change the way we communicate if we want to be heard. Great communicators are masters at this.

The only person who enjoys a lecture is the person giving it. Still, we continue to lecture and pontificate, steadfastly refusing to shift communication to match what is happening in our culture.

Great communication styles are always evolving. Keep up with them.

 ## EXERCISE:

SET THE TONE

Pick up your phone and call someone who you know has voicemail. Go ahead. I'll wait. Write down what their outgoing message says. I'll even wait for you to get a pen. I am nice that way.

(cue *Jeopardy* background music)

(Music matters. If the *Jaws* theme were playing right now you'd be nervous.)

I just called three voicemails. Here is what they say:

- *You have reached Sam's voicemail. Please leave your telephone number after the tone, and I will return your call.*

- *Hi. You have reached Susan, and I am unable to come to the phone right now. Please leave your number after the tone, and say it slowly. I will return your call at my earliest convenience.*

- *Thank you for calling Tim with Bradford Electric. Please leave your telephone number and the time that you called [this is stressed], and I will return your call shortly.*

Do these sound similar to the message you just listened to?

This is a great example of communicating in the past and not communicating to be heard.

Back when answering machines first came out, we had to tell people what to do. We needed to let them know to leave their message after the beep, otherwise, they wouldn't know when to speak.

Things have changed.

Back then, people needed to leave their phone numbers because we didn't have caller ID or electronic devices that stored hundreds of numbers. We had things called "phonebooks" with alphabetized tabs where we wrote down numbers in pencil in case someone moved. Remember, Wite-Out didn't exist back then either.

In the two hundred plus times I've called my friend Tim's voicemail, I have never mentioned the time of my call. He's never complained. His choice of outgoing message shows he isn't really communicating to be heard, and as a result, I never noticed what his message actually said until I did the test above.

Changing the way we communicate will increase listening. Increased listening results in better communication.

Communicating to be HEARD is the first step in any communication. It is a speaker's responsibility to get people to listen.

CHAPTER 11:
THERE IS NO FINISH LINE

The only way to be truly good at communication is to practice it every day and in every situation.

Great communication skills are not born—they are a practiced art. Remember, you can only change one person: Yourself. And that is sometimes impossible.

You cannot improve communication skills simply by reading about them. Just as we learn to ride a bike by sitting on the seat and pedaling like mad, so we must also take our new communication skills to the pavement for a regular test-drive. Unlike this analogy, we may not see immediate results from our efforts; moreover, we may never see our efforts and practice as a full-blown technicolor result.

I wonder how many of us would ride a bike if we fell off of it 90 percent of the time? This is why communication is so tough: There is no sure fire way to have great communication all the time.

In order to improve communication, we will sometimes need to "tack". On a sailboat, the best way to move forward can often be to circle back and pick up a better gust of wind. The same can be true for improving communication—by overcoming bad habits we can actually experience a temporary decrease in our overall perception of effectiveness.

I don't want to scare you into thinking all your hard work will have no result. It will. Here is my promise:

> **Great communication will blossom from the fertile soil of consistent practice. Keep in mind what fertile soil is made of! Mistakes and missteps are good—when we pay attention.**

When we consistently barrel through our communication, not correcting our inefficiencies, we emerge poorer listeners and communicators in the long run. We are more effective when we notice what we are doing and make course corrections as we go.

Since the last paragraphs were like verbal baklava—many layers of indirect meaning surrounding a core function of communication—I'll make things easier to understand by giving you a list. I know our popular culture likes lists, even if I don't. See, I am open to doing things I do not like just to get you to listen. I won't number them (I have to keep some aspect of my anti-list defiance).

Here is a list for you. Malcolm.*

So far, I've shown you great communication involves:

- A <u>consistent</u> practice of new skills and ideas around communication.

- An <u>acceptance</u> that we may be the only people in the room practicing to improve communication.

- The <u>realization</u> that we may never receive instant gratification, or even basic confirmation, that our efforts are creating results.

- The <u>willingness to continue</u> our practice anyway, even after discovering that the three points described above are true.

- The <u>understanding</u> that we may be 100 percent correct in what we are saying, while the '<u>way</u>' we say '<u>it</u>' has more impact on our effectiveness than the words we use.

- A <u>readiness</u> to work hard to first be <u>heard</u> by the person who is listening. (Read this one several times; it is, as Frank would say, the crux of the biscuit.)

- An <u>eagerness</u> to communicate in a fashion that allows us <u>to be heard</u>.

- The <u>ability to look at</u> our communication style and determine if it is damaging our message. Remember, people would rather do harm to themselves than do what a person they do not like or respect suggests.

- A <u>desire</u> to communicate in ways that lead others to <u>value</u> our message and <u>respect</u> their associations with us.

- The <u>acknowledgment</u> of the blatant truth: Miscommunication <u>will</u> happen. Our language, our society and this human spaceship we all share is set up in such a way that miscommunication is unavoidable.

- An <u>embracing</u> of the belief that conflict BUILDS relationships when done early and often.

- An <u>acceptance</u> that every interaction either BUILDS or REDUCES relationships.

- The <u>practice of rapport and listening</u> will decrease the probability of miscommunication. We are better communicators when we are better listeners.

- An <u>acceptance</u> that we are the only person we can truly <u>change</u>. For many, that is a big enough challenge. Communication is an intricate system of levers and pulleys; there is no graduation from the school of communication improvement. It is a lifelong commitment to addressing our own behavior.

- Willingness to be a great communicator: **Regardless of Result**.

*If you were wondering about Malcolm, the person I mentioned at the top of this list, he doesn't exist. When my niece Raquel was little, she thought "You're welcome" was "Malcolm." My entire family says "Malcolm" now instead of "You're welcome." Why do I write this here? The list got a little boring. I decided to hold your interest with a story. Another reason is I like the story, and my family will like it too. Keeps things a little more personal and interesting.

Have the self-discipline to communicate to be heard.

(Sometimes this involves doing things you don't feel like, like writing lists.)

CHAPTER 12:
YOU'RE NOT FOR EVERYBODY

Like I said in Chapter 5, people rarely listen or act upon what we say if they do not like us. This might have been misunderstood. Our job as great communicators is not to get everyone to like us. This is impossible and in fact could make people dislike us for trying.

If I do not like you, I will not listen to you no matter what you say. Sure, I might feign interest. If you have a super duper interesting bio, some audiences might listen. If you're just an average Josephine—forget it.

The audience is more likely to LISTEN to a person they feel rapport with.

When we reveal our true selves to the audience and do it in a memorable way, the audience is more likely to remember what we said. When a speaker integrates his or her personal and professional life in an interesting fashion, audiences want to listen. Being yourself will increase rapport and listening.

We are not for everybody.

A young woman in one of my sessions asked me to help her act older and calmer. I asked why.

She told me she recently applied for a job she didn't get. The company told her she didn't land the job because she acted too young and spunky. The wise human resources director instructed her to act more mature at her next interview and she'd have a better chance of being hired.

I refused to help her act older and calmer. That company was the WRONG place for her! The right company will not hire her if she acts older and calmer. The RIGHT company will not hire her if she acts differently than she really is.

We were able to harness her spunky energy and integrate it into her speaking style. She found her perfect job a few weeks later by simply being the wonderful woman she already is.

This is not just public speaking. An audience can be one person. I spent too many years trying to be like the people teacing me to be different than who I am. True success came when I refused to be what they wanted me to be.

The stuff you hide from others—start showing them.

Even though people listen more to those they like, trying to be liked by being different than your true self is never a good idea.

CHAPTER 13:

WE'RE ALL SQUARE PEGS

I am weird. I want you to know this.

If you don't believe me, call my voicemail. I change my message often, and it is usually unprofessional. What type of responses do I get?

- Hang-up and never call back. This person will never do business with such a weirdo. (I just saved me and them a lot of time.)

- Leave a message telling me they will not do business with me because of my out-going message. (See parenthesis above.)

- Laugh out loud first and then make a befuddled attempt to leave a message. These are my favorite. They usually forget to leave their number even though they know they are supposed to.

- Laugh out loud first, leave a perfect message and tell me how wonderful I am.

- Laugh and hang up. They then wait an hour or so and leave a message so I don't know it was them.

- Leave a normal message like nothing is going on.

Yes, I lose business because my messages are weird. I consider my outgoing message as a litmus test—as soon as a potential client hears my message they get to decide if they are the right fit for me. I don't have to do anything.

And my outgoing message isn't the only thing that's weird. You already know my business card has a funky title on it. I change my title all the time too. Some people hate this. Perhaps they want to know my title so they can decide how important I am. Others say my revolving titles are unprofessional. What does unprofessional mean?

It all started when I put "Friendly Neighborhood Bill Collector" on my business card when I started my collections company. I wanted folks to know I was different and my business card indicated this.

People loved it. So one day I had "Janitor" printed under my name. I did this in response to the title surfing I saw people do at Chamber of Commerce meetings. As this one elicited a mixed reaction, I decided to match my title to what I really did in my personal and professional life: I was an empathetic person. A helper.

My title: "Psychic Wet Nurse."

Too many eyes left the card for my chest—not exactly a good idea in business. So I came up with a new one.

"Princess." That one stuck for a long time, and I still rotate it in. People laughed. Some folks were REALLY offended. Feminists told me it was degrading. Folks informed me there was no way a high level political campaign would work with someone with that title on her card.

On a weekly basis, well-intentioned people began suggesting that if I would just bend a little to fit into that round hole, or pretend to in the beginning, I could do more good work in the world.

Fit in Christina. Get in the door Christina. Then you can be goofy. Once you are in they will accept what you are teaching. Infiltrate by wearing Khakis and a white shirt. This "fitting in" is killing America.

The melting pot is a great place for fondue—not for people.

I am bored easily. I have a short attention span. I am creative. I am weird. I am clearly also repetitive. Get used to that.

Keep what makes you different. Nourish it. Stand naked in it and do not flinch when others point and laugh. The people who are eclectic and different are better able to live their beliefs and change the world.

Remember the stuff you hid from others in high school? Well, today kids film that stuff and put it on MySpace.com for everyone to see. Transparency is the new black! (And that's a fashion reference!)

Be the square peg you are. You are interesting because you are different from everyone else. Your unique self gives others reason to listen.

CHAPTER 14:

FIRST DEPRESSIONS

We only get one chance to make a first impression.

This common saying, perhaps a byproduct of our over-stimulated culture, often causes communication problems. It takes courage to express individuality, and people who are worried about first impressions don't take chances.

Just how much input do we have when making a first impression and what does this have to do with communication?

Humans size each other up very quickly. This is an instinctual tendency harkening back to Neanderthal times. Usually, we decide who a person is and what they are about within the first five minutes of meeting them. Actually, we determine who they are during the first twenty seconds, and then spend the next four minutes and forty seconds looking for evidence to support our initial impression.

This well-worn theory is destroying us and organizations. It has been used to scare people into acting like someone they aren't. Professionalism, the stiffbacked-agenda-laden-perfect culture never existed and is the kiss of death now.

Since some humans are highly intuitive, they will have ample successes to continue this pattern throughout their lifetime. We reinforce this behavior because it has done us good in our past. Everyone has one or two loud examples of our intuition saving us from harm; more likely we have louder instances of ignoring the hairs standing up on the back of our necks and the negative experience that invariably follows.

Thus we continue to judge people—harshly at times. We are often wrong. When we make assumptions and evaluate a stranger's entire character according to those assumptions, we stop questioning and listening. Great communication requires constant questioning and focused listening; it also helps to correct our biological predisposition to judge others.

Who is to blame for this 'instinctive' behavior? Perhaps you have heard of the 'ancient brain' resting in our noggins. It exists as a nucleus in the brainstem called the locus ceruleus (also spelled locus caeruleus or coeruleus—Latin for "the blue spot"), and it is responsible for physiological responses to stress and panic. Home to our "fight or flight" response, it is our body's primitive, automatic, inborn alarm that prepares us to stand and fight or run like mad from perceived attack, harm, or threat to our survival.

Since we don't come across life or death issues so much in modern America, our blue spot has come up with a new way to stay busy: Judgment. Judgment—also known as assumption—closes off communication. The moment we decide who someone is, we shut the window to any new information they may present.

We must admit that we actually misjudge on occasion if we are ever going to overcome this communication crippling behavior. The choice is obvious: Keep judging and live with the consequence of weakened communication or stay open to all the information as it comes in and successfully actualize our communication goals.

Think of judgment as having a Rheostat switch—the special switches that let you adjust the light between off and on. So, rather than turning judgment off, you can learn to minutely vary the impact—the voltage—or strength of your judgment, just as you might dim the living room chandelier.

Being judged by others stifles our great individuality and communication.

Accept the fact that you are often being judged. Allow it and try not to change your behavior too much based on it. The person judging you could just be wrong or simply curious.

Our judging others stifles great communication.

When we judge others, we stop questioning and listening. Challenge your assumptions.

I'm depressed when I talk about impressions. They reduce listening and individuality.

First impressions are in the eye of the beholder. Practice challenging your first impressions—both the ones you have about others and the ones you wish to have about yourself.

CHAPTER 15:

BOXES ARE COFFINS

Fitting into a box robs creative energy. It is hard to remember the persona for each part of our life. You are far more interesting than any character you create. The things you don't tell people are fascinating too. I promise.

I know I am in a lucky position. Some readers will argue that they *must* fit in to keep their checkbooks from emptying. I don't have to do that because I have my own gig and am not beholden to a boss. This is because I am unemployable in my current form. There are others like me.

I challenge you to start something on the side. It is a way to counter-balance your need to remain another brick in the wall at work. Something on the side will satisfy your fears of being fired—allowing you to continue hiding your individuality in one place, while simultaneously giving you a safe place to explore being fully yourself. Write a book. Start a monthly event. Join a non-profit board. Something.

You don't have to fit in. I lost a huge opportunity during a campaign because I refused to die my hair a normal color and change my business card to conform to their expectations. Does that make me lose?

Yes and no. I lost the cache the big name client would have lent to my new business; I also got to stay true to my authentic self. I am okay with both because I was able to keep working to open new doors. This is my unique talent, and it allows me to continue creating ideas which positively impact the world.

Watch the movie *The Fountainhead* with Gary Cooper. Please. Pay close attention to the courtroom scene, in which the main character, an architect who refuses to fit in, says great innovators are always met with fierce opposition. He quips," The guy who invented fire was probably burned at the stake with it."

Challenge all assumptions that you have to fit in; they are only true in the short run.

CHAPTER 16:
WE HATE PHONIES,
WE HATE PERFORMANCE

Fear of first impressions is ruining individuality in our culture.

Over the past decade, "brand promise" has become a common buzzword in business. Serving as an organizational or individual promise to the customer, this concept is granted to every organization and every person. Whether these promises are kept or not, depends on how true they are in the first place. A brand promise is not a goal: It is the reality of what we are.

Why am I talking about brands in a communication book? Branding is not just for corporations anymore. Individuals can embrace this idea to help them craft their personal communications style. Organizations can use this concept to create internal and external communication programs.

The basic principal here is to remain congruent with just who we are. In the past, speech trainers convinced people to perform—to be different or better than the person they truly are. Most people shine more brightly when they are harnessing their power of self and not acting. Personal congruence is the goal.

One way to practice this idea is to notice how we act when we are with our dearest friends. This is usually the time when we aren't acting. We are laughing, sharing, philosophizing. Our bodies relax, and we trust the ease and communication that comes from true friendship. This is when we are most truly ourselves.

Remember, there is a difference between being yourself and being inauthentic. Some people are shy and quiet, and they can make a deep impression while engaging in communication. Conversely, others have public personas which reflect their overwhelming exuberance for life—not an act, just a bigger than life image. This is truly who they are—they can't hide it. Imagine the colorful variety of authentic communication styles that exist in the world. Isn't it amazing?

Celebrate differences! Be real. (If you are like me it might take you a minute to remember what real was before you created "the brilliant you" in junior high school.)

You seem a little bored. Perhaps I've been lecturing too much. Here's an exercise to vary your experience:

FINISHED FILES
ARE THE RESULT
OF YEARS OF FIELD
AND SCIENTIFIC
STUDY OF THE
EXPERTS

(Author of this fun exercise is unknown)

Give yourself one minute to count the number of "F's" in the sentence in the box above. Rules: Do not trace the letters with your hand, finger or pen. Instead, just use your eyes to read the sentence.

Write down your answer in the box below. (If you are in a bookstore, you might want to buy the book first.)

How many did you see? If we were in a room full of 20 people, we would have several difference answers.

Did you write down your answer? If so, go to the next page for the answer. If not, try it, you'll be surprised!

If you answered:

Less Than Four—You probably read the passage above aloud to yourself. Oratory people are more likely to believe what they hear than what they see. Reading aloud may have caused you to skip a few F's. Go back and see if you can find them. If you still can't find them, trace your finger backward on the sentence, looking at the letters instead of reading the words. You probably missed a few F's because they do not sound like F's. (Don't worry, this is a simple exercise to reveal perception and does not imply there is anything wrong with you.) For example, you may have overlooked the F in "of" is because it sounds like a "V". This example illustrates how those who read out loud or in their head tend to put more value on the things they hear.

Five To Seven—The rest most likely see five to nine Fs in the passage. In reality there are seven. Go ahead, go back and count.

Eight Or More—I wonder how you got more than there were. Did you add one for good measure? Or maybe you included the F in "Fun" at the bottom of the box. That F is not in the sentence so it doesn't count.

No matter how many times I do this exercise with a group, there is never a consistent result. I think it's interesting that a room full of highly intelligent people never reach the same answer—even though this is a tired exercise many have seen before.

Why the exercise? True, it is not as effective in a book as it is with a large group. And if you are one of the seven F answerers, you may be a wee bit bored. Yes, it seems obvious now, though not when you imagine eight of your peers coming up with a different answer than you. I use it to illustrate perspective.

We each have our own way of seeing things, so it's impossible to share the exact same perspective as the other humans on the planet. We notice different things, and that noticing forms our point of view. It helps to remember this when communicating with others.

And since these varying perspectives form communication, it is no wonder we miscommunicate so often.

Luckily, there is something you can do about it. We talked about it earlier, and we'll talk about it more in the next exercise. It involves going against your predisposed biology. Suspend judgment. Don't turn it off, just push pause for a moment.

When we judge, we reduce listening and questioning. We assume we know what the other person is about to say and what they are about. This assumption reduces communication to rubble.

Great communicators put their assumptions on hold and thirst for new proof.

EXERCISE:
HOW DO YOU COMBAT BIOLOGY?

As easy as I am trying to make it sound, we all know that pausing perception and assumption is not an easy task. Maybe this will help.

For the rest of the day, go through this mental process with each new person you meet.

- Notice the thoughts you have when introduced to a new person. Ask yourself the following questions:

    - Is there an Olympic Judge lurking around my subconscious watching with a critical eye for the perfect engagement or dismount?

    - Am I making assumptions based on limited information?

    - Do I focus the base of my opinion on the person's resume?

Listen closely to your answers, and as you do, practice looking for evidence that your initial opinion was incorrect. Be truly interested in the other person.

- Document your experiences. This is the part you will likely not do; and, the practice of making notes in a diary about your experiences will cause your cellular memory to make changes based on trends you see. This subconscious shift will result in better communication.

Why is it a good idea, to pause our perceptions?

For absolute, self-serving motives! People know when we are judging them. In the new relationship economy, judging is the kiss of death.

Remember, people will go against their own best interest if they feel manipulated or do not like you. Nobody likes being judged.

Example:
> Uwe was a miser. His staff laughed at him when he requested people limit their paper towel usage. He recycled everything. He was the wealthiest man they knew—and the cheapest. At his eulogy, his employees learned that his family lost everything—everything—in the concentration camps. He had survived a most dreadful situation of loss and waste. There was not a dry eye in the room as non-profit after non-profit leader sang the praises of this man who gave almost all his fortune to charity. Only after he died did his staff realize just how wrong they had been.

People know when we are judging them. It reduces listening.

Great communications occur when there is a free flow of ideas and language between the people involved. By suspending judgment, we allow for deeper discourse and more focused discussion. Effective communication results in better understanding and deeper relationships; it also furthers our personal and business goals.

CHAPTER 17:
WALK A MILE IN A MAN'S SHOES (HALF A BLOCK IF THE SHOES ARE FOUR INCH PUMPS)

It is not enough to recognize another person's outlook; we must also put ourselves in their place and try to see things from their point of view—or as Dale Carnegie would say "Try honestly to see things from the other person's point of view." [4]

People will listen more when we listen more. While we hear this phrase all the time, how often do we recognize that reduced judgement is the tour de force of the great communicator? The more we practice this art, the more likely we will have professional relationships that work.

When we pass judgment and use this limited information to decide who someone is, we are reducing listening. Not surprisingly, this causes strain in relationships from the start—causing hackles to rise, heels to go down. Not a very good way to start a working relationship or to get what we need in life.

It isn't enough just to see things from their side: Stop judging what their side is and <u>find out</u>! Stop putting people in boxes and start being fascinated. Drop your agenda and focus on the individual.

Become fascinated by understanding the other person's perspective. Even if you never truly get there, keep practicing.

 EXERCISE:

BEING FASCINATED

This isn't always easy. It takes practice and self-discipline. Practice? Doesn't that make us inauthentic? No. There is actually an easy way to do this on a daily basis. For the socially lazy (we've all been there), this will be a challenge.

Sit on the floor right now. Stretch your legs in front of you, knees together and straight. Now try to put your head on your knees without bending them. If you are able to do this without any pain, take your lower lip and pull it out and up over your head. (Thank you Carol Burnette for that exercise—it is how she described childbirth to men.)

With the right focus and attention, we can create elasticity in our interaction with other humans. You need one thing to practice this skill. (Don't worry, I won't ask you to put your head on your knees again.) From this moment forward, everyday, be fascinated with others. When you are fascinated with others, the world opens up.

1) Fascination breeds an alertness and energy that reduces nervousness and stress. The more you notice and interact with others, the more endorphins you create for yourself.

2) Fascination increases audience attention. Audiences know when someone is interested in them. They like it. It increases rapport, and increased rapport means better listening.

3) Humans are attracted to the story. When fascinated with those around us, we are better able to recall our stories in living detail. Stories are buzzing around us all the time, though we miss them if we're too busy focusing on our watch.

Yesterday was the first day of my book writing retreat. I made the agreement with myself that nothing or no one could interrupt this week of writing. I canceled all of my meetings except one with Dan. Dan simply would not let me cancel with him, and I must say I was a little irritated by this. Sitting in the restaurant waiting for him, a petite blond woman was seated next to me at a separate table. As I wrote a few notes, I started thinking about fascination. It is so easy to lose it when we are annoyed or short on time. I turned to the woman next to me and said, "I suppose if both of our dates stand us up we can have lunch together." She laughed, and we started talking about how we felt uncomfortable having lunch alone when we were in our 20's. Somehow the conversation moved to work and family. Then to our challenges with childbearing. Susie had experienced three miscarriages and a termination after her first son was born. At forty-six she finally decided it was time to stop. She shared experience and advice that moved me to tears as I considered my current struggle with infertility. In five minutes, this stranger had done what my friends and family were not able to do. She gave me hope. Hope that I could have another baby, and hope that I could survive if I did not. I was sad to see my lunch date out of the corner of my eye and thanked her. As our hands touched we both smiled comfortably. Our experiences are the texture for good talks. By being fascinated with the woman next to me, by choosing to interact rather than sit and fume, I am forever changed. And I also have an experience that can be crafted into a speech on a variety of topics from hope to relationships to diplomacy.

These two examples illustrate how fascination can lead to amazing discoveries, interactions, and experiences, and thereby provide vibrant details for your talks.

Being interested in others improves communication.

Last week I presented a Courageous Speaking Workshop. One hour before my presentation, I tiptoed into the room and put my computer and bag of tricks under the front table, as I would be rushing to set up after my last meeting. Leahl, an employee of the hotel, entered the room just as I was hiding the backpack. He gave me a little look and then made small talk. We chatted for a moment about the changes in the hotel industry since 911. I explained why I was leaving the backpack, and he waved his hand away—no worries. As I left the room, I realized the act of putting a backpack under a table in a downtown San Francisco hotel is now considered a suspicious act. If I were a man—particularly a man with a turban and an accent—Leahl would have behaved differently. Currently our culture is challenged, stuck trying to find balance between self preservation and stereotyping.

CHAPTER 18:

WATCH FOR WHAT IS RIGHT

Adopting a positive outlook works wonders in communication, especially since it shields you from miscommunication quagmires. I'm not just talking whistling a snappy tune on a foggy day: Actively watch for what is right and positive. Sometimes I have to create it as I did in that restaurant example.

Start paying attention to what you like about all people. That's all. So for now, your practice is WATCHING for what we like without saying a word about what we see. In a later chapter I will discuss techniques for vocalizing your positive viewpoints.

Maybe you don't want to be a warm friendly person who has empathy. You do not want to watch for what you like because you really do not like people. Okay. I hear ya.

How about I give it to you this way: Watching for what we like in people is actually self-serving. It makes our day a little brighter. We start noticing what is right in the world and this gives us a lighter skip in our step.

Maybe you don't care about skipping. Okay. Try this.

We are warm-blooded, tribal animals. We mimic what we focus on. There is an innate mechanism in the human animal that encourages mimicking. In fact, we actually copy what we see without even thinking about it. So, when we notice things we like in people, we draw these traits into our own being. Think of your eyes and mind as if they were magnets, taking your positive thoughts and using them to improve your own skills. This is not acting, it is biology. Seeing what is wonderful makes us wonderful.

Maybe that sounds cheesy to you. You're tough. I'll tack again.

Relationships will improve merely by focusing on what is right. We know when people do not like us. Our antennae go up when we are negatively judged. When we stop judging, antennae go down and positive communication gets easier.

Quick story to elucidate the point:

> Susan was alone in her office on a Sunday evening, enjoying some uninterrupted time as she completed a project. Grateful Dead tunes wafting from her iPod, she sat at her desk with her eyes closed typing away to the rhythm of Bob Weir's guitar. Suddenly she turned her chair and leapt to her feet, startled by her boss standing in the doorway. Somehow she sensed his presence even with her eyes and ears fully absorbed elsewhere.

No doubt this has happened to you. You are in traffic and turn to find someone staring at you. How did you know they were staring?

Just as Susan sensed her boss standing in the doorway and you sensed the lady staring two lanes over, people sense how we feel about them and will act accordingly. Even if we do not know enough about someone to like them, if we are truly interested and looking for positive clues, they will pick up on our good energy and tend to be more open.

I'm not suggesting that you become sycophants and drive others away with your incessant petting. The point here is to practice watching for what you like, and when that is easy enough, start noticing how your positive thoughts affect your day.

As I have said before (and will say again—this is important), we are in a relationship economy. If you live on an island and do not need to interact with others to communicate, perhaps you can skip this step. Though for most of us, relationships matter. The human relationship is the true currency.

Reflecting on my successful debt collection days, I now see that people paid me because they liked me. I am great at lobbying for a position because I find something I like about the representative before I walk in the door. Even if I don't tell people I like them, they sense it. And this makes my job easier—they are more likely to listen to a fan than an adversary.

Watching for what we like improves relationships. When we have a positive relationship, we are more likely to get a pass and another chance if there is a misunderstanding. When we have a positive relationship we are also less likely to be misunderstood.

In the book *Freakonomics*, Stephen Levitt cited studies statistically proving that doctors are more likely to be sued when they have a terrible bedside manner. Interesting.

My mother was an amazing pianist and an even better instructor. I asked her once when I was around eight years old what she did that made her so good—she said she watched for what she liked in her students' playing and told them often. She explained it made her a better pianist and the side benefit was she watched them get better too when she mentioned it.

My dad was able to transform a governmental agency when he **joined** it instead of protesting it. Positive works.

Being positive feels good, eases communication, and it can be good for the most important person in the room: You.

CHAPTER 19:
YOU SAY POTATO

In the early 70s, a communications professor conducted a comprehensive, far reaching study on communication behaviors. Like many research studies, there is much debate over what the study actually demonstrates. Most agree the study definitively proves that <u>how</u> we say things is very important.

Here's what Wikipedia says about the esteemed professor:

> *Albert Mehrabian (currently Professor Emeritus of Psychology, UCLA), has become known best by his publications on the relative importance of verbal and nonverbal messages. His findings on inconsistent messages of feelings and attitudes have been quoted throughout human communication seminars worldwide, and have also become known as the 7-38-55 Percent Rule.*

According to Mehrabian, there are three elements that go into our communication: Words, tone and voice. His research found words to account for 7 percent of the message, tone of voice accounts for 38 percent, and body language accounts for 55 percent of the message. These percentages are often abbreviated as the "3 Vs" for Verbal, Vocal & Visual.

Audiences can only remember a limited amount of information. <u>How</u> we say it has a major impact on the audiences' ability to <u>hear</u> what we are saying, and <u>how</u> we say it is critical if we wish the audience to <u>remember</u> anything we said.

This is everything I have told you about communication so far in a nutshell: The way you say things can be more important than the words you use. People will not listen to us (even if we are correct) if we are boring communicators. Similarly, when we are rude or hostile, folks will cross their arms and put invisible hands over their ears.

Okay, you are right. Fame and fortune also impacts whether folks listen to us. If we are in a position of power, others will feign listening because they have to. Is this really listening? I disagree with what Mehrabian and most professional communication peeps say about looks. Looks are no longer 35 percent. Things have changed. There ain't no way a crass red-head with poor grammar could have kept your attention this long if looks mattered that much. I'd say the new reality is:

> 7 percent Words
> 72 percent How
> 21 percent Looks

HOW you say the words matters most.

EXERCISE:

"HOW WE SAY IT" EXERCISE

I learned this exercise in third grade. My teacher Mrs. Hall had the class say this common nursery rhyme five times to prove her point about inflection. It's a good one.

Say the following sentence five times, putting emphasis on the bolded word in each version.

Mary had a little lamb.	Mary had the lamb—Bob didn't.
Mary **had** a little lamb.	Mary lost the lamb or no longer has it.
Mary had **a** little lamb.	Mary had just ONE little lamb.
Mary had a **little** lamb.	It was a little lamb, not a big one.
Mary had a little **lamb.**	It was definitely a lamb, not an iguana.

Make up a sentence of your own and try it. I just did. It works.

I never tried to steal your purse.	(Implies that someone else did.)
I **never** tried to steal your purse.	(Emphatic that I didn't steal it.)
I never **tried** to steal your purse.	(Implies I did steal it, I didn't just try.)
I never tried **to** steal your purse	(Doesn't really make sense.)
I never tried to **steal** your purse.	(I did something else with it.)
I never tried to steal **your** purse.	(I tried to steal someone else's purse.)
I never tried to steal your **purse.**	(I tried to steal something else.)

Here's another example of emphasis:

> *King Kong stood on the top of the Empire State Building. Fay Wray screamed, "Flying plane, Flying plane!" Kong gave her a quizzical look and said (assuming he could talk for our purposes), "Don't worry. I have no intention of flying a plane." Just then a flying plane hit him from behind. Poor big monkey.)*

Our language is set up to fail. It is no wonder miscommunication happens. Luckily, later in this book, I will talk about what to do when miscommunication happens and conflict occurs.

It is not what you say—it is how you say it. Don't fret over choosing the right words. Instead, practice how you say them.*

*Some words matter A LOT – we will address those later for dessert.

CHAPTER 20:
BEING NICE IS SELF-SERVING

Once, in the middle of a customer advocacy class I was teaching at a local hospital, a woman stood up and said: "I do not have time to be nice to everyone. I have enough friends. Let other people take care of themselves."

My response: *Remind me what you do for a living?*

Woman: *Customer Service.*

Christina: *Do you like people?*

Woman: *Not all people.*

Christina: *Got it. So, if there are a hundred people you do not know in a room. On average, how many of them do you like?*

Woman: *Two.*

Christina: *Remind me what you do for a living?*

Woman: *Customer Service. We have a lot of repeat customers so the room question wasn't fair.*

Christina: *Got it. If there are a hundred of your customers in a room, on average how many of them do you like?*

Woman: *Nine.*

Christina: *Remind me again what you do for a living?*

Woman: *Maybe I am in the wrong job.*

Christina: *Your call.*

Liking people makes the relationship economy so much richer. In my customer service classes, I teach folks to be <u>fascinated</u> with the person on the telephone or on the other side of the counter. In the example above I neglected to reinforce that being nice in customer communication is not only for the other person: It is a gift we give ourselves.

Listen, my parents were hippies. I remember thinking all of their friends were poor because they would sit around a circle and share the same cigarette. While *Kumbayah* singing was absent, there was a lot of love. I learned how to be nice, and it was easier. Don't worry, being nice to others isn't about becoming another Mother Teresa. I have found that the nicest collectors—those that are the most pleasant on the phone and truly like people—are consistently the top collectors.

I get away with a lot because people like me. It isn't manipulation. I truly like most people I meet. I can find something cool about anyone. (Except George Bush. I can find nothing favorable about that man. Never vote for someone who isn't concerned with history nor how he will be remembered in it.)

Whoops. That was not paid for by an independent expenditure, that one's free.

Communicating to be heard means some of you will stop reading because of my negative Bush comment; obviously I am not communicating to be heard—though I am being true to myself. And thus the yin and the yang of communication. I hope you continue reading anyway.

Actually, since writing my nasty-gram about Mr. Bush, I read a story about his childhood. He lost a little sister Robin to leukemia when she was three. From the reports I have heard—all hearsay—the family didn't really talk about it much. Makes me have some empathy for him now. See, I can find something I like.

If you want productive communication, start by making yourself comfortable. This makes it easier to notice positive things about the person. What do you like about your job? About others? About the room you're in? Uncover things about yourself that make you more present and engaged, even if it is a cup of coffee and a muffin, and use them until being nice becomes second nature.

Conversely, immediately alienating the person with crossed arms, deep frowns, Bush-bashing, blank stares, even if you believe this person to be your "adversary", is never a good way to start a meeting. These signals point to a dead end. You won't go anywhere interesting or productive in your communication with this attitude. We have all heard the philosopher's question: "Would you rather be right or happy?" On average, people say they'd rather be happy; even when their actions show they would rather be right.

Remember our earlier observation: People will harm themselves just to prove that a person they don't like is wrong. It is not our job to have everyone like us, though as part of our communication regimen we may as well try. Being nice is an opportunity—a chance for greater communication successes by creating true relationships with others.

Don't hate the customer service woman above for not liking people—she is just in the wrong job. The new relaitonhsip economy will be tough on her. Be nice.

Be fascinated with the other person. Find something you like about them.

 **EXAMPLE:**

IS IT LEGAL TO BE NICE?

As I've already mentioned, I started a collection agency with the goal of shifting the way corporate America deals with debt. My mission was to "Turn a Collection Call into a Sales Call." I wanted hospitals to extend patient care into the finance department.

My team and I used many techniques to show consumers that we were different. We sent get-well cards if they told us they were sick. We found employment hot lines and temp agencies in their area if they needed a job. We even hired a few consumers who lived nearby to come into our office and stuff mail. When we had a great telephone call with someone, we sent them thank you cards.

When a consumer disputed the bill, we tried to help them figure out whether they were right or not—even though we only got paid to collect. We knew if we helped them, they'd help us the next time. It was a quid pro quo kind of experiment.

It worked, and, subsequently, many of our "debtors" became clients. It was a nice thing. Things were good. Then we got sued. When we were served with the legal papers, my skin crawled and my stomach sank. I couldn't believe it. It was pretty serious, especially since our legal deductible was $5000—a hefty sum back then.

Then something really cool happened. I called our trade association. I had a lot of buddies in the group as I am a person who likes to make friends. One of them put in a good word, and the association covered our deductible.

I hired an attorney. He translated the many-page complaint for me. The attorney said we were being sued because (and I wrote this down at the time because it was so unbelievable) "by being nice you are beguiling the least sophisticated debtor into paying when he otherwise wouldn't."

Our company became the Delilah of the collection industry. Imagine, being sued for being nice. Fortunately, there's a happy ending: We won. See, you can be nice while collecting debt.

The story doesn't end there. It gets better. That single lawsuit created a tsunami of repercussions. It made me even more fascinated with other people, and them even more interested in me. I promise, in my next book, I'll share even more about what being nice and fascinated can do for you.

Communication guru's tout watching for what you like so you can manipulate others—No! You are doing it for you—remember, being nice is self-serving!

Your communication experience is a mirror. What is it reflecting?

 EXAMPLE:

A SUGAR-PAVED ROAD
LEADS TO PARADISE

Coaching a political candidate for public speaking is a challenge if I haven't witnessed the candidate in his/her natural habitat (i.e., behind the lectern). I like to have some idea of his or her style, personality, goals, strengths and weaknesses. Generally, before I agree to a coaching session, I try to catch at least one public presentation by the candidate—this helps me to know if I want to further the cause.

Once I scheduled an urgent meeting with a new candidate who had a pivotal speaking engagement the following day. I knew who he was, though we had never met directly. Hours before our meeting, my son became sick, and I had to take him to the doctor. I knew how critical public speaking skills were for this candidate, and I felt awful for missing the meeting and hurting his campaign efforts. I left a voicemail message with my apologies. The candidate left me the following message in return:

> *"I heard your concern for me in your voice. Please know that what is important right now is that little boy. We have all been there as parents and the last thing I want you to worry about is my silly race. We will work together when it is right for you. Please take care of you and your family. If there is anything you need, you tell me."*

I was impressed. When we met later, I retold the story to his campaign director, adding that I trusted this candidate from that telephone call. I committed to his campaign from that one heartfelt message. I changed my schedule around and found volunteers for his campaign. I did all this extra effort because I liked the guy.

I am afraid to write the next sentence for fear it could be used to manipulate others. Please use this information wisely. There are high-level people who would use this magic for evil purposes. I will not work with them.

Being nice to people has exponential rewards.

 **EXAMPLE:**

HOW MANY FINGERS
IN THAT WAVE?

There you are. Minding your own business. Driving your car to work and WHAMMO some other driver cuts you off in the rudest way.

What do you do? This is great practice for a great communicator.

I say out loud: "I HOPE YOU MAKE IT!"

I imagine they are racing to the bedside of their beloved/parent/grandparent who is dying. They are driving like that hoping to see their love for the last time. They have to cut people off as every second counts.

Sure, I have the right to flip them off. Sure, they are likely just being a rude jerk. And, who do you think finds more joy in their drive to or from work: Me or the one fingered salute guy?

Being nice has exponential rewards. All self-serving.

CHAPTER 21:
DON'T BE NICE
JUST TO MANIPULATE

I never tire of talking about being positive and watching for what you like. This is an almost spiritual practice. I do it every day—as often as I can. Walking down the street I assertively notice everything around me: The sky, an interesting building, the smile on a strangers face. There are many positive things to witness in our everyday world. All the guru's teach us to be positive. I know.

Still, I frequently remind others how this practice will make them better communicators.

- Watching a communicator and noticing what we like will make us mimic that behavior naturally. (We don't have to copy them; we are apes and naturally do this.)
- Humans have a sixth sense: We know when you're adoring us and when you have spectacles on your nose and your eyebrow up.
- Our day becomes a little brighter (and people will be more interested in talking with) us because we are positive.
- We notice great communication habits in others that we may want to practice for ourselves.

It is a rare human who will raise their hand when I ask the question, "Do you get enough positive feedback?" It is my personal quest to notice and loudly celebrate what is right and positive about a person.

As I said in earlier chapters, the first step on the road to great communication is to notice what is going right with a relationship, in the workplace or in the world. Now we have come to the second step: Verbalizing what we see.

This is when we learn to celebrate what is good about something or someone, and all the little things that make it so.

Positive feedback has long been used as a trick or tool in communication. THIS IS NOT what I am suggesting. Being verbal about what we notice stands alone. It isn't done to pave a road for future communication, to get another to go along with what we want, nor to pretend we are not irritated. It stands alone. All alone.

I have a rule. I send at least one card a week to folks I meet out there in the big blue marble. I do this for self-serving purposes. It deepens my relationships with people, and helps me be heard and remembered. More importantly, it reminds me to appreciate the amazing humans in my incredible life.

Start telling people what you like about them without wanting something. Just say it and walk away.

CHAPTER 22:
MANAGEMENT COURSES ARE DESTROYING POSITIVE FEEDBACK

Management 101 has irrefutably harmed positive feedback. Maybe even destroyed it. This is because managers are instructed to develop positive rapport before lowering the boom on an employee.

This is absolutely the wrong way to tell someone what you like about them. Flattery for the sake of "establishing rapport" will get you nowhere. Trust me.

You don't have to be a manager to be guilty of this negative behavior. Look at me, I'm accusing you, and I don't even know you. Am I right? I have never met anyone who has not used positive feedback to pave the road for negative feedback. It is a nasty tumor in our society that must be cut out of our communication. Today!

Example:
> Bob: *Hey Susan. I really like that you come to work on time every day and that you worked last Saturday,*

What is Bob's next word as a manager? You guessed it…

> Bob: *BUT, you are not hitting your goal and we need you to step up.*

> Susan: *[in her head] Bob believes I'm useless. He doesn't care about the extra time and effort I make to do this job right. He just said that to tell me what he really thinks about my work. I do not like or trust Bob.*

All Susan hears is the negative part of Bob's message. She too read the management book that states "give them positive feedback first to establish rapport, then give them the correction." She knows her manager fluffed her to cushion the bad news, thus turning his "positive" statement into a negative one.

This is not how we give positive feedback. Positive feedback to anyone, not just in a management situation, needs to stand <u>alone</u>.

In my office and in my life, I am always telling folks what I like about them. I draw little crowns atop my employees' names on the goal board when they do something exceptional (even if it's just a warm smile first thing in the morning). I don't say anything, I just do it. They notice.

Someone put up a sign at our back doorway that says "Reminder: Did you clock out?" I wrote under the "Reminder" sign: You are a fabulous, unique and precious human being. I'm glad you work here.

I also send notes to their homes. And not just when they hit a goal; I do it when their herculean efforts bring them close. My note doesn't say, too bad you didn't make it. My note says, you have hit the goal many, many times and you will again. I just need you to know how much your team loves you. Thank you for choosing the family of Allegory.

This is not just about management. This is in every area of our life. Never tell your partner how much you love them before asking them to clean the toilet.

Being positive has been used as a trick for too long. Just do it because it feels good or don't do it. I will never forget the thrill of my first standing ovation. A year later I found out the audience purposely gave <u>all</u> speakers a standing ovation to make them feel good. Kind of took the fun out of it for me.

Fake positive is worse than no positive.

Positive statements must STAND ALONE—never follow them up with a favor request, a negative or a corrective statement.

CHAPTER 23:

NO SUGARCOATING!

Being positive is not about sugarcoating! No you didn't catch me. In the example earlier, I said "sugar paving" not sugarcoating. There is a difference.

Humans can generally handle the truth—and truth telling is full of nuances. When used inappropriately, truth is a powerful weapon; when wielded with awareness and integrity, it is a highly effective tool. In the latter use, we aren't avoiding correction or conflict, we are being direct in order to build relationship rather than break it down.

Be reminded: In the 80's, an ill-conceived communication tool for leaders spread across the workplaces of America like a bad flu. Tell an employee something good, then point out what's wrong. This false "rapport building" is manipulative and based upon a flawed notion—that indirect speech has more influence than direct speech.

This is patently wrong. Adults are adults. We do not need others to sugarcoat what is not working, instead we need opportunities for growth. And growth only happens when listening is part of the communication formula. I can't hear you when you tell me how great my hair looks when you follow it by saying my feet smell. I would rather you just take me aside and say "your feet stink." Compliment my hair after I've changed my socks (and only if it looks nice).

We can be direct while coaching for correction. Being direct does not mean being offensive. It means being clear and free of prejudices and judgment—which is the case when we are centered and focused on our desire for a positive outcome. This leaves the other person open and able to provide us with details we may not have known without our having told the truth. Maybe I keep limburger in my shoes.

Here's a real example. Alicia came to work late three times in the past two weeks. Her manager sat her down in the office and said:

> Alicia, you are a good employee. You get your work done, and we like you. BUT, you keep coming in late which shows disrespect for the team. Please stop.

Alicia leaves the office unhappy and uninspired. What if the manager said:

> Alicia, I know you are interested in becoming management with this firm. I worry that your recent tardiness is going to stand in your way. Tell me what is happening. This isn't like you.

Near tears, Alicia tells her manager she has been coming in late because her mother, who has been living with her for over a year, is near death.

Which tactic encourages communication? Obviously, the method without sugarcoating allows the truth to come out, so that together, manager and team member can figure out a solution to her temporary tardiness problem. As leaders, we lead people, so we must communicate effectively.

Be direct, don't sugarcoat, and make it about what they want, not about you.

👁 EXAMPLE:

THE POSITIVE MEETING

Every day in my company, every employee has one job they must complete: They must watch out for a fellow employee, client or person doing something **that they like**. Their mandatory job is to catch a team member doing something great!

First thing in morning, the entire team stands in a circle in our common area. Each employee must go around the circle and share their positive observation with the team. The first fifty times we did this, it was uncomfortable for just about everyone. Then people got used to the idea. The following is an example of a positive meeting. These positives really happened.

James, welcomes everyone and starts with his positive:
> *Yesterday at around 3pm, I heard Christa on a telephone call. I could hear the customer screaming through the line. Christa not only kept her cool, she offered the person help and compassion. I will copy some of the stuff she did in that call and work on them with my wife when she is mad at me—like this morning! (Everyone laughs.)*

The entire circle looks at Christa and applauds. Everyone turns to the next person in circle, Carla:
> *This morning I was in a serious rush to get here on time. (Everyone laughs knowing Carla is usually a few minutes late.) The line was long downstairs, and I wasn't able to get a cup of coffee. I mentioned this to Tracy in the elevator, and she snuck downstairs and got me a cup while I punched in. Thank you Tracy.*

The entire circle looks at Tracy and applauds. Everyone then turns to the next person in the circle:
> *Last night was a bad night. My son was rushed to the emergency room, and there was quite a line to get in. I sat on the floor to nurse him and the guy behind the counter came running out to hand me a blanket to sit on. Now that's customer service!*

Everyone asks if her son is okay. The team is now aware of something that may impact her performance or attitude today. We know to cut her some slack should she seem upset; we know what is bothering her. The next person continues:
> *I had a hard time finding something positive yesterday. I'm not feeling well, and I'm tired. I do appreciate Bill the doorman—he is always so friendly when I come in. He makes me say hi!*

We applaud. A few people in the circle agree. Someone suggests we invite Bill to our office party at the end of the month. We like that. (We do invite him and he becomes a part of our family. He's still one.)

> *I bought a new car yesterday.*

We applaud. We ask what kind it is. What color? While this is good news, it isn't catching someone doing something great. We let it go this time and watch for Molly to catch someone doing something great in the next circle. If she doesn't, we'll remind her of the job she is forgetting to do. It's Christa's turn to give her positive:

> *I like this positive meeting. It takes a little bit of getting used to, and I like it. I did notice how helpful this entire team has been to me as I get used to my new job. Thank you.*

Office politics can kill the culture of an organization. By setting up a systemic focus on the positive (in each other and the world), we increase our effectiveness and disintegrate ugly rumors and politics.

Here's what you didn't know about the above meeting:

Right before our positives circle, James rushed by Christa in a hurry. He didn't look up or say hello. He was irritated and in his own world. His wife had dropped him off right in the middle of a fight. Man, he thought, that woman sure can push my buttons.

Christa is a new team member and was told yesterday that James was moved to the other side of the office in order to give Christa a more appropriate workspace. As he gruffly walked by, she decided he must be angry with her. Oh great. Office politics. It isn't her fault they moved him away from his buddies. This place is cliquish—it's like everyone is drinking the Kool-Aid anyway. Ugh.

It is really hard to be mad at someone if they tell everyone in the room how fantastic you are. Jame's comment in the positive meeting completely evaporated the bad road Christa was going down. She assumed he was being mean to her when he was really in a fight with his wife.

The funny thing is, this came from a negative experience. Supervising a collection agency in 1985, I called a meeting at the end of the day and simply asked everyone to say something great about the person standing next to them. I did it because our receptionist Martha had died unexpectantly, and I wanted everyone to connect in a human way. The meeting was incredible. We laughed, we cried, we connected in ways we had never done without alcohol. I got in trouble for that meeting. The owners daughter thought I was organizing a union and freaked out.

As a result, I didn't something like this again until years later. Positive scares people—just so you know. They think positive means you want something, you are selling something or you are manipulating. Be prepared.

Noticing what is right will improve relationships and your outlook.

CHAPTER 24:
LISTEN WITH YOUR EARS
NOT YOUR MOUTH

We think we are good listeners. Often we aren't.

Listening is the most important skill of communication. In the educational sessions I teach, I lead a segment that is four hours of listening practice. Consistently, folks fail listening tests in the beginning and, after a few hours of practice, improve these skills.

I see what you are doing. You are doing the "yeah yeah" thing. Got it. Listen more. Okay.

If only it was that simple. Here are some ideas for you to practice listening. Hey! I'm doing a list for you. See how I communicate to be heard?

- Only give advice if they ask for it—Giving advice is one way of abridging the other person's thoughts and rushing to some sort of conclusion. It is almost a control mechanism. Leave the advice giving to the paid professionals, and truly listen to the other person. (Unless of course, the person asks for advice.)

- Do not multitask when communicating—Checking emails while listening is not listening.

- Become fascinated with the other human—Make this a fun game.

- Ask questions and listen to the answers—Thirst to know more.

- Criticism doesn't belong on a to-do list—Do not coach people unless they ask. We have a mantra in business: **Build** instead of **fix**.

- Always ask right before giving advice—Even if someone says, "Hey, I need your advice" be sure and ask for permission just before giving it. "Are you sure you want my advice?"

Listening means you are not talking, typing or thinking about your response.

LISTEN WITHOUT PRE-FORMULATING YOUR RESPONSE

The first time I heard this concept was in 1976 at William Land Elementary. Our class was talking about the Civil Rights movement and my best friend, Lisa Wong, made a remark about the deep South.

I was from the deep South, and I didn't like what she was saying, so I blurted out my thoughts in the middle of her sentence. Sue Immig, my sixth grade teacher, knelt next to me and held my hand.

> Ms. Immig: *Chrissie, I know you lived in the South and your parents were really active in the Civil Rights movement. You are proud of them for this, right?*

> Chrissie: *Yes. [My lower lip starting to tremble.]*

> Ms. Immig: *I see that you are a good daughter and want to protect the name of your parents, is that right?*

> Chrissie: *Yes. [The tears were starting to come.]*

> Ms. Immig: *[Addressing the entire class] Children, this is an important thing we all need to learn. When something really matters to us, and especially when our feelings are involved, we change the way we listen. We listen to talk and give our side rather than to try understand what the other person is saying. When we do this, no one wins. Lisa, I know Chrissie is your best friend. Can you explain to her what you meant by what you said so she can understand?*

Lisa came over and gave me a big hug. She whispered in my ear how proud she was of what my parents tried to do and explained what she meant.

I tear up still when I share this story. Had Ms. Immig not stepped in I wonder if Lisa and I would have remained such close friends. If you know Ms. Sue Immig, please have her call me—I'd like to thank her for this essential lesson.

The story is more than the words. The lesson Ms. Immig shared lasts to this day. I remember telling my father about it when I got home, and he and I made a deal. My dad, who liked to play games with me (especially when they involved vocabulary lessons!), suggested we clap our hands whenever we felt the other person was truly listening. There was a lot of clapping in my house for the next few days.

I wonder what it sounds like in your house? In the office? How are you listening? I pinch my ear <u>hard</u> if I am nervous or not listening. It is incredible what it does to my body. I listen more when I feel that pinch on my ear.

Listen and your response will come naturally when it is your turn to talk.

EXAMPLE:

ADVICE IS NOT WHAT THEY WANT

As you will read in more depth later on, my niece is a brilliant child with cerebral palsy. She is confined to a wheelchair, and this was extremely tough for my sister and her family. Over the years, I called my sister many times to check in on her life and the progress of my niece. We have a special bond.

By now, you probably see me as a very positive person. I was more positive then. In my phone calls to my sister, I just blew sunshine through the receiver— talked about how blessed we were and gave my sister, an exhausted single mother of three, all sorts of unsolicited advice to get through it. One day, my sister, who rarely cries, hung up on me in the middle of one of my "head up young person" soliloquies. I heard her sob right before the phone went "click."

I sat stunned for a few minutes and realized how damn tough my sister was. I couldn't imagine being twenty-six-years-old and facing what she was facing—a disabled child, a toddler, a baby, a mortgage, and a divorce. She was doing it all on her own with no financial support and certainly no real emotional support from me.

I called her back and said something like, "I am an absolute ass. Everytime you call me I try to make you feel better by telling you positive things and giving stupid advice. Not once have I sat and cried with you—told you I can't imagine how difficult it is and how much I admire the job you are doing. I do. And I am so sorry. I want to listen. Let me try again."

From that moment on my sister and I became real friends. Truly. Our relationship grew into the kind of sibling relationship most humans dream of.

I finally stopped trying to fix what was unfixable and just listened to her. I was so afraid of actually admitting how hard it was for her—I thought my job was to convince her there was a bright side.

What she was going through sucked. My little blossoms of advice smelled more like crap than perfume, and she helped me find a new way to be supportive.

Listening without talking improves relationships. Advice is a shortcut to talking and real emotional commitment.

CHAPTER 25:
STOP NAME-BADGE SURFING

Stop name badge surfing. It is offensive and transparent. At every event I attend I feel sorry for the poor souls looking to see if the person they are talking to is important enough to warrant their affection. I often write the word "NOBODY" on my name tag. It makes it a lot easier for people to get me right away.

Here's a great example. I am at an event, and we are all milling about waiting for a famous person to speak. I am having a hard time connecting with people, as name badge surfing is high, human connection low. People are ignoring me in their hunt for someone who will take them up the ladder. After the speech, the famous person engages me, and we talk for a bit, catching up on a previous conversation and memo.

Suddenly, my stock price in the room shoots through the roof. People who had no time for me forty minutes ago hand me their cards and say "let's do lunch." Sad. I'm the same person with the same hair, only now I have cache—the biggest star in the room wanted to talk to me.

Fortunately for our self-respect, the new relationship economy does not like people who are only interested in others for self-serving purposes. It knows self-serving purposes are shallow and won't have lasting impact.

A friend of mine tested this theory at a function in San Francisco. She put "Swig"— the last name of a respected San Francisco philanthropist—on her name badge. She couldn't believe how well people she didn't know treated her. When they asked if she was related to "the Swigs" she responded, "No. I put the name on my nametag to test a friend's theory on name badge surfing. "Almost every person said, "Don't you just hate that!"

Hang on there Christina. You're being judgmental of me. There are a lot of names to memorize in the world. I only look at the name tag to help me remember.

Okay. I do that too. I do it while I am shaking hands and I tell them so. I look them in the eye and listen to their name before I check their badge.

Try not to judge the person nametag surfing. They are good people too.

All people are important. Be interested in every person you meet.

PART III

CONFLICT

CHAPTER 26:
YOU SEE A CAT, I SEE A RAVEN AND IT IS REALLY A UNICORN

We all come from different perspectives, and this is why miscommunication happens. It isn't that there is something wrong with us or with them: Human beings, when honest, see things differently.

Conflict and opposite beliefs are the sign of a healthy relationship.

Our communication comes from instinctual responses, experience, emotion and somatic responses. We aren't bad.

Expect and enjoy conflict—it means something better is being created.

STORY 1:
SILLY RABBIT, THAT'S WHY IT'S CALLED A *SLIP*

I'm nineteen-years-old, and I am standing with my knees knocking while speaking about a legislative bill. I was in a meeting with some California legislators, lobbyists and citizens. I dressed meticulously that day. As I recall, I wore a bright red coatdress with brass buttons and a plaid collar. I chose some black pointy-toed pumps to round out the outfit. I wanted so badly to look older than I was. I was channeling the tough exterior of Alexis Carrington (remember *Dynasty*?). Inside, I was absolutely terrified.

In those days, I avoided public speaking. I cowered at the mere glimpse of a lectern. One of my earliest public speaking traumas occurred when I was best man at my best friend's wedding. As we all know, the best man is supposed to give the toast, only I freaked out so much I got hives. The groom's big brother Bob ended up giving the toast while I stood aside in my tuxedo. This still makes me sad.

I was in Sacramento at the Capital that day to speak on behalf of my stepbrother Gary. I was also there for my Dad, for my brother Steve, for the guilt I had carried for years. It needed a voice. I needed a voice.

Years earlier, Gary pulled up to the Village Apartments just as I was about to run to the corner store for a Dr. Pepper. He was so happy to have his life back. His shoulder length hair was a mess, and I think he had bugs in his teeth from smiling so much on his motorcycle. He definitely had a hint of the prankster in his eyes. He was radiant.

He asked me if I wanted to go for a ride, and I immediately said no. To this day, I am not sure why I said no so quickly—I loved motorcycles. As he rode off I thought about chasing him down with a helmet. This encounter was the last time I saw Gary alive. He took a ride that weekend and went off the side of a cliff. He wasn't wearing his helmet.

No helmet.

Three years before I had a similar encounter with my stepbrother Steve. As he hopped on his motorcycle, I somehow convinced him to wear my mother's helmet. Since her helmet had daisy stickers on the back, we stood in his closet and peeled the stickers off one by one, stuck them on the door, so he could replace them when he returned. Lord knows he didn't want to look like a sissy.

On the curvy road ride to his girlfriend's house, he lost control of the bike. He left traces of his arms and chest on the road, taking out a cow in the process. Fortunately, he survived, though he had a quarter inch gash that circled his helmet from front to back. Whew! I remember watching him recover from a shoulder injury and pretty extensive road rash; it was a lot of pain to witness.

Unfortunately, Steve's close call didn't deter Gary from riding without a helmet. Probably because my family lived on motorcycles. I had learned how to ride a mini-bike when I was five; we did not like to wear helmets much.

I remember waking up on a Saturday to the sound of my stepmother crying. That day, as all the family gathered in our apartment talking about Gary and his rebellious nature, Gary's little boy said "Da Da" for the first time. It was bittersweet watching him weave around us testing the new words—so proud of himself.

At Gary's funeral we played songs like *Born under a Wandering Star*, *Rambling Man*, and *Freebird*. These were the songs that reminded us of him. Gary was truly a rambler, and he loved freedom and adventure more than anything. He first ran away at three, though it was more like he was running towards something. When he was four, he dug a hole under the fence to go fishing; at twelve, my stepmother found him in Nevada—a state away from his Sacramento home.

What I remember most about his funeral happened just before they closed Gary's casket. As my brothers tucked a fifth of Jack Daniels, a pack of Camels and some pot in Gary's pocket for the hereafter, I swear to you, I saw Gary's face change. The mischievous grin that lived on his face suddenly appeared. Beneath all the make-up he was getting ready for another adventure.

By now, you've probably guessed why I was at the capital. The helmet law. The room was full and unruly, people weren't listening to each other, and it was frothing with emotion. I sat in the middle of it all, without any coalition or affiliation. I just knew I wanted to say something. And remember what I said earlier—speaking in public was not something I did. I was terrified and having an awful time. Hives. Vomit. The works.

A few weeks before this event, my Grandmother had passed away. Her husband mailed me a box of her slips. Yes, lingerie. Standing in that room, tears brimming in my eyes, I was channeling Maude as I wore her white slip with light blue embroidery on the front panel under my coat dress. Grandma wore it in the 40s, and, though a little worn, it was exactly the right length, well made, and beautiful. I was trying to feel powerful that day.

When it was my turn, I stood up and told the story I just told you. I am not sure if anyone heard what I said. My voice shook and cracked, and I even cried a little as I tried to get a small group of people to know my brother—all in about two minutes. I told the story of Gary—of the day he drove off. I cried about how his absence left a hole in my family and left me scared to death. I cried for my regret in not saving him.

People were uncomfortable, though I could tell they were listening. The entire room was listening and applauded when I completed my two minutes.

Anyone who has ever found an old rubber band knows elastic deteriorates over time, and, as I turned to walk to my chair, the elastic that had seen my grandmother through decades decided to give way. I felt it and stood paralyzed as the slip fell down around my ankles. Unsure of what to do and somewhat hidden by the chairs around me, I decided to step out of the slip and keep walking. Big mistake. The heels of my pointy stilettos had broken down and become serrated, so the slip got stuck on my shoe and I had to reach down in front of everyone and pick up my shoe and the slip. As I hobbled to my chair with one shoe and no slip, my face turned redder than my dress.

I have told this story a million times. In my memory, there are 5000 people in the room, and they are all laughing and pointing at me. This moment formed the next decade of my life, and my imperfect memory of it stunted any future public speaking opportunities. And do you want to know something ironic? The more I sit in my dark closet and remember the actual event, the more I believe most people didn't even notice—and those who did gave me a ton of love and support and only teased me in caring ways.

It has taken me years of recounting this embarrassing moment to remember why I was there and why I had that slip on. These details create texture for this story and keep the attention of the listener.

Reliving a story means telling it in different ways as your memory wakes up. It wasn't until a year or so ago I realized the TRUE lesson of this story. It isn't storytelling, it isn't emoting, it isn't embarrassing moments. It is knowing myself better. What is my opinion on the helmet law? Do you know?

Thus begins our look at conflict. I will tell you my opinion later.

Listening is reduced in almost every conflict encounter we endure.

CHAPTER 27:
JUST AS CERTAIN AS THE SUN RISING IN THE MORNING: WE WILL HAVE MISCOMMUNICATION

Our language is set up to fail.
Miscommunication happens.
What are you going to do about it?

Accept that miscommunication will happen. The English language has many intricacies and nuances, setting us up for a veritable smorgasbord of misunderstanding. Lexical and syntactic ambiguity can either result in major catastrophes or annoying interactions.

Did you understand all that? Yeah, I had a hard time figuring what those sentences meant when I first wrote them too. Read them again.

Now do you understand? The following example makes it easy to understand why the English languange is so easily misunderstood:

> *A person in distress calls 911 and yells at the operator, "She hit the man with the cane." The operator asks the caller if he needs an ambulance or a squad car. The person on the line screams, "DUH! She ran him right over!" Obviously, from the caller's words, the 911 operator thought the woman hit the guy over the head with a cane.*

As I said in Chapter 16, perspective is different for everyone. Basically, there is no reality. There is only perspective. There is what happened, what you think happened, what they think happened and the intuitive melodrama background music playing in everybody's heads.

My acknowledgement of this makes me terrified to print this book. I fear my perspective will change tomorrow and my memories are flawed in some way. I am not the only one stifled by this.

Humans have a sixth sense that sometimes misses the target. We discern things that are not steeped in reality. Our past experiences can color our immediate ones, so that we may not be able to read the situation from an objective perspective. Of course, everyone has experienced the reverse of this, when we perceive something correctly, only to have the other person refuse to admit it. Maddening both ways.

Miscommunication causes conflict, so we need to become good at telling people they are standing on our foot. Many public speakers water down their effectiveness because they fear a tough question or do not want to experience conflict in the room. When we overcome our fear of conflict, we can become great public speakers. Or to put it a different way: A great communicator MUST be great at conflict.

Simple.

You will experience miscommunication—if you never do, someone isn't being honest.

CHAPTER 28:
YOU WANT TO KNOW WHEN YOU HAVE SPINACH IN YOUR TEETH

Ever look in the mirror and realize you have spinach in your teeth? Or poppy seed, fennel or some other offending hitchhiker? Your stomach sinks as you realize you haven't eaten for four hours, and during this period you've spoken face to face with at least seven others. Urgh!

You know they saw the spinach. Why didn't the first person (or the second, third, fourth and so on) say something? Did they even hear what you were saying to them or were they too distracted by your spinach?

If you are doing something that is keeping you from moving forward in your personal and professional life, don't you want to know about it? If you are standing on someone's foot, crushing the tiny bones in the little piggy that ate none, you'd want to know—right?

Most conflict is spinach in your teeth. See it that way. No big deal. Something we should deal with as soon as it gets stuck rather than waiting four hours or four days or four years. Relationships grow stronger when we discuss little conflicts rather than ignoring them until they build into big ugly ones.

If there isn't some kind of conflict going on in your life—someone is sandbagging. I will say again, if you agree with everything I'm saying in this book, one of us has a problem. You are drinking the Kool-Aid, or I am afraid to offend you by telling you exactly what I think. The same is true at work, at home, and everywhere you dwell.

It's no wonder our inability to communicate to be heard in conflict destroys relationships. The key is learning to identify the subtle changes that come over you when conflict arises. You can then learn to de-escalate the conflict by making subtle shifts in your speaking and listening. The coming chapters will guide you through this.

Conflict is good. It will offer the most growth in your relationships. Conflict is the beginning of innovation.

CHAPTER 29:

THE PATH
OF MOST RESISTANCE

Want to know something ironic? I hate conflict. I have spent most of my life devising clever ways of avoiding it, so I am the perfect person to tell you conflict must be accepted and dealt with. I know firsthand how conflict avoidance destroys relationships, causes unnecessary stress and dilutes the possibilities of grandeur in the world.

We were taught at an early age that tattletales are bad people. Who came up with this crazy idea? Perhaps the bullies of the world got together and hired a PR wordsmith to spin this odd belief system around tattling. It certainly isn't logical.

I kept my mouth shut most of my life. I did not want to accuse anyone of anything, so I let all my concerns and imaginings swim around in my head. As my mind grew more cluttered with swimming things, it sought fragments of information that confirmed my negative assessments. My conflicts increased. Organizations suffered because I stayed mute. Relationships broke. Things ended.

When I set my sights on the debt collection industry, I chose the path of most resistance. I did this for a reason I didn't realize at the time: I chose the industry that would force me into conflict and make me figure out how to handle it.

The harsh world of collections was my training ground. It inspired me to create unique ways to handle conflict positively, and, eventually, I came up with quantifiable methods for dealing with something I'd avoided my entire life.

All humans are walking around with a sign around their neck:

> *Please do not sugarcoat or manipulate me by aura-fluffing me. I trust you when you tell me, without a trick or script, that I am standing on your foot. This only works if you practice telling me the bad news without acting like a serial killer, a placating ninny or a verbal terrorist. HOW you tell me matters—just make sure you tell me. Don't push me around either—I'll push back in some way.*

What I learned in collections is "The 2 percent rule": Less than 2 percent of humans are bad people. The rest of us just created odd communication strategies to survive when we were kids. Forgive us. We want to be better. Stop pushing us around—we dig our heels in.

Having power over someone else (actual or perceived) is the worst thing that can happen to a great communicator.

BEING RIGHT IS NOT THE SAME AS BEING A GREAT COMMUNICATOR

Karen enjoyed her time on the board of directors for a local non-profit. Her stature in the community was excellent and long-standing. She prided herself on always being the voice of reason for the organization; the other board members relied on her insight and her unique perspective.

Because of a business trip, she was unable to attend the January board meeting so she called in via speakerphone. Toward the end of the meeting, the board began to discuss a community member's accusation that the board and the organization were not diverse. Karen listened and tried to remain calm and thoughtful. She recalled that this question had come up the year before and that the board had not done anything to address the issue fully.

One of the board members suggested they craft a message to the community stating the organization's commitment to diversity. Karen commented, "I am not sure we are committed—we haven't done anything this past year to …" She was interrupted. She took a deep breath and tried again, "Maybe the board should listen to…" She was interrupted again. At least four times total. It wasn't until later in the year she realized the interruptions weren't personal.

Then one of the women said, "We have to let the community know we are very committed to diversity…"

Karen could not take it anymore and burst out with, "That is bullshit! We are not committed. If we were committed we would have changed our behavior after talking about it last year."

Total silence. All of the hard work Karen had done to win the respect and favor of the organization went up in smoke. From that moment on, the organization did not include her in the inner circle and did not seek her counsel in their diversity presentation to the community. Karen was correct, the board's actions in the past year had not shown their commitment to diversity; and still she neglected to consider that the board members and the organization *felt* they were committed. No matter how right Karen was about the board's need for true action, the way she pointed it out alienated her from her fellow board members. Thus the issue of diversity was not truly addressed. Eventually, Karen was kicked off the board in a very unusual way. The organization suffered. So did Karen.

Karen is me. Is she you?

Have the discipline to speak so your ideas are heard and understood.

CHAPTER 30:
HACKLES UP...
HEELS DOWN

Humans become defensive when they sense folks do not agree with them. Their hackles go up and a physiological response of reduced listening and less clear speaking skills naturally follows. This is followed by more interrupting, less listening and more emotive communication.

Hackle control must be the goal for both parties in a conflict. We must control our own hackles so we are able to listen and understand. We must also communicate in a manner that helps others keep their hackles down. Hackle control is self-serving. If you truly want to improve your relationships, increase listening and get your ideas across, communicating to keep hackles down is paramount.

If you are mad and just want to attack someone verbally, cool. There are times when it feels good to vent your anger. You may have every right to blast someone: That person is a disrespectful, unconscious pig who doesn't deserve your kind attention to hackle control. Keep in mind that this is not great communication. Remember that philosophy from so many chapters ago: Would you rather be right or happy?

When we push folks around, pressure them, use force or try to manipulate them they will reduce their listening. To change a mind we must first be heard. We often forget the biological fact that a person listens less when their hackles are up.

Our Hackles UP reduces everyone's listening.

Their Hackles UP reduces their listening as they are defending.

Sugarcoating and pretending our hackles aren't up reduces listening. We really are transparent when we try to pretend we are not mad.

Conflict either improves or destroys relationships: There is no middle ground. Focus your attention on improving relationships through conflict. (Lack of conflict destroys relationships too.)

Communicate to be heard and focus on the long-term relationship.

CHAPTER 31:

THEY SMELL IT COMING
LIKE JEAN NATE AT
A JUNIOR HIGH SCHOOL DANCE

Let me repeat myself (in a different way). Have you ever been waiting in line at the grocery store and sensed someone staring at you? Quickly you snap your neck to the right and sure enough, they are. How'd ya know they were staring?

Think for a moment about a time when your sixth sense kicked in. What does it feel like to sense someone looking at you despite the absence of any audible or obvious physical cues. Kind of trippy, huh?

Human beings are basically animals. We are able to notice and feel things without being able to explain the reasons why. This is why fake or manipulative communication does not work. Others smell it the minute we open our mouths in an untrue way. Our actions become transparent and hackles go up, thus destroying any possibility for real communication. (I don't mean to belabor the point, though here it is again. So I'll belabor—**This is exactly why a step-by-step systems of pre-planned communication scripts rarely work.**)

Hackle control starts with *how* we say things. As the sixth sense radar operates in the background, other obstacles to successful communication are happening in the foreground. When conflict happens, many people generally go through a series of behaviors—audible and visual, verbal and non-verbal—that exacerbate the conflict. I call these behaviors **Neon Signs Of Disagreement**™.

Purposeful or accidental, neon signs of disagreement are words, actions, facial expressions, tone or gesticulations that come up during conflict. Neon Signs of Disagreement engage the hackles of the other person. They are like flashing red signs saying, "Hey You! Stop listening. I don't agree with you at all. Start working on your retort."

These neon signs of disagreement signal conflict is coming, even if neither party desires it! It takes training and discipline not to react when you see the other person going into conflict mode. Instead, most people enter the "ready position" when they encounter the neon signs. The ready position reduces listening and increases defensiveness.

Speak in a way that does not engage the ready position (yours or theirs).

GET "READY" FOR BAD NEWS

Kelly was in the training and event business. She got railroaded into organizing an event with a group (all of them volunteers) who didn't really care about making their event great. Despite this overwhelming obstacle, Kelly committed to making the event a success; after all, she was in the event business, and she had to live up to her brand.

At the first meeting, all the volunteers sat around the table. The vibe was an overwhelming "let's get this event off our backs with the least amount of effort." Every idea Kelly presented was shot down. Clearly the volunteer group had never read a book on communicating to be heard. She had to work hard to keep her defenses down and not feel offended.

Finally, Kelly decided to be transparent:

> *"Listen gang, I can't be the front man for an event that doesn't have some sparkle. I will help in the background—I just cannot be the MC if we don't add some pizzazz.*

> *I..." Kelly was interrupted.*

> *"This event is not about you, Kelly. Why are you making it about you."*

> *"I am not making this event about me," said a surprised Kelly.*

> *"Yes you are! You are saying if we don't do it your way you won't participate."*

Kelly retreated. She didn't take on the conflict and instead sat silent through the rest of the meeting. She attempted to salvage things by sending an email to the entire group. Using her best personal accountability language, she expressed her hurt feelings, stating she felt she had been treated rudely.

Email communication is often misunderstood, and her effort merely worsened the conflict. Their next meeting was fraught with accusations and more defensiveness. Nothing was resolved, and, in the end, the event did not turn out as Kelly would have liked.

Over a year later, Kelly still feels stung by the experience. Here's why: When she expressed her hurt feelings, the team responded defensively, accusing her of her being insensitive and self-serving. She did not feel heard.

When we go into conflict and someone expresses hurt, we must remember that feeling bad for hurting another **does not mean** we agree with their assessment. We need to learn to accept that these two states are not mutually exclusive. For some reason, people think they can avoid feeling bad for the hurt they've caused by convincing the other person that they're wrong in feeling hurt in the first place. Relationships are forever harmed when we bury our hurt feelings or reject the hurt feelings of others. We feel unsafe in our communication if we do not trust our feelings will be honored. As a result, we hold back our true thoughts. This creates barriers to communication, and over time, we build up grudges in our relationships.

Ours is a grudge holding culture. Grudges are insidious. They create negative patterns of interaction. We have all witnessed longtime-married couples taking swipes at each other over the smallest infraction—like who forgot to buy butter. This is because they have built up grudge walls between them. And to make things worse, grudges cripple relationships as they slowly chip away at their core.

Holding a grudge, simply put, is the opposite of forgiveness. As you read these words, what are you not forgiving? Is it time to forgive and move on?

In the example above, both sides handled conflict poorly, resulting in several communication violations. When you are done reading this book, revisit this exercise and see if you can identify the communication glitches. Extra credit if you come up with an alternate scenario in which clear communication made all parties feel heard.

Hint: Kelly was not communicating to be heard either.

Attacking a person's feelings without addressing what is wrong leads to the hackles going up. Once the hackles are up, everyone is in trouble. Forgiveness is the quickest way to being a great communicator.

CHAPTER 32:
NEON SIGNS OF DISAGREEMENT: NON-VERBAL

Non-Verbal cues happen before we ever open our mouths. It is obvious to the other person that we are not listening to their words: They read our body language. Since folks like lists, I'll give you another. Here is a list of non-verbal neon signs of disagreement:

- **Rigid body**—Stiff upper torso and rigid hands signal the conflict ready position. I often film when I am leading conflict role playing exercises, and the results are very powerful. Audiences can always pick out the people trying to turn conflict around. Their bodies give them away. An unmistakable stiffness occurs in their upper torso. They stand taller, don't use their neck, and turn with their entire body. It is a neon sign. Relax. Avoid hackles before speaking. If we put our shoulders up in tension, we are spinning our body into fight or flight mode.

- **Forgetting to breathe**—Stop holding your breath. Just breathe naturally. Now that I've mentioned it, go ahead and do it now. Doesn't it make you feel better! When people hold their breath, the rigid body engages. Now they have two red flashing neon signs. The other person goes on alert. This engages the fight or flight chemical to be released from our endocrine system. Once this chemical is in our body, our brain doesn't work as well as it should since all our blood has left our brain.

- **Fake smile**—I hate this one. I taught a group of security guards last week, and they told me how people yell "Rent-A-Cop" at them all the time. I asked how they responded, and they told me they smile and say thank you. I was surprised, as I wouldn't appreciate someone calling me a name. I suggested they reply more honestly, with something like, "Yes I am. I am paid to keep you and all the other customers safe." Actually, that isn't how I'd really respond. I'd simply say, "Ouch. That's not so nice." When people call me names, I rarely ignore it. Being a great communicator doesn't mean being a doormat. We can respond to it without making it a fight.

- **Shaking head while the person is talking**—This one is equally annoying. And not so subtle! It is as bad as interrupting the speaker in my opinion.

- **Squinting eyes**—In conflict, people often squint their eyes to show confusion or irritation. Open your eyes and listen to the person speaking. You will learn something. Really. Trust that your opinion and stance is strong enough to be watered down by their opinion. Search for ways you are wrong.

- **Angry or bored expression**—People read expressions, hence the saying "his face was an open book." What is your face doing during conflict? Is it scrunched up and angry? Are your lips pursed and your eyes roving the ceiling? If you want the other person to hear you, pay attention to what your face is expressing nonverbally. Your face should tell the other person, "keep talking, I'm listening." To show them you really want to hear more, um, really WANT to hear more.

- **Exasperated breath**—This is the opposite of breath holding, and it is technically a verbal neon sign, as it involves noise. Since it is breath, I am including it as a non-verbal sign. Ever talk to a teenager? They are masters of exasperated breath.

We do all sorts of things to mask our frustration or to show it. Rather than Harrumptf, we are better off asking questions and increasing listening.

Non-verbal cues are neon signs that don't match the nice little words of agreement coming out of your mouth. This reduces listening and relationship.

CHAPTER 33:
NEON SIGNS OF DISAGREEMENT: SOME WORDS MATTER A TON

Remember, when I talked about words themselves being less important than how they are expressed? I gave you some fancy formulas and broke it all down very simply to point out that the words themselves only account for only about seven percent of communication. Well, now I'm going to contradict myself: There are SOME words that matter a lot!

I call all of these verbal neon signs of disagreement **plague words**—as they tend to spread like plagues in organizations. If one person uses a plague word, others pick it and soon, the word is an office disease!

There are three categories of Neon Signs of Disagreement (NSD) plague words:

- Viruses—words like but, you, always, never.

- Dilution words —unsolicited subjective opinions, know-it-all facts, assumptions, projections, "you are wrong" statements.

- Tone of Voice—sarcastic, degrading, passive aggressive or ridiculing tones.

Avoid plague words, as they substantially decrease listening and dilute the effectiveness of your opinion.

CHAPTER 34:
THE "BUT" VIRUS

Samantha tells Bob, "I appreciate your opinion Bob, **but**…" We all know what comes after but. She is getting ready to tell Bob he's wrong. Bob knows this as soon as he hears the dreaded word. Whether intentional or not, Samantha has successfully negated all the nice things she said with one simple word.

BUT is a huge verbal sign to the other person that everything said before "but" was just an attempt at being nice and complimentary. The real news is coming, get ready for it:

> *Mr. Brownstone sits across from his employee Jessie Thompson, who eagerly awaits his review. "Jessie, you come in on time everyday, you are always cheerful and we love having you around here; BUT, your end product is often disorganized, you have a habit of procrastinating and we do not see that you have the quality we need to move this department forward.*

When we say something 'positive' in order to get something in return or soften bad news, people learn to not trust what we say. In the above leadership scenario, Jessie is an adult who can be coached to achieve better quality in her work. This is not what her manager conveys. As a result, Jessie misses the positive feedback and only hears the words that follow the but in the middle. Communication is compromised, and growth is stunted. I am writing an entire book right now (stay tuned) on how to give employee 'reviews.'

Rather than coupling it with criticism, positive feedback must be given when we notice things are going well. After stating the positives, we must **be quiet** and let the positive statements stand alone. When corrections and criticisms come separate, they will be better received because there will be more trust.

Keep in mind that this style of communication—stating a positive before a negative—worked in the early days. This is no longer true, as its transparency diluted its effectiveness. People commonly acknowledge its role as a manipulation tool. Real, effective communication doesn't require manipulation.

Some of you are really smart. You will remove **but** from your vocabulary only to replace it with some fancier words you found in a thesaurus, such as however, nevertheless, although, yet. Same thing. Avoid them too.

Grammarians of the world unite! I know in English class we were told to use the word "but". I understand that technically it might be grammatically more perfect to use but. Are you speaking to win a grammar award or to be heard?

Say these outloud.

> *I do see value in starting the meeting at 9:00 am; but, most people commute and need to come in at 10am.*

I agree with the value in starting the meeting at 9:00am, and our commuters need to come in at 10am.

Hear the difference? Same thing—I just am not telling the person they are wrong. Of course, only say I agree if I agree.

I moved from Doraville, Georgia to Sacramento California when I was nine years old. Miss Sane, my fifth grade teacher was in shock by how advanced I was in school. She wanted to move me ahead to Junior High. Instead she had me tested for the gifted program with a beautiful young Asian woman who's name I do not remember.

During the test this woman asked me all sorts of questions. English was a second language for her and we had difficulty understanding each other. It made us laugh and made the test take a lot longer than usual. She explained to me that in her native tongue they never verbally said BUT because it implied conflict. I still remember that lesson today. Remove the conflict SIGNAL words from your vocabulary.

But, Though, Actually, Yet, However, In my experience, you are wrong—they all mean the same thing.

Use <u>AND</u> instead of but. The sentence will get your point across without the offensive Neon Sign Of Disagreement that triggers reduced listening.

CHAPTER 35:
OTHER VIRUS WORDS

It isn't fair—but got its own chapter! Yes, there are other words that reduce listening too.

You

Quite often, "you" is a verbal finger point. We do not like when people point fingers at us, nor do we like know-it-alls. When we use "you" we imply the other person is other. Communication becomes a verbal us against them, and us against them means we are wearing different colored jerseys and therefore we must disagree.

I hate the word you, and I struggled with my editor over its use. I believe we is much more powerful tool in communication. I believe we denotes more inclusive language. Even though I am an "expert" I am still a part of we. "We need to treat customers like royalty" versus "You need to treat customers like royalty." Hear the difference. The word "you" makes it sound like a statement of blame, as in you are not treating the customers like royalty.

You sounds like an accusation even if you don't mean the "you" standing in front of you.

Always and Never

When we are frustrated or emotional, we tend to exaggerate. In conversation, the moment a person starts using words like, always, every time and never, it is a neon-sign that they are agitated and not really listening. They have moved toward a less effective speaking pattern. The other party reduces listening and starts thinking of times that negate the always or never over generalizations.

Sir and Ma'am

The words Ma'am and Sir have lost their positive connotation in contemporary communication use. Retail clerks use them when they are dealing with a hostile customer because keeping their job prevents them from using the word they really want to say. It is a rare human who can use ma'am and sir without it being a neon sign of disagreement.

Basically & Honestly

To be honest, blah blah blah. The other person thinks, "So, you're being honest with me now, are you?" Basically the person wonders if you forgot to think before you spoke. Get my point? These are filler words that don't serve much purpose other than to convey that the speaker is not quite sure about what he or she is saying.

Actually

Like basically and honestly, actually can mean disagreement or, when overused, be just plain annoying to listen to.

Can't

When we say "can't" the other person hears "won't". Can't is a fast track to a negative listening response. One way to avoid this undesirable result is to think in terms of what you can do when turning down a request. This is not about sugarcoating—it is about delivering your message clearly and positively so hackles don't go up.

I can't put pickles on your burger Sir.

vs

Here is what I can do, I will give you a ton of pickles on the side.

That is interesting

This was a great idea a couple of decades ago. Now folks know that "that is interesting" means, I disagree with you.

You are wrong

Giant Huge NEON sign to reduce listening.

If there was a way to …

…keep your phone costs down, you'd want to know about it wouldn't you? This one is tired and manipulative. Don't use it.

I appreciate your concern for…

This worked once. It has been over used and now causes hackles. "I understand" is the same thing. You might as well say, "I appreciate your concern for quality, which is why we are taking so long to finish this sentence." (wink)

I'd like to over explain here to make sure you get it. Using these words is like erecting a giant neon sign over your head that says, "HEY, please start formulating your response right now and reduce your listening. I am disagreeing with you!"

Certain words have more weight than other words, so be mindful in your communication.

CAN TRUMPS CAN'T

Sid stops by Richard's office and drops a pile of work on his desk. "Hey Rich, I need this by Monday. Thanks."

Richard already has way too much work to do. It is Friday and department heads have been dumping work on him all morning. With all the work piling on his desk, Richard begins to fear that he'll have to give up his weekend plans—and even then the work might not get completed.

So what does he do?

The Can't Way:
Richard looks at Sid and says, "Sorry man, I can't help you."

Sid's hackles go up, "Hey man, what do you mean can't? The Thompson account is counting on us and there is no I in team! Your job depends on it."

Sid walks away, and Richard picks up the phone to call his wife about missing dinner, the weekend and the wedding. He thinks under his breath, yeah buddy, there isn't an I in team—where'd you learn that, a management seminar? There may not be an I, there is a Me. Richard holds a grudge against Sid for the next seventeen years.

The Can Way:
Richard looks at Sid and says, "How exciting Sid. The Thompson account is going to be live again. Now, I'm here most of the weekend to keep the Brown account happy, I can have Thompson done by Tuesday at 5pm, how does that sound?"

Sid's hackles stay down and he says, "Forget about the Brown account. This one is more important—get it done first."

As Sid starts to walk away, Richard says, "Hold on Sid. Let's get Ben on the phone and clarify so we are both not left in the ringer if I drop Brown."

Richard calls Ben. "Hey Ben, Richard and Sid here. We have two projects competing for my time: Brown and Thompson. I have eight hours to put into one of them; they both need ten. What's your call?"

Bob says, "Drop the Brown account."

Richard says, "Got it. Let's get Janet in on this conversation so she hears from you that I am not going to work on her deadline."

Richard conference calls Janet, "Hi Janet, Richard, Sid and Bob here.

I've been told to focus on the Thompson account rather than the Brown account this weekend. I'll step off the call and let you and Bob work out the Brown timeline. Have a great weekend gang. I like chocolate donuts if you feel like sending some around on Sunday. "

Reality Check:

Richard comes in on Sunday afternoon. There are two files on his desk with a note: "Rich, I know you can do both. I believe in you. —Bob"

Richard gives Bob a call at home right away, "Hey Bob. I received your note. I have just enough time to handle the Thompson account and didn't know our Friday discussion had changed. Let's call Janet."

Get the gist? Over communicate in an upward spiral rather than a downward spiral. It is HOW we say it—not what we say. Being upbeat and over communicating will make the difference.

Super Reality Check:

Bob may not be a great person to work for if he constantly avoids direct communication and leaves cute little sticky notes basically saying "What I said on the phone Friday about this wasn't true. I was just avoiding conflict. You can do both. It doesn't matter to me if your personal life suffers."

I get that some of us are forced to work for folks like Bob. Does a great leader meet Richard at the firm on Sunday with chocolate donuts and say, "We are in a pickle. We must take care of both accounts—I led you astray. How can I help?" NO! A great leader calls Richard back right away on Friday afternoon and tells him the same thing. (If it absolutely must be done.) AND brings chocolate donuts on Sunday.

Begin with what you can do and move the conversation toward a strengthened relationship.

CHAPTER 36:
DILUTION WORDS: SAVE YOUR OPINION FOR THE END OF THE SENTENCE

If we start out sentences with our opinion, it puts the other party immediately into response mode. Response mode reduces listening.

Avoid using these phrases at the beginning of a sentence or at all:
- You are wrong.
- I disagree with you.
- I see it another way.
- You aren't seeing it right.
- If you'd just read the history.
- From my experience.

Using any of these phrases is tantamount to saying: I'm about to disagree with you, so go ahead and formulate your response to what you think I'm saying instead of listening to what I'm actually saying. Got that?

To illustrate the point, imagine this communication scenario:

"You are wrong Susie. The best way to land this account is actually to offer a lower price."
(Susie stops listening at the end of the first sentence.)

or:

"Susie, you are right about people being focused on the service level. In my experience…"
(I caught ya! You thought I was going to tell you to say "in my experience." Never. "In my experience" is another way of saying, hey stupid, I'm right and you're wrong!)

try this:

"Susie, I agree with you about customers having different buying motives. Price is often the only way we can get them to answer the door. How about if we give a competitive price and lead with how much time the customer is going to save when they implement our system…"

What is my opinion on the helmet law? Remember my story about Gary? Do you know for sure what it is?

Because I didn't put my opinion first, the entire room was listening to what I said. Had I put my opinion first, half the room would have begun formulating their response instead of listening to why I believed what I believed. You still don't know.

Communicate to be heard rather than to express opinions.

CHAPTER 37:
DILUTION WORDS:
THE OTHER BUTS

I have a friend who knows more about Middle Eastern politics than anyone I know. The man can really explain the history of the conflict in terms that a person can understand and also have a healthy debate.

My friend also has a tendency to use modifiers and generalized statements that decrease listening. Sitting around a campfire, I heard my friend say to an eager crowd of young liberals thirsting for more information about the Middle East, "If people would just read the history, they'd know what I am talking about." Folks started fighting him on his assertion they did not read history. Then he interrupted, "People just don't want to face the facts."

From that moment on, everyone fought him on his statements and stopped listening to his intelligent opinion on the Middle East. After hours of this heated—and not by the fire—debate, it became clear that most everyone agreed with his assessment, once they waded through their personal offense at his generalized statements.

Even though words are only about 7 percent of the communication pie, there are some powerful words that can constructively influence the actual ratio of listening to the message being presented.

Modifiers, brash assumptions and generalized statements about the audience will alienate people and reduce relationship and listening. Stop accusing and start communicating.

CHAPTER 38:
DILUTION AD NAUSEUM

There are other words that dilute your message. I call these the wishy washy words because they weaken your communication and make you appear manipulative and fake, especially when you overuse them.

I get the most conflict when I teach this stuff. It is usually from the guy in the back left-hand corner with his arms crossed. He has been taught to not say things directly to give people the feeling they have a say in what is going on.

It worked in the 70's when no one knew the system, now it just waters down our effectiveness.

These phrases and words are:
- I think...
- I feel...
- I believe...
- If...
- I want you to...
- We need to...
- You said...(repeating what you heard).

In the 70's we created a communications paradigm using phrases like "I think" and "I feel" to water down the aggressiveness of our communication. Listen carefully: it doesn't work anymore! Once people catch on, these phrases lose their effectiveness. Putting "I think" in front of a sentence now means there is room for doubt.

In the 70's women were moving up the corporate ladder and starting to sit at the table in boardrooms. Someone thought it was a good idea to teach men to water down their 'powerful' statements by putting "I think" in front of the sentence. It is offensive now. I am strong enough to just take your thoughts on the matter without you watering them down with "I think". I know you think it. You are saying it.

For example, take these two sentences.

I think we need to end the war in Iraq.

Really? You think so? Or isn't it better to state,

We must end the war in Iraq.

Saying I think , I feel, if or I believe means there is another equal option. Start making bold statements:
- *If you vote for me...* (if?) becomes: *When you vote for me...*

- *I'd like to be that president...*(so would a lot of people!) becomes: *I'll be that*

President…

- *I believe we should abandon our manufacturing of the buggy whip*—becomes: *We must abandon our manufacturing of the buggy whip; the horseless carriage is removing our market.*

- *I want you to take out your business card and give it to another person in the room*—becomes: *Take out your business card and give it to another person in the room.*

Proper use of I think, I believe, I feel

- *I think we should turn left* (if you are unsure which way to go).

- *I believe I can fly* (This is also the title of a great song. It is effectively saying "I Believe"; the song is a powerful expression of faith and belief).

- *I feel hurt by your comment that I am making this all about me.*

Wishy-washy words reduce effectiveness and listening.

CHAPTER 39:
TONE DOWN THE ATTITUDE

Tone is everything. Even without saying the actual words, people often call each other names with their degrading or disrespectful tones. There is a wide palette of tones, such as sarcastic, passive aggressive, cold and calculating, ridiculing, and so on. You know when this neon sign is flashing at you.

I often see the passive aggressive tone being used during conflict in the professional arena. This is the one where the person slows down his speaking, pauses a lot and gets a ridiculing smirk on his face. It is a dead give away. If you do it, stop now. Everybody is on to you.

When you pretend you are calmer and switch into so-called "professional mode", it doesn't work either. Calmer cannot be faked. You are either calm or you are not. The false calm reminds me of the scariest kind of serial killers—the ones who continue to talk nice while they hack you to bits. Try not to be a serial killer.

When I was a young woman, I was leading a meeting about a controversial topic. One of the attendees kept addressing me in sarcastic and degrading tones. I continued to be clear and kind in my communication, and finally the attendee lost his cool and called me a "bitch" in front of everyone. I looked at him and said, "You know, you may be right. We can talk about that after the meeting. The real issue here is not a personality trait of mine—it is whether we want to do something to protect our businesses from…" The room burst out in applause.

Everyone was suffering from his neon sign of disagreement, and we were all relieved when his disrespectful tone was put to rest.

Do you like when folks are passive aggressive or placating? Neither does anyone else. This hurts relationship. **A reduced relationship reduces listening. To change a mind, make a sale or change the world: We must first be heard.**

Uber-professional tones reduce relationship. When in conflict, communicate the same way you do with your friends on a good day. There is no reason for verbal and physical requests that reduce listening.

Watch your tone.

◉ EXAMPLE:
THE VERBAL EQUIVALENT TO THE HAND IN THE ELBOW GESTURE

Political campaigns are wrought with opinion. Part of my job is to give my view and let the campaign team make a decision based on their candidate and their plan.

One of my clients was coming in for a second meeting. This candidate brought the campaign manager and two more team members. I requested everyone be present for the communication coaching so it would become a campaign thing—not a candidate thing.

At one point, I mentioned to the campaign manager an idea I had about the bio on the website for the candidate. The bio started with the candidate's history as an executive in the hedge fund industry. At the time, the newspapers were frothing about a hedge fund short-selling scandal, and every day some new negative piece of information emerged about the hedge fund industry. So, I suggested, given the current climate, I'd start with another place in her bio. Yes, include the hedge fund industry, just don't lead with it.

The Campaign Manager was visibly ticked. Her face got red. She leaned forward with a very negative expression and tone. The two other people in the room held their breath. I could see it coming.

> *"That is interesting, Christina." She seethed. It is hard to describe the venom in her voice. She was clearly angry. She spoke slowly and deliberately, "I appreciate your, uh, what shall we call it, intuition [said with disdain], we have done research with the experts [said like a snakebite], our information clearly indicates you are wrong. Thank you for your thoughts. I appreciate them."*

The entire room held their breath. Her team was frozen. I laughed and said, "Intuition trumps data." I said this in a friendly tone and then went on to talk about other things. Not angry. Not bruised.

The point of this story is not about me being right nor about what the experts claim. In fact, she may be 100 percent right in her poorly communicated assertion (though she's lucky I heard her!)—that is not the issue. I am perhaps unimportant. Her candidate is the one who will suffer. Why? Her team will not tell her the truth. They are afraid of her wrath.

Her candidate will lose elections because of this communication style. Her team will not tell her what they really think—they will not tell her if there is spinach in the candidate's teeth for fear of losing their job and losing her respect. This will happen time and time again until she learns to accept and appreciate conflict and contrary opinions.

Here is how it must go :

> *"Have you seen the newspapers lately? I suggest you do not lead with the hedge fund industry, as it is garnering a lot of negative press right now."*

> *"Really. Tell me more about that…"*

Responding to a contrary opinion with an inquisitive "tell me more" attitude will result in stronger relationships and better data. When we close ourselves off to new information we end up investing all our money into an Edsel or the last buggy whip company.

I need to repeat the point of this chapter. When we are offensive in the way we receive new information, we will reduce the new information we get. We may then step in front of a bus and no one will stop us for fear of reprisal. Not good!

Meet contrary opinions with a happy desire for more information. Ask questions.

HACKLES AND NEON SIGNS

It is hard to describe tone in a written document. The example below can be misconstrued if read in the wrong tone.

Bill: *Hey Carla. I noticed that while I was speaking during the meeting yesterday, you were writing emails on your Blackberry. It felt like what I was saying was not important. Was it?*
- If Bill speaks the above in a casual, non-accusatory tone, Carla is more likely to listen. The moment we say YOU in a sentence, folks will take it as accusation. By asking a question, Bill brought the tone (and Carla's hackles) down.

Carla: *Bill, I use my Blackberry to take notes, I wasn't checking emails.*
- Is this true? Is she lying? Bill might think he knows. If he actually saw an email screen, now is the time to let her know. He needs to choose how important this conflict is at this point: Should he go in for round two or set an agreement regarding future protocol?

Bill: *Ok Carla. At the next meeting, please inform everyone that you are taking notes on your Blackberry so others know you are listening to them. Sound good?*
- To keep the team together, Bill decided to drop the email screen question and take his issue to the higher cause. Maybe the story ends there or maybe not.

Carla: *I don't think it's necessary Bill. You are the only one who noticed.*
- Bill must decide how to react.

Bill: *You are wrong Carla. Others noticed, and it hurts our team.*
- This is direct and isn't sugarcoating, though I doubt if Bill would purposefully give Carla a NEON sign. By starting his comment with "you are wrong", Bill puts Carla into response mode, and she stops listening. She may not even hear the team part. So perhaps Bill could respond this way:

Bill: *Perhaps I am the only person who noticed, and maybe everyone noticed. Let's not take the risk of damaging the team's communication by neglecting to mention it.*
- Speak in terms of benefits—not accusations. As a manager Bill could add a goalpost comment such as "Carla, you want to run this department some day, and we want to make sure the team knows you are a good listener."

I am still a little ruffled by Bill ignoring the lie if there was one. Once I saw an employee emailing during a staff meeting, and I simply stopped and addressed it on the spot, asking "Carla" if the email she was checking could wait? Avoidance is sometimes a long term tactic and other times it's conflict avoidance. Tone really matters in these situations. Having a truly light heart sets tone and keeps communication flowing.

See conflict as an opportunity to improve your relationships. Realize that sometimes you will have find the joy in crawing on your belly over broken glass to understand the other human better.

Speak in the same tones you do when you talk about the weather or some other neutral subject. Talk to the person in the same way you talk to your closest friends. Do not fall into the trap of changing your tone during conflict. This is a neon sign that tells folks to get ready for a fight.

To truly build relationships Bill needs to know what Carla wants to be—what her goals are. The moment Bill becomes a coach rather than a superior the more likely Carla will respond. More about that in the next book.

To have a great tone—loosen your grip on control and anger.

CHAPTER 40:
PRINCESS PISSY PANTS WILL CREATE MORE WHOOPS

I am running a new business, serving on a couple of boards, raising a toddler, teaching at a preschool and traveling way too much. And guess what: Today I am stressed. Five minutes is a really long luxury of time in my world.

I have folks working with me who handle my calendar, appointments and everything I do. If they save me five minutes, I have more time to write and teach.

As a start-up company with multiple roads to carve, we are all carrying multiple responsibilities. We have full calendars, long to-do lists, and many people to call back. Mistakes happen. Here are a few:

- I arrive at an event and do not have the phone numbers for the contact person.
- I do not have the confirmation number to check-in to my flight on-line.
- I find out ten-minutes before I am to teach that the title of the presentation is different from what I have on my information sheet.
- The wrong teaching materials are packed in my bag.
- A giant bottle of dish soap (used in one of my exercises) explodes in my bag from the air pressure.
- I have no business cards.

Being frustrated over mistakes does nothing for anyone. Having a positive attitude does. I have a mantra: RALLY. When a mistake happens I say this mantra in my head:

RALLY, RALLY, RALLY...

Innovation comes from adversity. When a mistake happens, I make the best of it in the moment. Then, I set about creating a process to ensure the mistake doesn't happen again. Thus, my second mantra (after I've rallied) is:

I am surrounded by great talented people. Our processes need some work.

Every mistake is an opportunity to fix something.

Please understand, adopting a positive mantra is critical. The first twenty-eight seconds of the situation, I am FRUSTRATED. I start making assumptions about my team and begin hurling myself down a stupid, destructive path.

Then comes RALLY, RALLY, RALLY. It works. I rally. The situation turns around, and things work out great in the end. Then I devote time to creating a better process, and I shoot off an email to my team, outlining the corrective process I have come up with, and hopefully keep the mistake from ever happening again.

Of course, my team wants to over-apologize, feeling bad and imagining I am really upset with them over their mistake. I always circle back and say, "I am not fussed"—reiterating how this mistake helps us make better processes for the future.

Bad processes destroy confidence over time. Great and talented people will start to become the opposite of what they are because of a bad process. And this is a different topic—for now, I gotta get back to being a great communicator.

Anger and frustration over mistakes often results in more mistakes and less magic. Find a way to toss the frustration and get back to building a solution.

CHAPTER 41:
INTERRUPT ME,
WILL YOU?

We have all had a brilliant or conflict-trumping thought in the middle of a heated conversation. Sometimes we bide our time until the opportunity to speak arises. More often we blurt out our thought, whether someone else is talking or not. While it is hard to contain passionate feelings, such interruptions escalate conflict and reduce listening.

Pay attention to two things:

- **Am I being interrupted?**—Notice when you're being interrupted and take a breath and interrupt your own natural response to interruptions. Then you can still be calmed, relaxed and a great communicator.

    Hey Walter, can I say something really quick? I really want to hear what you have to say and understand your point of view. One thing I know about me is when I am interrupted, I tend to get my hackles up and stop listening as well. Let's start over. I'll let you finish—you let me finish. Okay?

- **Am I interrupting?**—Notice when you are interrupting. Say something about it. Call attention to it and ask for help to stop.

    Hey, I just interrupted you. How rude of me. I'm really sorry. Please go ahead and finish your thought.

Oh, and one other thing. Stop judging people for interrupting. They may have learned to communicate in an environment which required them to interrupt if they wanted to be part of the conversation. It is how they survived. They don't mean to be rude. Talk to them about it when things are groovy—i.e., when they are happy and not interrupting.

Notice interruptions as they occur and call attention to them in a clear and understanding manner.

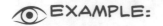

AIKIDO THAT ATTACK

Translated as "the way of harmonious spirit", *Aikido* (ahy-kee-doh) is a Japanese martial art developed by Morihei Ueshiba as a synthesis of his martial studies, philosophy and religious beliefs. Ueshiba's goal was to create an art practitioners could use to defend themselves without injuring their attacker.

Consisting primarily of body throws and joint-locking techniques, aikido emphasizes joining with an attack and redirecting the attacker's energy, as opposed to meeting force with force. It is more than physical fitness, as it also accentuates mental training, controlled relaxation and development of spirit (or *ki* in Japanese).[5]

Aikido is a wonderful metaphor for communication. Even if you are an aikido communication master, you will encounter disruptive and hurtful communication thrown at you from others. Great communicators must choose which attacks to confront, which ones to let wash over them, and which ones to akido and use for good.

> *Talulah was the first female and the youngest person to serve as the President of a national trade association. It was her first public appearance as President, and she was nervous. Everything was going fine until a controversial topic came up, and the group fell into a heated debate. Tempers were high, and listening fell by the wayside. One member dominated the floor, and kept interrupting others. For the third time that morning, Talulah used her gavel and interrupted Mel as he spouted his opinions. She braced herself, and, this time, she stated an unpopular opinion:*
>
> *"I disagree with you Mel, if we are going to sustain our industry, we need to put some money into consumer protection."*
>
> *"Talulah, you are being an inexperienced moron," replied Mel.*

Not surprisingly, the room erupted in a collective gasp. Talulah had a few options in response—confront, ignore, aikido. Which one would you use?

Confront
"Mel, It is not okay for you to call anyone here names. Let's keep it professional."

Ignore
"Mel, the legislators will continue to attack us until we do something REAL that protects consumers in our state. This bill does that."

Aikido
"Mel, you may be right about that. We can discuss my inexperience at the

bar after the meeting. The real issue is how we can sustain our businesses with all the negative attention directed at us by the public. This bill will…"

or

"Mel, the legislators agree with your assessment of me. In fact, they think the same of everyone in this room. This bill will transform the negative opinions about our industry and…"

If you think quick on your feet, aikido is always the right response to an attack. Later in this book we talk about how to practice aikido moves in communication.

Ignoring an attack is for chumps and those stuck in the 80's. Make the attack work for you and use it for good.

CHAPTER 42:
DO YOU REALLY NEED TO TELL THEM THE BABY IS UGLY?

In conflict, setting priorities in truth telling is the ultimate challenge. A great communicator chooses the most important things to discuss and lets the others go.

It is infeasible and undesirable to address every nuance of a moment. Most conversations are ongoing and long-term, and they must be treated as such. When we try working out every detail of a conflict at once, we lose our effectiveness. Sometimes in the heat of battle, it is best to take a break and come back to the conflict when hackles are down.

> *Tom, you never listen to me! I always have to remind you to pick up the dry cleaning, and I am sick of it. Ever since we met you have treated me like a maid. It is time you grow up little boy and start taking responsibility for this family. I will not be your slave. I must be some sort of chump for putting up with this!*

There are so many things to respond to in this paragraph. Tom has every right to jump in and point out a few things, such as:

NEVER—This a word that is rarely true and certainly not in the example above. Tom can easily counter that point: *If I never listened to you I wouldn't have heard what you just said.*

ALWAYS—Another dyno-word, easily refuted when Tom references the Tuesday three weeks prior when he picked up the dry cleaning without being reminded.

EVER SINCE I MET YOU—A maid? He can point out that time three months ago when he scrubbed the house from floor to ceiling.

TIME TO GROW UP—Tom can cite examples of how responsible he actually is, such as how he pays his share of the bills on time, how he cares for their daughter and how he changes the oil in her car.

SLAVE—Tom can talk about the ways *he* is actually the slave, such as changing the oil in the car, retiling the kitchen floor and cleaning up the dog poop.

CHUMP—This is a real blow. He can talk about how *he* is really the chump and clearly they should get a divorce right away!

Tom thinks about what his wife is really saying and decides to be the clearest communicator he can in the moment:

> *You're right Claire. I understand why you are mad. I don't know why I keep*

forgetting to pickup the dry cleaning. I'll go get it right now and put next week's pick up date in my calendar so I'll remember. How's that sound?

Great communicators know how important it is to be heard, and they make their decisions accordingly. Tom may still feel bugged about being called names, and, if he doesn't air his feelings, he may build resentments that will come out in future arguments. Being a good communicator, Tom doesn't vent his frustration over name calling when hackles are up. Instead, when things are calm, he brings up the ugly baby in a different way.

Hey Claire, I've been thinking about the fight we had earlier, remember the one about me being a dope and forgetting the laundry again? I wonder if we can work on name calling. I've been bugged since that conversation about the slave comment. Can we both work on not calling each other names? I don't want to teach little Karlie to copy our behavior.*

**Of course, Tom needs to say this in his own words—rather than follow my script!

Set up agreements before a fight on how both parties are going to help each other increase listening.

CHAPTER 43:
DON'T PRETEND YOU ARE NOT MAD

Conflict is generally uncomfortable, especially when hackles are up and we are flashing neon signs of disagreement. Conflict becomes even more uncomfortable when we pretend we are not upset and revert to a hyper-controlled manner of speech.

Do not pretend you are not mad. Accept it. Call attention to it. And also recognize that you may be too upset to really listen. If so, ask for a break and clear your head:

> *You are important to me. I want to hear what you have to say. I am also really upset about this, and my hackles are up. I am not listening as intently as I could, and I fear I am missing what you are trying to tell me. Can we take a ten-minute break? I'm going to run around the block and come back willing to listen to your point of view. How does that sound?*

If this sounds weird and unnatural to you, try something else:

> *I am very angry that humans are allowing toxic substances to be used in creating children's toys. I am looking to this legislative body to help protect the six million toddlers in our state from unsafe toys. Will you help me protect them?*

If this sounds too direct:

> *Clearly, I am upset about this. It is really difficult for me, and I want to resolve the issue. Can we talk about it?*

When I allow myself to stay angry at someone over a period of time, my frustration leads to poor communication that will ebb away at the relationship. To cleanse myself of such destructive anger, I am honest about my anger and look for positive ways to clear my head and get it out in the open. Mantras are very helpful. Depending on the situation, I use:

- Rally.
- Listen for the gems.
- What if they are right. Find out.
- Loosen my heart.
- Usually the more irritated and defensive I am, the more likely they have a point.

Pretending you are not upset when you really are blocks true communication.

CHAPTER 44:
IF SOMEONE SNAPS YOUR BRA, SAY SOMETHING ABOUT IT

I hesitated to put this one in here, though I think it is especially important for the female professionals—many of whom have been taught to ignore inappropriate behavior! Sometimes we simply must confront the other person and hit them on the nose with a rolled up newspaper. When we avoid confrontation, we are not great communicators—we are chumps.

Years ago, a highly regarded man in my industry grabbed my boob in front a bunch of people. I was so shocked I simply walked away and avoided him from that moment on. I never said anything. It still bothers me. Several people saw it—no one said or did anything.

Every time I was in a room with this man, I threw daggers his way. He mortified me. I also worried that the people who witnessed his act assumed I was his girlfriend. When his wife contacted me to say something at his funeral, I lied and made up a silly excuse. People were angry with me for declining to speak at his funeral. It seemed I was important to him.

This wasn't the first inappropriate situation to come my way. As a young female executive in the 1980s, I received a number of rude innuendos and salacious gestures. It got so obnoxious that I couldn't ignore it any longer. The solution I came up with is direct, simple and very effective. I'll describe it in a story:

> *The Masher Senator and I were the only two people riding in an elevator at the Capitol Building. I had heard about this guy, so I was ready when he moved toward me and peered down my shirt in a hunt for cleavage. (I was a slight young woman, and he had to look hard.) Then leaning into me, he put his arm on my arm and asked if I wanted to go out for a drink. Gross.*

> *"WHAT are you doing?!" I said in a loud mother voice with direct eye contact.*

> *"NOTHING!," he yelped as he quickly snapped his arm away and moved to the other side of the elevator.*

Invoking a strong maternal voice works every time. It keeps you from being a victim and puts the other person on their heels. They respond as if they are five years old and being scolded by their mother.

If someone is coming at you with a knife, admiring the beauty of the handle will do nothing for you. Great communicators do not allow anyone to stab them.

You must tell people to get off your foot if they are stepping on your toe!

CHAPTER 45:
OH! IT'S YOU AGAIN

If it has happened once, chances are it will happen again. Every communication is an opportunity to practice for the next one. Use your experience with similar situations to create stock solutions—what I call pre-solutions—for common communication experiences.

When you devise ways to respond to common misunderstandings or errors, you can enter into communication and negate conflict with more confidence. I am not suggesting you craft messages that avoid responsibility; instead, come up with a message that helps the other person stay open to communication.

For example, if Joanna's passion is frequently being mistaken for anger, she can offer a pre-solution at the first sign of misunderstanding:

> "I'm sorry if my intensity is overwhelming, Trevor. Imagine what it is like being me! Please do not mistake it for anger."

As she develops relationships with people, they will see this is truly how she is.

Often organizations have conflict patterns that arise over and over again, such as team members not cleaning up the conference room or neglecting to pick up the phone when the receptionist is on the other line. Pre-solutions work because we have the discussion before there is a problem. People are better listeners before there is conflict.

Pre-solutions are smart in public speaking too. You already know the questions you don't want to answer. Figure out how to answer them now—before the question comes from the audience. You know it will!

Prepare ahead of time for all potential situations.

 **EXAMPLE:**

PRE-SOLUTIONS

As Stacey hung up the phone, her co-workers laughed and teased her about getting a call from "another customer who brightens the room by leaving it." It was the second time that week a client had called to yell and scream about charges on their bill—and it was only Tuesday! Why did they always call screaming?

Upon closer examination Stacey discovers why: Clients are angry because they signed a contract with a law partner and a junior attorney was working on their case. She decides that the firm should rethink its practice of using other attorneys on cases; the clients just don't like it. This situation is a perfect candidate for a Pre-Solution.

Stacey approaches one of the partners for more information. She asks him why the firm puts junior attorney's on cases negotiated with a partner. The partner explains that his billing rate is $600 per hour, so it is far more cost efficient for the client when a lower paid attorney handles the steps that require less expertise, such as doing research for precedents. This keeps the client's bills down considerably.

Stacey is glad she asked, as now she has the info she needs to create a pre-solution—one that will keep angry client calls away from her desk. During the relationship interview with a new client, Stacey introduces herself and explains their billing practices. One thing she made sure the client knew about was their cost saving measures:

> *When possible, our law firm uses junior attorneys in the firm to do the more basic research. This will keep your costs down and your quality up. You will see this on your statement. Please know that Mr. Ralson, a partner in the firm, is handling your case when his expertise is needed. It is our way of delivering superior results at a good price.*

A pre-solution is telling the client the firm's billing policy is a benefit to them— i.e., a positive—before there is an issue.

Create solutions to problems before they happen. Be ready.

CHAPTER 46:
CALL ATTENTION TO WHAT IS GOING ON IN THE ROOM

Decades ago I was watching a play, standing room only, with a good friend. He had gas. It was awful. He looked at me after a minute or two of the offending odor and said, "Wow. This is great! No one knows it is me!" I laughed. "Um. Sweetheart. Everyone knows it is you: You are the only person smiling right now." He looked around the cabaret floor and noticed everyone else was grimacing and gagging. Whoops.

Pretending is not an option for great communicators. Whether it is pretending to be someone else, pretending we aren't upset, or pretending a situation isn't happening, we won't do it. It is simply against our better judgment.

Years ago, I took a class to become a minister. A woman in the class, Marty, said something that I bring to every meeting, communication or relationship:

I don't see you so don't pretend to be there.

What? This kind of veiled communication happens on a daily basis. We notice there is something going on in the room and we ignore it. Perhaps we are too afraid of conflict or don't want to embarrass anyone. Maybe we don't have time or couldn't care less. More likely we don't trust ourselves and fear that quizzical "what the heck are you talking about" look. So, instead of using our voices and stating the obvious, we stop listening and push on through.

Now you know. Trust yourself. Start talking about what is going on in the room. Often. You'll be amazed at how much brighter everything becomes. True, you might be wrong. Your assumptions about the feelings or motivations of others will be off base sometimes. It is okay, you've opened up the room for more honesty and discussion.

If you discover your assumptions about the room are wrong a lot, good. This teaches you to pay closer attention to your sensors. Perhaps you have outmoded patterns of communication that cause you to distrust or misread others. By expressing your observations, you learn to overcome these patterns and trust more freely.

Or

If your observations point to a sickness in the communication of the team, you can ask questions and try to get to the root of it. Often. It is true, people won't always fess up to the bigger issue. They may dodge and duck, insisting there is nothing else going on. Even in seemingly insurmountable situations such as these, you can pay attention to people's answers and listen with understanding.

With patience you may even find a door waiting to be pried open.

Or

If your observations are spot on, you can speak openly about them, in the same way you do with your closest friends. Trust that speaking your observations will make a difference. Remember, the way you say the words is as important as the words themselves.

Examples of calling attention to what is happening in the room:

- Hey, I notice the room got quiet all the sudden, what's up?

- Uh oh. Did I just offend you?

- Hi gang. I am late. It is rude. I am sorry.

- I am sensing I just said something wrong. Did I?

- I promised to have this to you by 3pm today. It is 11:30am right now, and I'm certain I won't meet that deadline. (Let them know before the deadline. Never let a deadline go by without saying something.)

- I sense this meeting is going on too long and everyone is getting bored. Am I right?

- Hey gang. We are on a tight deadline, and I feel our energy getting low. Will a five minute refresher break help? We gotta get this done.

- If you agree with everything I have said, one of us has a problem. Either you are drinking the Kool-aid and just going along with what you hear or I am not risking offending you by saying what I really think. (I use this one a lot to get folks debating.)

- We have been debating this issue for hours. Here's a 3x5 card. If you had to vote right now, what would you vote? Write it on the card. (I have done this over a hundred times and 95 percent of the time it ends the debate.)

- Honey, is this the wrong time to talk about this? I am sensing it is, though I might just be over-sensitive.

- Honey, I just bit your head off. Not okay. I'm sorry. (This one works great in relationships.)

Of course, there are a few key rules of conduct for calling attention to problems in the room. They should be obvious to you by now. Can you guess what they are?

- Speak in such a way that your ideas are heard.
- Be your natural self.
- Do not attack individuals nor the organization.

- Have pre-solutions to anticipated attacks on you and your policies.
- Practice questions beforehand.
- Listen carefully to what others have to say.
- Remain neutral and learn from your observations.
- Avoid using the word YOU.

Calling attention to what is going on in the room helps everyone. If someone is frustrated or annoyed, the room already knows it. We can shift this room-sucking energy by bringing up the elephant in a pragmatic, non-dramatic way. Remember—even with finely honed communication techniques and our best intentions—our efforts sometimes fail. Be prepared. Transparency may freak people out. That is okay. To become great communicators, we have to get used to transparency, especially when things get tough.

Verbally address any communication weirdness in the room.

EXAMPLE:

THE ARTCAR ATE MY HOMEWORK

A decade ago I ventured up to Point Arena, California to work on an art project. While I've long forgotten the details of the project, I clearly remember meeting a woman who breathed and walked artistry in her life.

She was sitting on the ground beneath a homemade jungle gym wearing a decorated bra on outside of her t-shirt. Her clothing was decorated with sewn fabric, and it was stitched to perfection. She was affixing shells and little pieces of beach glass onto a travel coffee cup. When she was finished, she stood and stretched and did some hanging yoga from the jungle gym. I watched in awe as she contorted her body and continued to talk with me in such an open way.

I have watched her transform the drabbest things into works of art. Her vehicle into bio-diesel artcar. A drunken mob into artisans. Words on paper into magic. I was lucky enough to get her to agree to be the editor of my book. We started our working relationship, and it continued to launch my ideas onto paper.

I am in a hurry, and I want to get this book done. I have been in labor with it for too long and need it out of me. A team member organizes a production meeting with the book team. Our editor calls in, and we are ready to move forward.

At the start of the call, our editor lets us know she went to the West Coast Artcar Fest instead of working on the edits. She had the audacity to take four days off! She hadn't realized that her finished edits were the reason for our meeting. She immediately apologizes, though her entire voice and energy go into feeling bad mode. The air is thick with ick.

This happens all the time in communication. Someone didn't know what the expectation was. Or the person did know and fell short of it. Or they tried to get there and feel they fell short of it. All too often, the person setting the expectations has an overwhelming desire to feel right about the other person being wrong. We want the other person to feel all the ways they have let us down.

Why? What does guilt and apology really do for anyone in such moments? When one person feels bad, everyone feels bad. In the example described above, the conference call became a totally different entity as she apologized. Everyone sat straighter and stiffer. One person stared at the ground, another out the window. We were not connecting. Tension took over.

Great communicators have a choice in situations like these. I have said it before, I will say it again: You can be happy or you can be right. As soon as I realized the ick was creeping in, I checked in with myself to determine if I was fussed about her playing hooky from her editing duties. Would my being fussed serve any purpose or work in the teams favor somehow? I thought about my editor's apology. It was genuine. She wanted to get the book done as much as I did.

The conversation momentarily drifted to other things, and I thought to myself, wait a minute—this entire book is about perspective. All my editor did was go out and get some perspective so she could swarm on the book. Frustration, anger, annoyance serve no purpose; such emotions only drag us all down into the muck and mire of defeat.

> *I interrupted the conversation, acknowledged her apology and got rid of the ick before it took everyone over. I told my editor and everyone on the call, "I am not fussed by the ArtCar Fest. I consider it perspective swarming. So now, let's just birth this damn book! No more wallowing in I'm-sorry-world." The mood immediately lightened up. We took a collective breath and abandoned the regrets and failings of the past. Only then were we fully present to be productive.*

Lamenting, worrying and being upset does not birth a baby. Pushing does. I have sat in countless meetings and watched CEOs, board chairs and team members—who just *have to be right*—go to great lengths to make the person in the hot seat feel bad for falling short of expectations. This is rarely the path to synergy and brilliance.

If I actually *was fussed* about something, of course I wouldn't sugarcoat it. If a person keeps stepping on my feet, I say ouch. Only I try to do so in a calm and clear way—even if they don't want to talk with me. Most of the time though, my minor annoyance pales in comparison to the work that needs to be done.

Call attention to the ick in a conversation. Deal with it right away. Have forgiveness. Move through and past it—verbally and energetically.

CHAPTER 47:
NEGATIVES ARE ALWAYS POSITIVES

A woman's organization surveyed its members to obtain feedback after a weekend event. On one of the surveys, a woman wrote, "Do not allow babies in the room. They are very distracting."

One of the speakers—a volunteer who gives at least twenty hours a week to the organization—brought her baby to the event. The baby was teething and having a tough day. Though in another room with her dad, the baby's cries could be heard muffled through the walls of the building.

The women reviewing the surveys were incensed. How rude! How dare she complain about a woman who volunteered to give up her weekend to be there and teach them something! The emotions escalated. Things got heated.

Fortunately, one of the board members stepped in and told the group to take a deep breath and remember that the survey was conducted to get opinions. She pointed out that this opinion was important and needed to be addressed without all the emotion. She looked at Carol and said, "Thank you for volunteering your time as a speaker, and I know this comment could be considered a slap in the face to you. We certainly don't want you to feel it speaks for everyone in the room."

This comment did speak to the greater issue—the issue this organization was formed to address: Being a woman in a professional world. For 86 percent of women, this means having children. Many women multitask in today's world, juggling jobs, social engagements, higher learning and childcare, and these women often have to make unpopular choices—like bringing a baby to a meeting.

With skill and careful listening, the board was able to see the unpopular survey answers as an opportunity to further define the organizations mission and role in the lives of its female constituency. Some questions came up:

- Should our organization be providing childcare to our members so they can attend these events?
- Should our organization draw attention to the reality that many women cannot afford nannies or steady childcare and therefore must bring their kids?
- Should our organization take a moment and directly address childcare options with members so folks understand what is taking place and how to deal with it?

With emotion out of the equation, the board was poised to take their organization to a whole new level. Instead of being angry with the woman who wrote this on the survey, we must embrace her for saying it.

They came to a consensus: If members (or speakers) had to make the choice between attending a session or not attending due to a lack of childcare, members should be encouraged to bring their children. The group agreed that if children began to distract the meeting, they'd call attention to it and try to mitigate before it was survey time. If children became an interruption, they would look into providing childcare for members in need. By handling the situation calmly, the women of the board were happy and closer because of their proactive stance.

To be clear, this conflict improved the organization. Because some woman had the guts to give her honest opinion on the baby in the room the organization developed its core belief about supporting women AND a policy of no talking about people when they aren't in the room. Thank you to the survey writer.

Conflict is good! The naysayer in the room is there to improve your message.

Life is an ongoing opportunity to improve relationships through positive and direct communication.

SAVE THE SPACE SHUTTLE

Scott loved California. As an engineer at the Nelson Corporation, Scott was transferred to the state and made responsible for inspecting microchips manufactured for the aerospace industry. His good friend Rob, a real party boy, had held the job before him; he told Scott the job was a cake-walk.

Standing in the clean room sporting a sterile white suit, Scott wiped a trickle of sweat off his forehead. He took a deep breath and acknowledged he was seeing a flaw in a late stage production item. As he reviewed several more chips, it became clear he'd stumbled onto a huge problem—one that would cost millions of dollars to remedy. His discovery might even destroy the project entirely.

Publicly acknowledging this problem now would cause a serious strain in his company, and it might cost Rob his job. Remaining silent about this obvious chip flaw could result in lost lives and a future space shuttle disaster. Scott made an easy choice.

In a rather heated meeting, Scott's boss and his friend Rob wanted to ignore Scott's discovery. They told him the company's responsibility ended the moment Luxan signed off on the chips last month. If the client didn't notice, it wasn't their responsibility anymore—the contract says so. By staying quiet, the company would save millions of dollars.

Scott was unbendable. He refused to have his name attached to such an error, and he went over his boss's head and revealed the error. In the short term, Scott lost two friends and his sweet deal out in California. In the long term, when Scott's written report of the chip flaw reached a top executive, the company chose complete transparency with their client.

In the end, good citizenship won out, and it became clear that client transparency was a core value for the Nelson Corporation. Scott was reinstated in California, and the entire lot of defective chips was destroyed. The project was delayed rather than scrapped. The client's order was eventually fulfilled, and the company continued to do business with Nelson.

As a result of this incident, the Nelson Corporation developed a training manual reflecting a philosophy of openness and disclosure. These training materials teach managers how to present bad news to a client. They also outline ways to address issues of quality with possible methods of correction and redress. Furthermore, all employees must sign a document requiring them to inform the CEO if anyone tries to cover up a mistake. Not only is this the moral thing to do, it also helps employees navigate difficult situations by circumventing the obvious pitfalls in company hierarchy. This way their corporate goals of quality and transparency are insured.

The right thing is the right thing—even if you lose your job because of it.

CHAPTER 48:
EXPRESSING CONCERN IN AN EMAIL IS LIKE A HANGNAIL

Avoid expressing concern by email.

The English language is full of traps for written misunderstanding. No matter how hard we work at clear communication, we must admit our language is simply set up wonky; there is no getting around it.

As this book is showing you, there are proven techniques to mitigate these misunderstandings and make your communication easier. Got a pen? Add this one to your list: Never express deep concern via email. Trust me, you are asking for trouble. Deep concern can be conveyed much more clearly face to face.

My sister and I email a lot, and I often find her response to my emails to be harsh or offensive. Nine times out of ten she doesn't mean them that way. If I call her and say, "hey what's up? Are you mad at me?" she'll be surprised at my interpretation. Sometimes I get her to read these emails out loud to me, and I am always amazed at how much more positive they sound in her voice. It isn't her writing that is the problem —it is my reading.

We can try extra hard to make sure our email isn't perceived negatively, and it still will be. Letting someone know they have fallen short of expectations—or that there is a problem—will be read without all the subtle nuances of positive relationship communication. What is meant as concern and caring can be misread as hostile and frustrated. And you know what happens when people perceive criticism and hostility: They don't listen.

And one more thing (though this one should be obvious): Express concern for another person directly to that person. Don't send an email and cc everybody who may have a stake in the issue. There is no reason to 'process' with co-workers or family-members. This is unfair to everyone and creates mistrust.

Stop copying everyone on the emails where you are pointing out a shortfall or misstep. Just stop sending these by email at all.

Avoid expressing concern through email—do it in person or by phone.

NO MATTER HOW MANY EMOTICONS YOU ADD, THEY WILL READ IT AS A COLON AND A LEFT PARENTHESIS

Smedley was interested in an arranged marriage over the internet. His wife died, and now he was raising six children all by himself. He wanted to meet someone who loved children and didn't have, or was unable to have, any of her own. He adamantly did not want any more children.

On the online service he subscribed to he met Tatiana. She seemed like a perfect fit, especially since it said right on her bio, "She cannot bear children."

It wasn't until she arrived that he learned the sad truth, "She cannot bear children." She can't tolerate them at all. In fact, she <u>hates</u> them. It turned out his six children hated her too.

Email will be misread. Period. Do not express concern or they will read :(when you meant :) and you will want a \-/.

CHAPTER 49:
MATCH OR EXCEED THEIR CONCERN FOR A PROBLEM

Mistakes happen. Things do not always go the way we plan. When a person complains or talks about their frustration over a problem, match or exceed their concern for the issue.

As you know, conflict arises when people don't feel heard. Even if they are being heard, they may not realize it if we don't adequately express our concern and understanding for the issue. When this happens, the hurt person may turn to yelling and screaming (and offending!) to get his or her needs met.

Or maybe we are just in the middle of someone else's bad day. We have all had a bad day and acted ridiculously.

Read the last two sentences again. Keep this in mind. Bad behavior does not always equal a bad person. We tend to forget that.

Instead of acting more calm (or using verbal neon signs like "sir" and "ma'am" to worsen the situation), try and match or exceed their concern. This only works when you truly share their concern:

> "Oh MY GOSH! That is NOT okay and NOT how we do business. How frustrating. Here is what I can do right now to address this issue for you."

Here's another example: Richard's team made a mistake. A client had asked them not to list an account, and not only did they list it, they contacted the account to collect the past due amount noted on the account. When the client contacted the company's client service department and let them know of the error, the rep was shocked and upset about the error. "This type of error is not okay, and I am very upset for you. You deserve better service, and I intend to make it right. Here is what we can do immediately…" The client interrupted and said, "Hey, mistakes happen. Relax."

It doesn't matter <u>how</u> someone is telling you they are upset, if they deserve to be upset, feel bad about them being upset. Emote a little Spock. Just because the message is wrapped up in barbed wire doesn't mean it isn't a message you need to hear.

Listen carefully for the emotion of the situation and, if you share it, show it.

POWERPLAYS CREATE
COMMUNICATION BLACKOUTS

Sitting at the breakfast table with his wife and two kids, Jeff flips through the paper grinning from ear to ear. It's been less than a year since he was laid off from his corporate job, and even though things got pretty scary financially at one point, he hit the mother lode with his new business venture. He couldn't believe his innovative idea was making him and his family wealthy so quickly. They'd paid off all their bills, paid off the house and set aside an amount equal to 50 percent of his old income into a college/retirement account. This was already a great day.

Meanwhile, Preston grumbles to himself as he logs onto the automated dialer system at the AVC Collection Agency. It just didn't seem fair to work on a Saturday morning; no one is going to be home anyway. His manager reminded him that he was 32 percent off his goal pace and that he better get some payments in full—Today!

Jeff jumps at the phone and quickly swallows his mouthful of cereal.

Jeff: *Hello?*

Preston: *[In an irritated voice] May I speak with Jeff Tomlin?*

Jeff: *You got him.*

Preston: *This is an attempt to collect a debt and any information obtained will be used for that purpose. We have a bill here for $516.32 for Amazon Dental. I am calling to get your credit card number for payment in full.*

Jeff: *Hold on there partner. Wasn't my insurance supposed to cover this?*

Preston: *[More irritated] Listen Sir, it is not my job to know your insurance policy. That is between you and them. The balance is due now, and the doctor has been waiting a long time for you to make good on your obligation. I am ready for that credit card number.*

Jeff: *You can appreciate that a person needs to first check with…*

Preston: *[interrupts him with a loud and indignant tone] Sir, your time to do all that was two months ago. Now you need to make good on your debt.*

Jeff: *What is your n…*

Preston: *[Again, loud and authoritarian] Pay the bill Sir!!!*

Jeff: *There is no need to get…*

Preston: *Pay the bill Sir or I will destroy your credit.*

Jeff hangs up the phone and tells his startled wife that no matter what happens they are NEVER to pay the dental bill. His sits down and writes a letter to the dentist telling him why. Preston doesn't reach his goal and loses his job and benefits, failing to recognize that if he'd communicated to Jeff in a clearer, calmer way, Jeff would have gladly paid the bill. Jeff had the money.

In this example, Preston is clearly a person who brightens the room by leaving it. We know not to communicate this way, don't we? If only! I have sat in meeting after meeting and watched humans, just like you and me (and sometimes maybe even you and me) communicate this way. People's hackles go up, and the group stops listening. This is not good communication.

People will harm themselves because they do not like a person. Jeff will ruin his credit rather than pay such a jerk. You must be careful in the way you communicate. Remember, people will do the opposite of what is good for them if they do not like you, feel manipulated by you or feel you are false.

👁 EXAMPLE:

A PROTON WALKS INTO A BAR (POSITIVE AGREEMENT)

A skill that works well for effective communication is something I call the "positive agreement."

I stumbled on it by accident. A friend I have known for a few years has an undeniably positive effect on people. He walks into the room and the people in it are immediately drawn to him— in a good way. This fascinated me, so of course I started paying attention to his speaking style. I didn't follow him around or anything, I just watched to see what it was he was doing that worked so well.

I began to notice that he always found something positive in what other people were saying. He had a genuine respect for others' opinions and this translated into a natural interest. He listened and responded affirmatively to things he agreed with, and let people know their ideas mattered. He never interrupted.

He did not manipulate others with fluffing accolades. This is transparent and offensive. Nor did he go through a laundry list of the things he agreed with. Instead he spoke in natural communication rhythm of positive agreement: He listened and responded verbally.

Here is an example to illustrate the details of positive agreement. Justin and Jasmine are talking with Bob, a consultant who will be leading their executive retreat. Jasmine is surprised to learn that she and Justin have a different concept for the function. It is imperative that they reach an agreement today so the retreat planning can move forward.

STRUGGLE	POSITIVE AGREEMENT
Bob: *Tell me your needs for the retreat.*	Bob: *Tell me your needs for the retreat.*
Jasmine: *Our executives need a complete makeover. They are not working well as a team and seem to argue over everything. We need this retreat to be a serious bonding session.*	Jasmine: *Our executives need a complete makeover. They are not working well as a team and seem to argue over everything. We need this retreat to be a serious bonding session.*
Justin: *I disagree. The executives just need some skills based learning around reading a balance sheet.*	Justin: *I agree with Jasmine. Our meetings tend to have a lot of disagreement. I wonder if some skills-based learning around basic business tools would help the team as well? Sometimes frustration happens when we all do not have the same tools to do the job. Jasmine, what do you think?*
Jasmine: *I am shocked you say this Justin! Have you failed to notice how silly our meetings are with everyone fighting...*	
Justin: *Jasmine, you always overreact. That's just the way boys are...*	Jasmine: *Hmm. I can see your point. I wonder if there's a way to do both?*
Jasmine: *[interrupting with an increasingly loud voice] What? I can't believe you just said that Justin. This is typical of this organization...*	Justin: *Great idea Jasmine. Do you agree that we need to craft the bonding portion to include some sort of skill-based learning so we don't lose them?*
(Now both people are behind their lines in the sand and not connecting or relating. The consultant sits back and wonders how to use this to his advantage.)	Jasmine: *That would be my worst fear. Let's come up with a plan. Bob, what can you offer?*
	Bob: *We can definitely work in both goals. I'll bring in one of my folks to do the balance sheet work and, when we are through, we can do skill learning exercises on communication and conflict.*

In the struggle scenario, Justin and Jasmine lob negative statements, peppering their conflict with neon signs like "always" and "never". Once we hear, "you always say things like that" or "you never listen to me" we know communication has disintegrated.

In the positive agreement scenario, Justin and Jasmine consistently back up their personal goals for the retreat with an affirmation of the other's wishes. This is an excellent tool and works brilliantly providing we really mean the positives we're stating. It takes practice to see things through a positive lens, and even more discipline to extract elements that we're genuinely positive about.

Some communications classes teach people to use this technique as a trick or tool. They encourage people to pretend to like something or to fake being interested. This is manipulation not positive agreement—it will not work. Only agree when you are truly in agreement with the basic tenor of what the other person says.

Let me say it again: For this to be effective we must truly search for what we like about what the person is saying and doing. If we decide to mention it—we can only do so if we truly believe it.

When someone is speaking, listen for the things you agree with and let them know.

CHAPTER 50:
SKIP THIS ONE IF YOU NEED TO BE RIGHT ALL THE TIME

The subject of this chapter is hard for some people to stomach. In fact, it might not be for you. I think you can handle it though. Perhaps you should go get an antacid first.

Are you ready? In the heat of battle—especially when conflict is mired in accusations and no one is listening—stop accusing and start looking for ways you are wrong.

What? Give in? Give them ammunition!? No way Christina! That is just bad strategy.

Not true. Take a look at the familiar examples from previous chapters, and you'll see how effective owning up to our faults can be. Imagine these communication scenarios:

- *"You know, now that I think of it, it was wrong for me to accuse you of checking email during the meeting. I shouldn't have assumed the worst about you when I know you to be a good listener. Let's inform everyone who was in the meeting that you weren't checking emails, just in case someone else in the room jumped to the same conclusion as I did. Okay?"*

  "Bill, I was checking emails, and I was also trying to listen to you. Bad habit. Thanks for telling me."

and

- *"You are right. I did forget to pick up the dry cleaning. That is not okay. I want to do better for us...."*

  "Oh my gosh! I just yelled at you over the dry cleaning! That is not okay. I don't think that was in our vows honey. I am sorry. You do so much, and I guess I am really frustrated by the insane amount of stuff on both of our to do lists. Remember back when we were in college and we could just hang out on the weekends? I miss that."

When you notice someone's hackles up, look for ways you may have triggered them. If you were wrong, admit it. Accept that they may use this against you, though chances are the other person will feel relieved by your honesty, and you will both grow as communicators.

Be outspoken about your failings.

CHAPTER 51:
LET THEM WIN

Yes, you heard me; I said let them win. If you are anything like me, this is a really hard thing to do. It's worth it, especially when arguing over trivial issues or at least about stuff less relevant to the bigger picture. You will be amazed at the positive communication shift that occurs when you simply let the other person have their perspective.

> *Sonny and Sandy were deep in an argument over who forgot to order the copier toner. They had a huge proposal due in one-hour, and the copier ran out of the precious liquid. After five minutes of blame, Sonny stopped, looked and Sandy and said, "You know what, you are right. Maybe I did forget to get the toner. How about I rush down to Kinko's and get the job done." Sandy stopped in her tracks—dumbstruck. "Hey, don't worry about it—it just as easily could have been me. I'll work on the graphs while you're gone. Thanks Sonny."*

The example above really happened (don't worry, I changed the names!). As Sonny shows us, it is far easier to just end the argument and work toward a solution. I do this one a lot in trivial situations. To repeat a favorite mantra, I'd rather be happy than right. Happy stops the argument.

Letting the other person win works wonders when backseat driving. Instead of telling the driver that I am right and he should have gone left, I just let it go. If he says, see I told you we should have gone right, I simply respond with something like, well, I'm glad you know where we're going. Then I distract us with a comment about the moon or the weather. Together, we let the water roll off our collective duck back. Of course, this only works if I am truly able to let go of my desire to be right.

We all have our tipping point. If letting someone be right stores up an arsenal of hackles, it's defeating the purpose. The reason? Unexpressed frustrations, i.e. stored hackles, have to come out eventually. Maybe not at that missed right hand turn; just watch out when they don't hear you ask them to pass the salt at the dinner table.

Letting them win can build great relationships and pave fantastic future conversations—providing you don't hold a grudge.

CHAPTER 52:
SPEAK DIRECTLY TO THE PERSON YOU'RE IN CONFLICT WITH

Processing a conflict with the person you are in conflict with is a great idea. Finding a disinterested third party to process with is not.

    Processing is gossiping.
    Venting is also gossiping.
    Gossiping is gossiping even if you only listen to it.

Gossiping is relationship deteriorating and thus reduces listening.

I can be 100 percent wrong about something and still find three people who'll tell me I'm right. They cannot know the full story if they only hear my perspective, so their opinion just doesn't matter.

I have a rule in my office. I will be a third party to a conflict if the person who comes to me truly wants to repair their relationship and needs my help in perspective. They must be honest as they talk with me, speaking in positives and looking for their own role in the conflict. Rule number two: At the end of our discussion, we invite the other person into the office so they know what is going on.

This type of transparency creates some uncomfortable moments, yes. It also lets everyone know that favoritism and backstabbing are not allowed.

Only talk about people when they are in the room. (The one exception is if you are saying an adoring thing or being interviewed by the police.)

When you are angry or in conflict with another person, tell them directly. Stop being a gossip.

CHAPTER 53:
BOXERS DO IT,
YOU SHOULD TOO

Ever been to a boxing match? I haven't. Though I do remember the movie *Rocky*, so I am familiar with a key element of the match: The bell rings and a break happens.

While conflict is not a boxing match, many of us make it that way. Remember, if the relationship is long-term, we do not want to knock out our opponent. We want to speak in a way that our thoughts and ideas are heard. Our goal is not to win; it is to communicate.

Remember: Hackles up, heels down.

When we find ourselves acting like we are in the ring during a conflict, we need to hear the bell. When we are unable to communicate to be heard, we need to hear the bell. When our body is rigid and we've stopped breathing, we need to hear the bell.

The bell says, "Hey you. Take a break will ya."

I call this the "round method" of conflict. You will come back to the discussion. You just need a little time to sit on the sidelines with your inner coach and get your head straight. Your words serve as the other person's bell too:

- *Hey, I have my feathers ruffled, and I am having a hard time listening. I want to hear what you have to say. Can we take a 15-minute break and come back together ready to resolve this?*

Listen for the bell (yours or theirs) and ask for a break. Only spit if someone has a bucket in front of you.

CHAPTER 54:
MAKE CONFLICT AGREEMENTS
WHEN EVERYONE IS HAPPY

This one seems so simple doesn't it? Have agreements about how things will go in conflict before there is a conflict. Let's look at the last example and imagine the other person doesn't want to take a break.

- *Hey, I have my feathers ruffled, and I am having a hard time listening. I want to hear what you have to say. Can we take a 15-minute break and come back together ready to resolve this?*

- *You always do that! I want to resolve it right now.*

- *Okay. Just know if you make me continue, I am not being a very good listener.*

Not exactly the desired outcome; even though the other person knows what state you're in, it doesn't really help you take a break. This is why, especially in close relationships, it is best to make agreements about conflict when things are going really great. Talk about how you handle conflict while you are sitting on the back porch watching the sunset, or over late night after work pizza.

> *Hey honey, I am in this relationship for the long term. When we are in a heated argument, I sometimes need to take a break in the middle. It helps me stop responding to you and start **listening** to what you are really trying to tell me. Can we agree now to take composure breaks when things get tough in future arguments or can we come up with another idea? What do you think?*

In my company we had a rule about interrupting. We all agreed that interrupting was rude and no one should do it. Well, we all know how forgetful humans can be, so after a while people started interrupting each other again. Irritation rose, and relationships suffered. When I observed an interruptee interrupting the interrupter to tell them they interrupted, I came up with a plan, and at the next staff meeting, I told a joke.

Christina: *Knock Knock.*

Staff: *Who's there.*

Christina: *Interrupting cow.*

Them: *Interrup…*

Christina: *(interrupting) MOO!!!*

Everyone laughed at my interrupting cow, and I suggested we start using "MOO" when we felt interrupted. The first few times we did this everyone laughed. The next few times we used it, people still laughed. It changed everything. We had agreed on something and found a fun way of dealing with it. When people heard MOO they knew to stop and it was fun. People were heard. Nobody was angry. What a reprieve!

Every new employee was taught the MOO lesson. It became a part of our corporate culture—and it improved our fun.

Talk about past conflict and errors in communication when everyone is sitting on the porch drinking mint juleps. It will be much easier (and more fun).

CHAPTER 55:
IS YOUR KILT LONG ENOUGH?
FLAGWORDS™

Miscommunication happens. Remember, communication is an intricate system of levers and pulleys that can either build or destroy a relationship, so it is important to learn how to use them properly.

I should have mentioned this early: Conflict either improves or reduces relationships. There are really only two options. Improve or fail. Improving is the best option—stop fixing and start building.

One way I have learned to do this is through the use of Flagwords™. I came up with the idea of flagwords in order to create a fun and inoffensive way of calling a "flag on the play" in normal communication. Flagwords help to keep us transparent and honest in our communication. They keep us from blurting out negative statements and opinions about what we don't like. Flagwords are an effective way to keep hackles down.

Remember my MOO example in the previous chapter? People were getting upset about being interrupted all the time. Before I came up with "MOO" as our flagword, interruptees had two choices. One, hold up a hand up and say, "hey, you just interrupted me", thus forcing the other person into apology or defense and subsequently shifting the energy in the room and stifling the free flowing exchange of ideas. Two, ignore the interruption and sit in silence, annoyed and distracted by being interrupted. Neither of these are very good solutions, as they serve to worsen the conflict.

Here is an example of how one of my team members used the MOO-word to call a flag on a miscommunication.

> Christa: *"Yes, I think this client is…"*
> Bob: *"We already know all about this client! I think we should…"*
> Christa: *"MOO." Everybody laughs.*
> Bob: *"Sorry, Christa. It is your turn to talk. Please continue."*
> Christa: *"So, like I said, this client is very particular in their needs…"*

When Christa was interrupted, she sidestepped choices one and two, and simply said "MOO". Bob knew the flagword and was able to stop himself and still laugh about it. Both were able to get their points across eventually, and frustration and acrimony were completely avoided.

This one little thing transformed our company culture for the better. Every new employee was told the joke and taught the Flagword™.

Come up with Flagwords™ to remedy negative patterns of miscommunication. Decide on these flagwords when everyone is getting along. Humor helps.

 EXAMPLE:

WHY FLAGWORDS™ WORK FOR A FORTUNE 100 COMPANY

A client of mine lost four million dollars in one day. He went from a $2 million profit to a $2 million loss in one day because the company lacked a process for logging in returned products. This loss was discovered by my client the day he discovered this procedural error, and much to his surprise, he also discovered many of his staff knew about it and, not thinking it their responsibility, said nothing.

He asked me to visit his company and see if I could get a pulse on the employee culture; he wanted me to help him figure out how such a large error could go uncorrected for so long. In my first meeting with his employees, it became glaringly clear that his team didn't fight him on anything. They simply agreed with any proposal or statement he came up with. There was a lot of approbation—not enough naysaying. They were definitely on the Kool-Aid!

At the lunch break, I asked him if he was willing to help me in an experiment in order to illustrate the point to his team. He nodded yes, and I asked him if he would put a piece of spinach in his teeth. This time he smiled and nodded, and we carefully lodged the green item in his choppers and went back in the meeting. He spoke for five minutes and not one person mentioned to him that he had this item in his teeth. I called for a break. Certainly at the break someone would privately go up to him and tell him. No one did. Not one person.

When we all came back together, I said, "Raise your hand if you saw spinach in Rall's teeth." Every single person giggled and raised a hand. My point was made. Why didn't they say anything? They were afraid of upsetting him. Then the real discussion finally began.

We devised a "spinach skit", and told the team that if the company has "spinach in its teeth", Rall wants to know about it—even if it isn't pretty. At a later meeting, we even passed out packages of spinach seeds and told the team to throw down a seed packet right before they disagreed with something Rall was saying or if they had bad news.

It worked, and this simple exercise allowed Rall to accept the true facts with humor & grace while encouraging his employees to speak out when they believed they had valuable input. New team members were taught the spinach flagword, and the culture was transformed.

Of course, flagwords work in personal relationships too. For example, after much begging, whining and dining, I finally convinced my very successful, sought after sister to leave her well paid and benefited corporate job to join my little company. My sister is my best friend, and we do have our moments in conflict.

After making up after a hearty row, we made a joke about how we say "remember" right before a loaded sentence—how it served as a little verbal shot over the bow alerting the other person that something terrible was coming. Together, we transformed "remember" into a flagword, and it became a humorous way for us to point out potential points of frustration in our communication. It worked famously.

I can tell you, my sister and I are closer now that she is working with me. (I can also tell you that without her my company would have failed. She rocks.) We communicate much better than ever. People say not to hire friends and family. They are wrong.

We don't hire friends and family because we are bad at conflict. Friends and family tend to have the same worth ethic and values as we do. We like them.

Hire friends and family **and** get great at conflict.

Flagwords improve communication and create more joy in professional and personal relationships.

CHAPTER 56:
LAW AND LOGIC
VS EMOTION AND RELATIONSHIP

This chapter is my gift to all the law firms in the world. I do a lot of work in the professional service industry and find law firms have a unique dynamic.

Think of a steam engine for a moment. Coal is shoved into the stove to stoke the fire to run the engine. The output is steam, and the result is locomotion. (While this is super basic, you get the analogy.)

In legal firms, logic and law are both input and result at the same time. This is unique and even seems to defy nature. This is the way it is. Law makes logic; logic makes law.

Law firms also specialize in conflict—it is their business. They are great at this product, and their clients love them for it. Though legal employees still want emotion and relationship even in a conflict-based, law and logic environment. If an imbalance develops between the needs of clients and the needs of employees, great communication can be compromised (even mediocre communication for that matter). Team members do not like it when they see their bosses treat clients better than they treat them.

Think of the wife of a police officer who makes his living telling people what do to. He does this all day long, then out of habit, comes home and tells her what to make for dinner. Maybe she already made dinner, or doesn't feel having spaghetti and meatballs for the second time that week. If he wants a peaceful, functioning home life, he has to take off his daytime persona with his uniform. It will work wonders for his relationship.

Imbalance causes poor communication—period. Treat employees like you treat your best clients. They are essential to your business and will thrive under these conditions.

Look around you and notice how your line of business is helping and how it is hindering great communication.

 EXAMPLE:

ROSEMARY BEADS

My mother's side of the family is very Catholic. (Yes, it is grammatically correct to put very in front of a religion in my family, we have nuns and a priest or two floating around in our clan.)

My mother made all the clothes for my sister and me. She would sew elaborate outfits with bell-bottoms and crazy colors. My sister and I were only two years apart, so people often thought we were twins. I especially remember one particular "sisters" outfit. It was an orange long dress with a white lace collar and a grey velvet belt. It was our church outfit. And whenever we wore it, the priest picked us out of the pews and had us—as twins of the congregation—do something in front of the group, such as carry a candle down the isle, sing a song, etc.

While we sort of welcomed the extra attention, we sometimes wished we could just stay in the pew and make faces at the two bratty boys who lived in our apartment complex. (These boys teased us all the time, especially when they found out our swimsuits—mine a frog motif, Leta's a flower motif—were actually underwear sets. Thanks mom.)

Well, I have to tell you, I was in love with my Aunt Rosemary, my mother's sister. She was everything I wanted to be when I grew up. Beautiful, a school teacher—and she always took us to see cool stuff. In a lot of ways, Aunt Rosemary was my church—the center of my universe. And she had an interesting necklace that she let me play with. When my older relatives saw me doing this, they said I was playing with "Rosemary's beads." So that is what I called them. Everyone seemed to giggle a little when I said it.

One fine morning at church, the priest asked my sister and me to come to the front pew and sit during the "wafer ceremony" (that is what we really called it). As I sat there, I noticed several woman nearby playing with Rosemary beads!!! Then the priest actually said "Rosemary beads" in his sermon. I couldn't believe how popular and famous my Aunt Rosemary was. Here we were at a church she has never been to, and everybody knew her and her beads!

I was beaming. I saw Aunt Rosemary in this new light. She was famous. When the service was over, I told the priest—in a very important tone—"Rosemary is MY aunt by the way." I will never forget the look he gave me. He didn't seem impressed at all.

It didn't matter. I was on Cloud Nine, just like all the angels I read about in Sunday School. I was the niece of a famous person. Rosemary.

I bragged about it to the bratty boys when I saw Rosemary beads on their mother's yellow-flowered, dining room tablecloth. I can still hear their laughter and see them pointing and holding their stomach as they made sure I knew how stupid I was. ROSARY beads stupid. ROSARY.

I never talked to the priest again. I was so embarrassed. I was really glad when we moved away from San Diego. Really glad. In some ways I was mad at Rosemary too. I don't know why.

Embarrassment is a communication stopper. Ridicule, disdain, fingerpointing—they all inhibit relationships and great communication. I was afraid to speak in public in part because of this silly experience when I was a kid.

The best way to deal with mistakes and embarrassing moments is to use them as material in communicating. People love stories and over time the sting will wear out of them.

Let go of, laugh about and improve on the past.

CHAPTER 57:
PLEASE IS NOT
THE ONLY MAGIC WORD

One of my dearest friends has a little boy who is one year older than my son. This is very fortuitous for me, as I get to watch her go first in every step of parenting. Observing her mother her son has taught me volumes, and, consequently, I was much better prepared when Sebastian entered our lives. (Plus every few months I get a big bag of hardly worn, little boy clothes and shoes.)

My friend is very creative, and she comes up with cute little code words for her son. Some of these words are made up specifically for her toddler, and they make me laugh out loud when I hear her husband use these commands on her without realizing it. This system of language can really help a kid understand quickly what the heck mom is talking about. I think this is a very effective parenting technique, and I have learned to emulate it at my house.

One of the code words she says a lot is "magic." You see, "please" is a magic word, and by saying "magic" she is teaching her son to use the word please when asking for something. It works really well, and he is a very polite little boy.

Why is this relevant? I have been in the business world for a long time. I have spent many years on non-profit boards. I no longer believe that please is the only magic word. When we want something from someone, it is easy to be nice. Please, is nice, and please is often self-serving. We say please to get what we want.

The real magic word is "sorry." We do not hear this word enough in our culture. I watched two people destroy an organization over their refusal to say "I'm sorry". For those who haven't been to Mother Theresa school, it is impossible to forgive without these magic words.

Due to rampant lawsuits in the 80's, corporations became afraid of saying they were sorry—sorry might mean liability. Instead, they carefully selected their words and refused to emote or acknowledge sorrow over a tragedy.

Being sorry does not mean we are wrong. If my son cries over my refusal to give him a bottle in the middle of the day, I am very sorry he feels bad. It makes me cry too. I want to give him the bottle, and my refusal makes him identify me as the cause of his pain. The greater pain would be letting him suck on a bottle until he is twelve-years-old.

If I am laying off a great employee, I am sorry. It may not be my decision; perhaps I am merely the messenger. Regardless of my role, it does not mean that I cannot feel his or her pain or that I cannot have genuine sorrow over the situation. I can say "I am sorry" and mean it.

Of course, to be effective, the magic word must be felt as it is spoken. You must feel the sorrow—whether it was created by you inadvertently or by acknowledging that some things are totally outside your control. Feel it. Say it.

The next step in effectiveness is to practice forgiveness—when you hear "I am sorry" or when you say "I am sorry." Forgiveness is the real sentiment behind this magic word. If we truly want to heal a relationship and stay in it long term, we must learn to forgive—ourselves, others, things under our control, things outside it. Until we forgive, we are stuck in the past. Our communication is stifled and not clean.

Forgiveness or lack thereof is truly the cause of most miscommunication and unhappiness. Lack of forgiveness is responsible for at least 65 percent of the unhappiness in the world. Aaah, that, is another book entirely.

Better communication can be achieved through four easy steps: Feel, Feel Sorry, Say "Sorry", Forgive.

PART IV
PUBLIC SPEAKING

CHAPTER 58:
PUBLIC SPEAKING EXERCISE

Get a pen. Yes, now. Go ahead and write in this book. If you are reading this book in a bookstore you might want to pay for it before you do what I am suggesting.

If you have skipped ahead and didn't read the Foundation and Conflict Sections, you will not get the true benefit of the chapters in the Public Speaking Section. This is because the building blocks of public speaking are covered in the earlier sections. Go back and start from the beginning, you will come back to this page. I promise.

Everyone else write down a topic you speak (or wish to speak) about often as well as the main point of the speech. Write no more than a couple of sentences for each.

One topic I have or need to speak about is:

The main point I am trying to make when I talk about this subject is:

A secondary point I am trying to make when I talk about this subject:

We will refer back to this page later.

CHAPTER 59:

WHY ME?

I guess you've noticed. There is no comma or string of special capital letters after my name. Sure, I went to college. I even graduated. I studied Economics at San Francisco State University, and this degree gives me no license to tell you how to speak in public. Some folks imagine a degree in Economics means I am good at math, have a strategic mind or that I am good at analyzing.

I'd like you to believe that. In reality, I wanted to be a Chemist. Dr. Coke in high school convinced me that I was to be the next Madam Curie. I tried being a Chemistry major for a while and ended up switching majors mid-term.

I selected Economics for one reason. I had to figure out how to earn a living, take care of my Parkinson's-stricken dad, and still have time to go to school. I needed a major that supported my lack of time as well as my innate ability to debate theory. A counselor suggested economics.

The key to economics is the ability to know enough facts to deliver a convincing argument. We all know the cliché about economists: They never agree. Instead, they argue opinion then back it up with "facts." I did super well in economics without really needing to study much. I was glad.

All this talk about education is making me bored. In truth, school did not teach me enough information to put into a public speaking book. As much as I loved my public speaking professor, he and the public speaking textbooks he used discounted my natural desire to tell stories. Instead, I was instructed to drive my key points while keeping my humor and entertainment in the back closet. My creativity was not celebrated and my natural style was bound in a verbal brace of professionalism that made it hard to breathe.

Every communication class I took tried to make me into something else. It nearly killed me—all that acting and professionalism.

Hold on there Nellie! By professionalism I mean that cold, austere, distant perfection you would never be with your closest friends. (I do not mean the professionalism that calls people back and spell-checks documents before sending them.)

Guess what? I started doing my own thing, and my professor didn't like it so much; my classmates raved about it. I let my natural voice come through, I used stories and humor and I still drove home the key points of my message. We all felt alive afterwards rather than tired and bored.

I'll never forget the first time I made the entire room crack up for a full minute: I said, "When I was a kid I thought my parents' friends were really poor. They all sat in a circle and smoked the same cigarette."

Did you laugh at that one again? It still makes me laugh, and I was elated by the initial response to that quip. I caught a bug that day.

Here's a secret. Public speaking is an outdated term. Get rid of it. I only use it here because you do. The real term is **Rapport Speaking**. Audiences listen to the people they have rapport with.

Rapport does not mean we have to make them like us. Folks do listen better to people they like. (Unless they are married to them. Snicker.) Rapport means communicating to be heard. Figuring out ways to engage the listener.

Having rapport with an audience increases listening. Communicating to be heard is an ingredient of Rapport.

CHAPTER 60:
PLAY IT AGAIN, SAM

In a previous chapter I talked about something really important. I have mentioned it before, and it is worth repeating—again and again. Perhaps because it seems too easy for people to get the enormity of it:

> *Be the exact same person you are with your closest friends, on a great day, when speaking to an audience.*

Done. Simple. This is rapport speaking. In fact, before any kind of communication, even conflict, be the exact same person you are with your closest friends on a great day when speaking to an audience.

And now comes the real question: How to make it so? That is what this book is for.

It is truly difficult to be the same great person you are when your face is red, your palms are sweating and you're standing in front of a room full of people who are clearly judging you. And if knees start knocking…oh boy…look out…here comes:

Mr. Ice Professional (Wo)Man

Also known as MIPM. MIPM is not a super hero. Male or female, he is a cold, nefarious villain who will destroy your ability to communicate to be heard. He has no emotion, is terrible at telling stories, and he is hard to look at, let alone pay attention to. Make him go away. He is not your friend.

Sounds too easy doesn't it?

Remember: Your unique and singular experience makes you the perfect person (and the only person) to present your ideas. The audience wants to hear the perspective of the speaker—you! You may as well give them an audiotape, cd or book if the real you isn't going to show up and present to them. <u>You</u> are who they want.

Please keep in mind that your experience has created your perspective. It is relevant and will hold the audience better than charts and graphs. Tell your story. Be engaging and attentive. Listen to yourself as you speak. And most of all, be you— acting is the kiss of death.

To be a great communicator: Be you on a good day.

CHAPTER 61:
BE CONGRUENT
AND BE A BEACON

Like a lot of things in this book, some things are so important I can't stop saying them. Verne Harnish gave me advice on child rearing once: Have very few rules and repeat them often. Good advice.

The guiding principles of this book are repeated in different ways. Such as the one mentioned in the previous chapter: Be the person you really are on a great day. The last thing an audience wants is a person to come grumping into a room and only "turn-on" when the spotlight hits them.

Another guiding principal is to observe what makes others successful communicators. Whether it's a huge crowd or one on one, you must watch for what you like about other speakers. Take note of what works for them. This practice will enhance your relationships with others and, more importantly, you will become a better public speaker as your cellular memory imitates good speaking behavior.

Hold on there Nellie! I am NOT suggesting you mimic anyone. We are warm-blooded, tribal animals—we act like who we are around and who we watch automatically. When we watch for what we like we automatically start doing it.

Siblings are often told they look alike. My sister and I look alike because we act alike.

I am not suggesting you pretend to be someone else. Think of it this way: If you notice Rebecca has great gestures, you won't have to think about gesturing—you will automatically start doing it. Remember, you are a natural monkey. If you are too critical as you watch other folks—you'll start picking up those habits. If you count the number of times a person says "UM" you will automatically increase the number of times you say UM. Our subconscious only knows yes and cannot distinguish between a "positive" and a "negative."

There are exceptions. For instance, there's a sales trainer I know who's a grumpy guy. Before his speeches, he looks at his notes and pays no attention to the current speaker or the room in general. He has every right to do what he wants, even if others in the room may perceive him as rude and inconsiderate. Perhaps he is.

Then, the minute he steps up to the microphone it is clear that his behavior is perfectly suited to who he really is. He is Mr Grumpy Guy with a really great message, and he stays true to character throughout the whole speech. He talks about how he is not a people person and that the audience should not expect to like him. He tells the audience important things that make a difference in their lives. Because it is in congruence with who he is, it works. He breaks every communication rule in the book and remains super successful.

The message? Do not listen to people who are trying to get you to be different than who you are.

Be congruent with who you <u>really</u> are.

YOUR PROFESSIONALISM IS KILLING YOU..

CHAPTER 62:
DON'T JUST SAY IT,
DISPLAY IT

When talking about an emotion during a talk, relive that emotion. Be thankful when thanking a speaker. Be sad when talking about something sad. If you say you are excited, ya better look it.

Audiences always notice how words are said. If the speaker doesn't have any emotional connection to his or her words, the audience will walk away and forget the whole experience. The speaker didn't care enough to feel it, why should they?

Bridging the emotional gap is often tough to do. It's challenging to live one's emotion in front of a bunch of people we've never met before—especially since we've always been taught that as long as we <u>say</u> the right thing we'll be okay.

I have this cool exercise I do when teaching the use of emotion in customer service. Okay, I'll listen to myself. Calling something cool is not the same as describing it. Let me describe it, then you can decide if it is cool.

When dealing with angry customers, listen to their complaint; when they're finished say:

> *How frustrating for you. I will do everything in my power to make this right, ma'am.*

I ask the room if these words are okay in a customer service platform. Most of the room agrees that the words seem positive and relationship building. I then play an audiotape of these words. The person reciting them is flat lined. They are reading a script. Is that good customer service? Next, I show them these words:

> *I hear your concerns for quality. I share your concerns. I will look into this for you and call you tomorrow.*

The room feels these words sound like good customer service. Then, when I play back the tape, they see the person reciting them is not flat lined, she is passive aggressive. Is that good customer service? No. Next, I show them this:

> *You sound frustrated. I am too. If you give me just a moment I can get the answer you need.*

Everyone agrees this wording is awful. Clearly not good customer service. Then I play the audio tape, and the <u>way</u> the person says this sentence actually feels more positive than the first two. The how makes a wrongly worded response seem acceptable.

Here's another example. I am in a business group. One of our members from another state passed away. A few of us asked the person running the program if he'd make mention of our fellow colleague and take a moment to remember him. This is what he said:

> *"I only mention Mr. Smith as he was a member. If you know him and want to say something, please raise your hand."*

It was done in the most callous way. Shocking really. It made the guy seem cold and crass; when really he's a sweet pea—though we had to give him credit for not pretending to be upset. Had he tried to use emotive words, he probably would have seemed like an android and hurt rapport with the group; instead, he told the truth, and we all loved him for it.

When using words like excited, <u>be</u> excited. Don't <u>act</u> excited. Acting excited smells like the gilled creatures tossed around in Pikes Fish Market in Seattle.

When using an emotive word, <u>be</u> that emotion or don't use the word.

CHAPTER 63:
BE THE WORD
YOU ARE SAYING

I'm sure you've noticed that I talk a lot about <u>how</u> things need to be said. It is easy to say, "just deliver it better and you will be a better speaker." Is it easy to do?

Sometimes. One easy way to improve your <u>how</u> is to <u>be</u> the word you are saying. Yesterday I dropped by the childcare provider in my building to see if I could get my son Sebastian on the wait list. When I walked up to the counter, two employees were standing nearby talking. They gave me a look and one of them begrudgingly came over to help me.

Now, I am Susie Sunshine, and it is my job to have positive interactions with other humans. I introduced myself to the woman at the counter. She started looking for the forms, and, while looking down at her paper and still shuffling, she said with frustration, "it's nice to meet you too." She gruffly handed me the forms, and I asked her if I should drop the packet off at this facility. She cut me off, "You should mail it or at least call before coming by."

My point? It was clear she was irritated that I dropped by. There is no reason to say "nice to meet you" if you don't mean the words. I didn't believe her, so I was not surprised when she snapped at my question. Looking down and being grumpy does not nice to meet you make.

The same is true in public speaking. "It's great to be here." Really? I hear this all the time, and too often I don't believe it. Either they don't seem so happy to be where they are, or they seem a bit too excited. They start with a BANG and then taper off the more they talk. This doesn't work either. Sometimes it is their glued on smile that gives them away. Only smile if you feel like it. Fake smiles are a neon sign to the audience. They make us look like serial killers or like we are selling something nobody wants.

What if you have to speak when you aren't feeling it? What if I am about to deliver a big talk, and my employee calls to tell me he missed an important deadline? Do I address the audience with the same frustrated tone I had with my employee fifteen minutes prior to speaking? No way! And I don't paste on a fake smile either. Instead, I figure out how to get back in the zone and let my frustration go for the time being. Usually this requires physical movement and/or chatting up everyone in the room until I forget that now I'm not going to be able to deliver that talk in Rome.

I'll say it this way: Match your emotion to your words when speaking. "It is nice to meet you" means you are happy to meet the person. If you are not happy to meet them, don't say it. I am not taking my son to the childcare center in my office building because of Mary Contrary. After my initial encounter, I began observing the place, and I am shocked at how unhappy the employees are there. Unhappy employees mean unhappy kids at a preschool; so I found a fabulous place for my son that is a little inconvenient for me—though well worth the effort. The preschool team loves their job, and he loves it there. It is obvious.*

If you are not excited, do not pretend that you are. When you use an emotional word, make sure it matches your true emotional state.

*(Later on in this book, remember this chapter when I talk about typecasting.)

CHAPTER 64:
GIVE THEM
THE SNOT BUBBLE

Allow your emotion to come through. Do not stifle it. If you cry- cry.

Women generally fight me on this one. They remind me that presidential hopeful Pat Schroeder cried in her now famous 1987 exploratory candidate speech. She was attacked and criticized for those tears. I am told it ruined her career.

Really? People freaked out? Oh my gosh! Do you want the person with their finger on the button that emotional? Do you want to vote for someone who will cry? I do.

Humans cry. Get over it. Tears are a show of strength not of weakness. How a person deals with their crying makes all the difference. I am one strong fother mucker. I challenge anyone to have ovaries as strong as mine. I tear up at least once a day. I cry.

I don't apologize for it, and it is not weakness. Male candidates now use crying to show their 'softer' side. It works for men. It works for women to. In the Human Currency Culture, hiding from our emotions destroys us in the eyes of others. Remember, if you are talking about an emotion, live it. Do not shy away from being human.

I know what you are thinking. Howard Dean. It's all over YouTube—the "Scream" that lost the presidency. Only it wasn't that scream that lost the presidency. It was his reaction to it. Imagine if he had he looked in the camera the next day and said, "Yes, I screamed. I am not the only person screaming. The American people are screaming to be heard. I am just the one holding the microphone. The American people are screaming for clean elections. Screaming for an end to the war in Iraq. Screaming for universal healthcare for all." The "Scream" would have transformed into a positive. Instead, he shied away from his true self and lost the nomination.

You get the picture. His silent shame and unspoken apology allowed his detractors to whip up a storm of negativity against him. It would have been much better had he simply made fun of himself while talking about how helpless a voter feels when they realize their vote didn't count. He lost momentum because he shifted into Ice Man Professional mode instead of staying true to Howard Dean.

You need another example?

Go to YouTube.com and search "Hillary Clinton's Evil Men" comment.

Notice how her first response made the question go away. The crowd loved it. Not surprisingly, her comment excited the media, and everyone wanted to know if she was referring to her husband Bill Clinton when she said she knew plenty of evil men. Instead of telling the media to relax and draw their own conclusions, she first tried to cover up her comment, then she snapped in a fun loving way, "You tell me to lighten up and be funny. Now I do and I am being psychoanalyzed."

The pirhanas stopped circling the tank and let it be. She was herself. It is when we shy away from our true selves we lose.

Here's another angle on emotion: Speakers often avoid talking about the really deep stuff because they're afraid of choking up. Forget that. If you choke up—good. It means you are harnessing all the power of the relationship economy. Here is what ya do if this happens to you:

1. Do not apologize for tearing up.
2. Take a physical step forward while looking someone in the audience in the eye.
3. Stop talking. Take a moment and breathe. Look at the audience.
4. If you can move, move again. Take a step forward, not back. Do not turn away. These subtle things will help you maintain your strength through this process.
5. If there is a lump in your throat, move. Cough. Say something. Push through that lump. Think of that lump as a lump of sugar. Ever see what happens when liquid meets a square scratchy painful lump of sugar? It melts. The same is true for that lump in your through. Letting the tears come out of your eyes will move that lump. Breathe toward it not away from it.
6. The next step depends on your personality. Here are some examples of things I've said or heard others use:
   a. "For some reason, I am having a moment up here." The audience laughs, the speaker laughs, the mood shifts and the speaker continues where he or she left off.
   b. "I cried when Wham broke up too."
   c. Stand and look around the room. Wait for your tears to dry up.
   d. "Damn, My jacket is dry clean only."
   e. Stretch. Yes, right there in front of everyone. The endorphins will help you.
   f. Breathe.
   g. End your speech. Once, while giving a eulogy, it became clear that I could not continue. So I simply said, "Thank you Grandpa—for teaching me to take risks." Even if no one else understood what I meant that day, Grandpa did.
   h. Speak louder. There is something about increasing your volume that quells the emotion of things.
   i. "I hope I am not the only one in the room who smells the onions."
7. Again, <u>do not</u> apologize. I am a snot bubble, so I crack jokes to make my tears more palatable to myself and others. It works for me. I am not apologizing for crying nor am I making light of it.

I am doing what I always do when faced with emotional trauma—I make it funny. If this is not who you are, then don't do it!

8. Find your authentic response.
9. Each time you talk about the subject it will get easier. If you plan to deliver a speech that has emotional content, deliver it out loud to a few people before the big day.

If you are like my son (i.e., male), forgive this next sentence; it will seem judgmental and finger-pointy, though it isn't meant that way. Women create life. We carry a future being in our womb and go through incredible pain to bring it into the world. This miracle is really astounding when you sit and think about it. (Yes, men provide the sperm; their part ends in fun, the woman's in ouch!) Thank goodness we have the emotional expressiveness to endure this incredible journey of life giving. We need our tears.

My point is that the woman's movement had a downside—it encouraged women to go into the work place and act like men. Crying makes some men uncomfortable, so we were taught to avoid it.

What we aren't taught is that your discomfort is interesting and needs to be dealt with—by professionals in the workplace. Remember, your professionalism is killing the real you! When women in the workplace start acting as real as they are with their closest friends, the world will be a happier place. Even men will feel more comfortable.

This is not a female/male thing. As I look out into audiences today—men tear up just as much as women.

And here is the deal: In the new relationship economy great communicators talk about the things that do make them tear up. Audiences (remember an audience can be one person) want more transparency. We want to know the real you.

Crying is a beautiful thing. Do not avoid or apologize for it.

CHAPTER 65:
DON'T BE HUMBLE,
YOU AIN'T THAT GREAT

My dad used to say this to me when I was a child. I didn't really get it until years later.

The saying came back to me recently as I skimmed through an article in the *San Francisco Chronicle* about a kid in China who's posting video of himself playing his guitar on YouTube.com. Everyone says he is the next Jimi Hendrix, despite the fact that he plays with his face hidden by a baseball hat and claims he's a six out of ten in terms of his ability to play. The article talks about how American kids have too much self-esteem—they think they are better than they are.

Similarly, a friend recently told me that Americans are seen globally as people with too much bravado. He said we are perceived as taking credit for things we have little to do with. He warned me to be aware of this opinion when I speak internationally. With that in my head I tried to reduce my bravado and thereby did not do as well as I usually do.

Confidence can impair public speaking. Too little confidence causes speakers to hold back what they truly know; it also causes nerves to wreck havoc on their body and voice. Too much confidence causes speakers to deliver boring lectures, as well as falsely assume the rest of the audience gives a rip about their egohead topic.

Ironically, being humble can actually be ego: I am so great I need to act like I am not so you don't feel bad about being so pitiful. Of course, this isn't always the case, though I have seen it plenty of times in my professional and personal relationships.

Perfection is a tricky ideal in our culture. We do not like people who act perfect. We do not like people who have a great big smelly ego either. We like people who are humble.

Humility can be a trap. When overgrown egos act like they don't know how great they are, we smell a rat. Anything canned or pretend puts us in a position of incongruence. And by now you know incongruence reduces our body's ability to communicate with our brain and keeps us from communicating to be heard.

True humility comes from the awareness that greatness is the result of hard work and great discipline. People who are humble understand the fleeting nature of praise and are always working away in the background to become better at something they are already good at. Some of the greatest people I know are amazingly humble.

My dad used to tell me, Do not be humble—you ain't that great. If you sit and think about it, that comment is a beautiful, effective way to convince a little girl to be "all that."

Humility is only a good thing when you believe it.

 **EXERCISE:**

DA BODY DON'T LIE

You will need two friends for this one. (If you don't have any, you might want to re-read the conflict section; it might improve your communication style!) Of course, you can also use two co-workers, your dentist and her assistant, the guy who bags your groceries and the cashier or just two folks from your family. The possibilities are endless—as long as three people participate. This exercise takes about three minutes to complete and about ten minutes to discuss the results.

Do not read ahead. This is critical. Hand the book to one of your exercise buddies. For it to work, only one person reads about the exercise; the other two are victims of the unknown. It's kind of exciting.

*******************************START********************************

Hi. You have just been handed this book to perform an exercise. It is critical you follow the steps exactly. Ask the two people involved in the exercise to sit and relax while you read.

Read until you encounter the word "**END**"—then perform the exercise.

Ask the two people to stand and face each other and look each other in the eye. (Remember, you are supposed to read all the way through before doing this.)

Ask Person 1 (the person who handed you the book) if it would be okay for you to apply a little pressure to his arm. If Person 1 says no because of an arm or shoulder injury, you will need to use Person 2 as the example. If both people have injuries, stop reading and hand the book to one of them, so you can be the example.

Assuming Person 1 is physically able (and a man for the purposes of this exercise), ask him to extend both arms out horizontal to the floor. They should look like this:

Ask him which hand is the strongest? Go to that arm. (Remember, the two participants are facing each other and making eye contact, and you are standing beside—not in front of—them next to the arm that is the strongest.)

Tell Person 1 to use all his strength to resist your pushing and keep his arm straight. You must push on his strongest arm and try to get his hand to touch the side of his thigh.

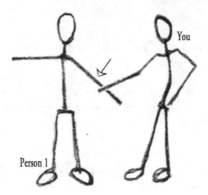

Person 1

You

Start pushing for about three seconds; he should be able to resist you. Then ask him to say, "I AM _____." You need to fill in the blank with something that is the opposite of what the person is. For example, "I am female" if Person 1 is male, or "I am male" if she is female. While saying this opposite statement, Person 1 will not be able to resist you and his hand will go down easily.

[Note of warning: I had someone complain about this in a class in San Francisco. He said telling a person to state they were male or female was offensive and insensitive to gay and transgender people. Yep. It might be. If a similar challenge presents itself in your situation, ask Person 1 to tell you a least favorite food before starting the exercise. It has to be a food that they are severely allergic to or absolutely hate. Most people have one. If the person says it is gouda cheese, the opposite statement would be "I love gouda cheese." It isn't as effective as the gender example—sex does sell after all.]

After successfully pushing down Person 1's arm without hurting him, walk to the other side of his body. This time announce you will push on the weakest arm and ask another question. Tell him to resist.

While pushing on his arm (the arm that is a little tired now due to being up in the air for so long) ask him to say a congruent statement—the opposite of what they just said, i.e., their true gender. "I am male" if Person 1 is male; "I am female" if Person 1 is female.

Most participants can resist the pushing quite easily when making a congruent statement. Visually, it is clear, especially since you are pushing with the same veracity as you did with the "stronger" arm. People are unable to resist when telling a lie and able to resist with a weaker limb when telling the truth. It works every time.

*********************************END*****************************
(Now do the exercise then come back and debrief as a group.)

Debrief:

- Person 1 will always feel like you are not pushing as hard on the weaker hand even though you are.

- This is a great tool if you have teenagers: Were you at the library? Yes. (Swunk! "Swunk" is the swooshing sound of a weak arm crashing against the thigh.)

- The body loses strength when you lie. Incongruence is lying to the body, the body can not tell the difference. In other words a lying body is a weak body. Our brain is part of our body. When we "act"in front of a room we are not using this machine to its optimal level.

- This exercise is a demonstration of kinesiology. Read about it on Wikipedia: http://en.wikipedia.org/wiki/Kinesiology

- Being who you are with your closest friends, engages every part of your body. You become a fine well-oiled machine, and your brain works better and words come easier.

- Being humble is not always being congruent.

- Not being humble may make people dislike you. You will need to decide how you feel about that.

- When speaking, you must also recognize the specific great work of others. This is not thanking people. It is sincere and specific acknowledgement. This gives others a chance to share the spotlight, thus counteracts the impact of your seeming overly confident (i.e., arrogant) and omniscient (wink wink).

Your mouth works better when your brain isn't focused on pretending to be something you are not.

Pretending to be anything (thankful, humble, confident) does not a great communicator make. You must be who and what you really are.

P.S. I first saw an exercise like this during 5th grade summer camp. I had to sell greeting cards to earn enough money to go and caught the entrepreneurial bug when I saw how easy it was to do. During camp a counselor used an exercise like this to describe how aligned our minds and bodies need to be when physically competing. I sucked at the race thing we were doing—I got really excited about this message. And now, I am crediting a camp counselor (who's name I cannot recall).

CHAPTER 66:
RELATIONSHIPS MATTER

Remember, today's audiences want to know the quirks and nuances of the speaker. They also want to interact in a dynamic way with any experience they are involved in. Let them know you. This is not being vulnerable. It is being real.

As poet Diane DiPrima says, "I'd rather be hated for who I am than loved for who I am not."

It saves everyone a lot of time when we act like who we are. There are people who will not like you because you admit that you secretly listen to Brittany Spears. So what. They are being judgmental; they probably would find a reason not to like you regardless of how many boxes you put yourself in for them. Your friends love you for being a cheese ball—it makes you who you are.

Think about this for a moment. I finally learned to stop trying to be for everyone. I am not. My talent trumps their judgment every time.

Again, only 2 percent of humans are simply bad people. I pray you never meet one of them in a dark alley. The rest of us just have some bad communication behavior we created after years of trying to survive. Figuring out how to build relationships with the audience will increase their listening skills. Not pandering, not falsehood— trust that their internal quest will shift things.

Relationships matter. The more they know the real you, the more likely they will listen to you.

CHAPTER 67:

WHO IS
IN THE ROOM

Blah blah blah. Speech coaches always talk about this one, and it's how politicians get a bad rap. The problem starts when the speaker is too focused on pandering to the audience rather than on understanding who they are talking to.

When I say "who", I don't mean proper nouns—not the name of the group and not even what they care about. I mean who is in the room—the individual people. How they listen and what they listen for. Which brings us around to listening again. Have you noticed how this happens? I hope so, otherwise you haven't really been reading this book.

Everyone learned some version of the following, and we still forget it when we are in front of a room.

There are four main types of listeners: **Visual Listeners, Oratory Listeners, Tactile Listeners, and Kinesthetic Listeners.** And to be heard, you must craft your talk to connect with all four types.

See Listeners:
These are the "I need to see it to listen" people. Power Point or flip charts work wonders for these folks (See Chapter 118 on page 272 for Power Point Tips). By providing some visual cues, they will listen, hear and remember.

Hear Listeners:
These are the "what I hear makes me listen" people. They learn by hearing and are the most straightforward listeners. When possible, interact with them so they can talk too. It is also a good idea to provide some oratory stimulus such as music; they will listen, hear and remember.

Touch Listeners:
These are the "I need to mess with something to listen" people. Some folks must have something in their hands to pay attention. I have been known to put Play-Doh on chairs before a talk so those that need to can connect with me by making a Play-Doh animal. Getting these folks to connect with other audience members through eye contact and handshaking will also increase their listening ability. By providing some tactile interaction, they will listen, hear and remember. (The thing in their hands doesn't have to relate at all to the speaker.)

Play Listeners:
These are the "make me do something to make me listen" people. Relevant exercises are great for this type of listener. (Be careful with games. Games have been overused and actually bore audiences now if they are not firmly rooted in some lesson.) By providing some kinesthetic engagement, they will listen, hear and remember.

Now the big question. What are audiences listening for? There are 101,324 categories of what people listen for in a talk. We will list some of the categories here:

<u>Activity People</u>—they are goal oriented and like:
- Goals
- Detail
- Completion

<u>Information People</u>—they are information junkies and like:
- Statistics and Research
- Analysis
- Proof

<u>Agenda People</u>—they are clock sensitive, impatient with tangents and like:
- Schedules
- Starting and ending on time
- Agendas and answers

<u>But People</u>—they are devil's advocates and like:
- Disproving theories
- Road testing
- Interactive dialog (tend to start most sentences with "but")
- Lots of Q&A (LOVE these people, they help you get better)

<u>People People</u>—they care about feelings and want to see:
- Mood
- Relationship
- Inclusiveness

Every room presents a myriad of listening types. Great speakers are like hearing magnets, incorporating multiple perspectives and sensitivities in their presentation to enhance listening.

Communicating to be heard means touching on all listeners.

Remember the song *Chopsticks*? You know, the piano tune a lot of us learned to play when we were young. It is basically a repetition of notes. Have you ever listened to the album featuring famous musicians covering *Chopsticks*? Greats like Dr John, Johnny Cash, Foo Fighters, Grateful Dead, AC/DC, Sting, Thelonious Monk, and others doing their version of chopsticks. You haven't heard it? That's because it doesn't exist. *Chopsticks* is boring. So are most speeches.

To communicate to be heard in the relationship economy, you must hit on all cylinders with the different types of listeners. Sprinkle in things for each type—vary things.

Craft your talks to gain the attention of diverse types of listeners and increase the listening.

(Remember, to change a mind, you must first be heard.)

YOUR PROFESSIONALISM IS KILLING YOU...............................

CHAPTER 68:
OPEN FOR WHO?

The opening of a public speech is the first few minutes of a speaker's airtime before an audience. Can you guess what the speaker's purpose should be during these opening minutes?

Please write down your answer here. I made a cute little box for you:

```
┌─────────────────────────────────────────────────────────────────┐
│                                                                   │
│                                                                   │
│                                                                   │
│                                                                   │
└─────────────────────────────────────────────────────────────────┘
```

I hope you got the answer right, though I'll be surprised if you did. I have asked this question thousands of times and usually get the following answers:

- To engage the audience
- To set the agenda
- To thank the audience for coming
- To tell a joke
- To say something to put the audience at ease
- To thank the person who introduced me
- To ask a rhetorical question
- To keep from throwing up

These are all really nice goals for the opening minutes, and they are all wrong. They were all pounded into my head as a way to gain better rapport with the audience and in reality this did not make me a better speaker. It made me a better pretender.

I have only had one audience member get this one right; if you are reading this right now, congratulations!

The purpose of the opening is for the speaker≠—you—to make yourself feel most comfortable. This is the time to do whatever it takes to kill the professional android who wants to step into your body and deliver your talk for you. It is the time for you to relax and allow yourself to simply be you. Whatever loosens the chocking grip of professionalism. Stop hiding behind that suit! That suit does not make the audience like or trust you. Enron execs wore suits.

What gets you into your natural place of communicating? Does telling stories about your kids work for you? Reading poems? Telling a joke? Spreadsheets? Do whatever it is that makes you the most comfortable and you will naturally get the attention of the audience.

Opening with a story works for most people—providing the story is being relived as it is told. I can pretty much guarantee that thanking the last speaker is as interesting to the audience as it is to you—not very!

If starting with a story, don't open with:

> *I am going to start with a story about…*

Yuck. Don't tell them what you are going to do: Just do it! Have the courage to grab the microphone and start painting. You can show them what they are seeing later.

> *It was summer 1979 and I am standing on the railroad tracks. It is blistering hot and a train is barreling toward me. My brother Craig has one arm, and my brother Steve has the other arm…"*

Start **in** the story not **about** the story. We have all been taught to tell stories in public speaking—telling stories is not enough. Get a time machine and put yourself back IN the story and find all the details you forgot. I was taught to keep my stories to two minutes!—no way! A well told story has so much detail—it is the detail of those stories that built your perspective. Find them.

Starting this way immediately gets the audience's attention. By the time you are eight seconds into reliving your story, you're so focused on what you are saying you're talking to the audience like it's a room full of your closest friends. When your story is over, you can easily bridge over to your subject, and its relevance will become apparent.

<u>I need to say this again</u>. Please stop telling the audience what you are about to do. We do not like it. We want you to sweep us into your experience, perspective, morning stop off at the coffee shop—something!

<u>Oh, yeah, one more thing</u>: Starting with a story is not the only way to start. Please do not misunderstand. I am not teaching you a communication trick, nor do I want you to become known as the speaker who always starts with a story. Story telling is simply one human being communicating with another. Its fun. (Later in the book we will discuss other ways of opening a talk.)

Let's go back to my helmet story example for a moment.

By starting with a personal story, I accomplished two things: I showed myself as an expert in my topic and became more naturally myself. No one knew the story of my life with Gary better than I did so I could tell it with confidence. This confidence gave me the needed courage to relive my story with detail and emphasis, which helped me access the person I am with my closest friends. And about eight seconds into it, I became me—not an actress, not a "public speaker"—just me. I didn't start by telling the audience their opinion was wrong, nor did I start with my opinion—so everyone was listening.

I was not mimicking something I learned in speech class. My purpose for being there wasn't to change minds. It was to voice the experience of my stepbrother. It wasn't until years later that I learned my approach was a public speaking technique.

I'll bet you still don't know my opinion on the helmet law. This is because, just like in that room so many years ago, I'm not giving you any neon signs of disagreement by voicing an agenda with my story. People listened to me then because I simply relayed a story that formed my perspective.

You may think you know—you don't. This means you will keep listening to me until you hear it. Okay. I won't make you wonder anymore. Here is how I ended that talk:

> *I miss Gary. His loss left a hole in my family, and I am here to speak for him. The last time I checked I live in the United States of America and unless you are going to monitor the cholesterol of every person in this room, high cholesterol kills more people than not wearing a helmet, this law is un-American. It defies the basic principle we all believe in: Freedom. Freedom. This law has got to go.*

Folks applauded. Even the other side. I was talking about a fundamental principle we all believe in.

Want to know the coolest thing about all this? It's self-serving as hell: Opening your talks from your personal perspective causes you, the public speaker, to get into your skin and be yourself. Want to know the other cool thing? Audiences love it too. Audiences are individuals. Individuals have friends. When friends get together, friends swap stories. By starting with a story, you make the audience feel like they are swapping stories with their friends. You are happy and the audience is happy.

Think about it. What do you do when you get together with your friends? You swap stories. Stories are the transactional medium* of relationship in our culture. Stories create rapport and rapport increases listening. Voila!

(My best friend and I can tell the same story over and over again and never tire of it. We rerun these stories to create understanding and learning. Okay, it is also very entertaining.)

Open your talks in a manner that relaxes you and makes you feel your subject.

(*transactional medium.. geez, I guess my inner economist is showing!)

CHAPTER 69:

DROWNING,
NOT WAVING

Ever see someone try to get the attention of 1000 people? How do they do it? Do they jump up and down? Yell and scream into a microphone? Do they yell "PLEASE STOP!"?

Unless it's a punk rock club, such crude attention grabbing antics merely serve to turn folks off—especially those who are already listening. Remember, it is the relationship economy, and the goal is to develop rapport not alienate a potential audience.

I was taught to take a moment and pause when I found myself before an unruly audience; just stare at them and folks will automatically stop talking. It works. It is fun as well.

One of the most powerful things you can do in front of a room is nothing. Well, not really nothing: I actually mean standing silently at the lectern and looking around purposefully at the eyes in the room—willing the audience to be silent. Believe me, this show of confidence and poise will get the attention of the audience faster than hopping up and down ever will.

As my work became more focused on communication and relationships, I noticed that these situations opened up an even more meaningful opportunity. Something we can learn and apply to ALL TYPES of communication.

I struggled deciding where to put this idea in this book. Did it belong in the Foundation Section? The Conflict Section? The Public Speaking Section? Then I realized it belongs everywhere, as it is essential for good communication of any kind. I know, you are saying— get on with it already! What is it?

Ask for help. Human beings like to help. Ideally, this is the reason we give advice (you've already learned that giving advice can also be an excuse not to listen).

I am a short woman. I do not command much presence physically. I have a small voice. It is a bit high—not Snow White high or anything, just an octave above normal. (When I was seventeen I tried smoking so I could have a Lauren Bacall voice, and smoking just made me vomit—no matter how hard I tried! So I am stuck with this voice.)

Here's what I do. I stand up at the lectern with one arm up and ask for help. Asking for help gets people's attention. In a calm voice I repeat,

- Please help me get the attention of the room.
- If you can hear me talking, please help me get the attention of the room.

YOUR PROFESSIONALISM IS KILLING YOU...

- If the person next to you is talking, please ask them to help me get the attention of the room. (People laugh.)
- If the person next to you is still talking, please take their wine glass away, and ask them to help me get the attention of the room.
- If the person next to you is still talking and they are talking to you, we are all watching you. (More people laugh).

This works because the audience wants to know what others are laughing at. They stop talking to find out.

It's incredible how quickly this works.

Sometimes I ask people to do something as well:

- If you hear me talking, please take a seat.
- If you hear me talking, please walk to the left side of the room.
- If you hear me talking, please clap once.
- If you heard that clapping, please clap twice.
- If I ask you to applaud again, I am just trying to get a standing ovation.

People really laugh at the last one. I have fun with this. I don't get frustrated or weird if folks aren't listening. Instead, I laugh and make those who're listening laugh with me. They relax. It's cool. It is much better than yelling "order" at the room.

The cool thing is—if you can get the audience to laugh while other folks are straggling in, still holding conversations and ignoring you—they will be more likely to listen quicker next time. Why? They want to know what was so funny. They realize they've missed something.

Never start talking unless the room is quiet and paying attention to you. Do not try to talk over the drunk revelers in the back. Sometimes this will take exceptional patience. In such cases, I walk to the back of the room and speak directly to the talkers.

In extreme cases, I even resort to overtly sarcastic comments and then talk about how sarcasm severs rapport:

> Can I ask this audience a question? I am not sure if it is true here in Alabama like it is true on the West Coast. Is it considered rude here to talk while someone else is talking?

I laugh, the audience laughs, then I mention how sarcasm is not the best communication tool even though it is really effective. People laugh again, perhaps more nervously this time. I ask them if they know of any better ways to get the attention of the folks in the back. Generally, the room becomes quiet.

Let me reiterate so you don't think I'm advocating bad communication practices:

> The sarcasm ticket only works if you then use it as a lesson to point out what doesn't work. Or if you are really great at sarcastic humor and build relationships

with the way you use it.

Asking for help works in conflict too. If we are sincere in our request for help, it soothes hackles and makes listening easier.

- Help me understand this.
- Help me see through my anger.
- Help me see this differently.

This works wonders in the middle of a fight:

Hold on Antonia. I hear your voice rising, and I fear I am not listening as well as I should. Can you help me?

Asking for help works as long as you truly mean it; it doesn't if you are faking it.

CHAPTER 70:
NAME DRIPPING

Speakers often look for shortcuts to gain the respect and the attention of the audience. Name dropping is one of these shortcuts, and lazy speakers often resort to this worn-out trick in order to prove they are worth listening to. I have fallen prey to this. It is a trap.

I will not tell you who I've taught. I will not read a bio to you or try to get you to listen to me because of who I am or who I am associated with. Why? Because your instant validation and respect mean I don't have to show you how great I am at communicating. I am more effective when you see me at my best, not when you put me there automatically, just because I know so and so.

The bigger the name, the less the audience requires that person to be a great speaker. Bill Clinton could walk on stage and read the ingredients off the back of a cereal box (or play mediocre saxophone) and folks would still be excited about him.

Something happens to us when we get the automatic approval of the audience. Our commitment to communicating to be heard decreases. Whether consciously or not, many speakers who know they "have the audience" won't work as hard. (The same is true of leaders in organizations, when we have power over people our commitment to communicating to be heard decreases.)

I have been victim of this slacker attitude myself. It has hurt me in the past, and I work to avoid it at all cost. When it is clear that my audience adores me before I even open my mouth, I try even harder to hit it out of the park. It doesn't matter if they were impressed by an earlier presentation, a video, or word of mouth, I intend to give them my most authentic, boldly communicating self.

I used to brag a bit about people I trained. If a big name client said it was okay, I would sometimes drop his or her name. This seemed to make it easier for me to get gigs. I would never trade on a client's name if they were averse to it—whether it was contractual or a simple verbal agreement. There were more than a few clients who didn't care, and some who openly endorsed my training and encouraged me to drop their name whenever necessary.

A celebrity endorsement is almost by definition a business generator. "If Blah blah blah loved it, why, just think what it'll do for me!" Look at all the celebrity photos packed onto the walls of restaurants, hair salons and clubs.

There is nothing inherently wrong with having big name clients or receiving celebrity endorsements. The danger lies in the trap of giving your all—your 110 percent—to the "special" engagements (those attended by big names), while slacking off for the more run of the mill audiences.

This happened to me, and when audiences approved of me the moment I said hello, I didn't try as hard to hit the mark. I had already impressed them, so I didn't bother to be great. Then one day I realized I only gave that extra push for really tough or prestigious audiences, which meant I was shortchanging my home base. Not only was this rude, it was also hindering my integrity and my innovation.

I am grateful this piece of information presented itself, as it made me rethink my policy of selected name dropping as well as discontinue my habit of only working hard for the "special audiences." Now I look into the faces of each member of any audience and see a roomful of "celebrities."

The truth is <u>everyone</u> deserves your very best whether they're big shots or not. Remember, we are all important to somebody—some are just going about it more unassumingly than others. The most important person I taught is someone no one knows. I am more impressed by working with her than anyone you have heard of. The relationship economy is repelled by special treatment.

I love entering a roomful of arms-crossed, unsmiling people and transforming it into a roomful of smiling, standing, wildly applauding people. Accomplishing this on the merits of your personality and the content of your presentation is one of the greatest feelings in the world. Okay, that's not entirely true; giving birth, narrowly avoiding death by accident, watching your child grow are also right up there on the feeling meter. So let me qualify my statement by saying, as a speaker there are no greater feelings. Well, maybe also when someone contacts you after a presentation and says you really changed their life—that is a really great feeling too.

It is okay to drip or sprinkle who you are and what you have done into your presentations. Just don't front load with your resume. Instead, weave this information in as you talk—it is a much more powerful way to let the audience know you.

Treat every public presentation as if the audience was paying you $100,000 to get them to listen.

CHAPTER 71:
TEMPLATES MAKE EVERYTHING VANILLA

I have already mentioned that templates are overused in our culture. They block authentic communication. Recall the story about John the lobbyist in the Foundation Section?

Templates are worthy of mention in the Public Speech section because speech templates—specific processes, protocols or methods of speech delivery—will bore audiences after awhile.

Speakers need to offer a kaleidoscope of ideas. Mix and match them up. Luckily, unlike the Garaminals clothing line (which I wore in the 70s), you don't have to worry too much about clashing—they all match. Inspire the audience with variation and good fun, and you have a winning formula for grabbing attention and achieving public speaking success.

I often start my speeches with a story. Beginning my talks this way gets me into my groove so I can stop trembling. I vary my stories and rarely relive one the same way twice. I try not to have a formula (and sometimes I do). I also have a few stories that include audience participation. Now and then, I simply ask people to get up and do a group exercise right out the gate. In fact, I do a certain exercise with every single audience I talk to because it works so amazingly well.

I suppose my real point is to give you permission to do what works for you—to do what feels right in the moment as long as it comes from inside you and not from an emotionless third party template. If you are excited about it, most likely it's working.

Oh, and please avoid the guy at the end who wants to tell you the three things you could have done to be better. He might be wrong.

Vary things. Keep your talks interesting for you and the audience.

CHAPTER 72:
THE ONLY PERSON WHO LIKES THE LECTURE IS THE PERSON GIVING IT™

I have referred to this before; now I must elaborate on it. Here is the deal: **The ONLY person who likes the lecture is the person giving it**. Period.

- Humans do not like to be told what to do.
- We do not like to sit still and hear someone talk without any opportunity for interaction.
- Most humans would rather talk than listen.
- We are our own favorite topic.
- Editorializing causes audiences to nod off mentally.
- We simply cannot listen as long as we used to.
- Entertainment is not enough—we want to learn something.

These points have always been true—even more so in the relationship economy. Communicating to be heard is the goal of any conversation. When we talk too much, the ears across the table begin to droop. They cannot stay focused through the droning.

In public speaking (any communication really), avoid lecturing and telling. Instead, vary the way you are communicating information.

We are taught at an early age to lecture. Picture sticking a funnel in someone's ear (be careful though). Even if we don't exactly visualize it this way, this is what we'd like to do. We want a funnel that will take all the information we are blathering on about (the wide part of the funnel) and streamline the information into their ear without spilling a drop. We try to do this when we lecture.

Unfortunately (for both the lecturer and the lectured), it doesn't work that way. Communication is fast. In public speaking, we need to communication to be heard first. Your job is to stop lecturing and do a verbal soft-shoe so others continue listening. People like to be engaged.

Think back to your favorite teachers in school. Were they the ones who read from the book and droned on in legalese about the Magna Carta? Or were they the ones who wove history into interesting tales of the struggles for freedoms? The ones who sometimes wore funny costumes or showed movies to illustrate their point; the ones who brought in a guitar and got the whole class to sing folk songs of the American Revolution.

The answer is obvious: We learned the most from the teachers who simply shared their love of a subject rather than beating us over the head with it. So again, this highlights one of our very important communication tenets:

It is usually not what we say: It is how we say it. Words are often lost; how they are spoken is often remembered.

This is why speakers who read to audiences are less effective in today's communication culture. What you wrote sitting at your desk is already stale and does not speak to the people sitting directly in front of you. Even if your pre-crafted speech is well written and well delivered, it will never be as interesting and engaging as <u>Rapport Speaking</u>.

The words on this page are 2 percent of the real message from me. Come hear me speak sometime, you will get what I mean.

Where did I learn this? My 3rd grade teacher Miss Hall. She had us move our desks around, work in groups, do crafts and she even promised us we could get rid of our desks for the rest of the year if we worked as a team and hit certain targets. It was amazing how much all the kids helped each other so we could make that happen. We were so proud the day we walked in and she handed us giant ice cream containers to put our stuff in. We scrambled under the tables, sat on the floor and had an amazing few weeks without desks. She had the rapt attention of every kid in that room because she rarely lectured.

Mix-up the way you give your message. Read some. Tell stories. Give analogies. Spout metaphors. Sing if you have to.

CHAPTER 73:
EXPOSITORY SPEAKING IS A NEEDLE IN THE EYE

For the love of god, do not present an expository essay! NEVER EVER EVER!

By expository essay, I mean telling audiences what you are going to tell them, telling them, and then telling them what you told them. This is a needle in the eye to audiences.

During my freshman year of high school, I was introduced to the expository essay. I was informed that this formula of writing would be used for every essay I wrote from then on.

This nifty little recipe has been passed down through the ages (along with starched uniforms and corporal punishment). It informs a (typically) underpaid teacher what to expect, and it gives students a basic formula for underachieving. Hmmmmm. Okay maybe some of you believe it works in some essay writing (though I am not convinced), it absolutely doesn't work when talking to an audience.

According to my unscientific research, roughly 11 percent of audiences need an agenda of some kind. That means 89 percent don't need to know your agenda or the target of your talk. So, your aim is to satisfy the first group and keep the second group from falling asleep.

To do this, I quickly provide a brief and basic agenda for those who need it. I do not tell them what I am going to say, I simply present the targets of the talk and make a brief statement and direct them to the PowerPoint road map on the overhead. Then I move on to the fun part.

Interacting with the audience is much better than designing a rigid agenda. Everybody will be more alert and interested if you devise creative ways to actively involve the room with you and your presentation. The main purpose of a presentation is for you—the speaker—to give your perspective on a subject. You have the microphone because they want to know what you have to say. They don't want to hear pithy leadership sayings lifted from an 80's era motivational poster.

A great speaker will energize audiences and leave them with a connection that encourages a desire to learn even more about the subject. There's no need to literally pound home various points.

When you say, "Here is what happened" and "Now, let me tell you what that means" the audience doesn't get to engage their own creative listening. You are telling them what to think, so why bother to think for themselves?

Certainly you must use some research to fill out your knowledge; and audiences only want to hear about the words of some guy who died a thousand years ago or the newspaper article if you make it your own. In other words, weave your research into an interesting metaphor or story. Make your talk You. Your perspective. Your story. Let audiences hear why you believe what you believe.

Give them more than they bargained for. Surprise them. Talk to them. Ask them to interact, to comment, to connect emotionally as well as intellectually with what you are saying. Details help you do this. When you relive a story with tons of details, the entire horizon of the human emotional experience opens up their listening. A greater understanding will grow—and audience's will be left with a deeper understanding and resonance—if you allow the audience to discover their connection to your words in their own way.

Expository editorializing and speaking formulas raise the YPH's (Yawn's Per Hour) and will bore the audience. Instead, use metaphors, stories and analogies to enhance listening and understanding.

CHAPTER 74:
LEAVE THE *PEANUTS* TEACHER AT HOME

Our goal in public speaking MUST be to be heard. We often think about what we want to say rather than how we say it. Hopefully you've noticed this book talks a lot about communicating to be heard. For me, the most difficult part of writing this book is finding a tone that doesn't come out feeling like a lecture to me—and as you know, the only person who likes a lecture is the person giving it.

When speaking in front of groups, I have noticed the longer I talk, the less people listen. It is as if I have become an adult in the *Peanuts'* cartoon. Remember how Charlie Brown, Lucy, and Linus sat in the classroom and the teacher just droned on and on in her bassoon voice, "Wohhh Wohhh Wohhh." Well, most CEO's sound like this when talking to their team.

Politicians are worse.

Human connection is critical in our current communication economy. Human interaction creates more human connection and thereby more listening.

If you get the urge to lecture, send a memo. Folks will pay more attention to a memo then they will to a lecture. Memos are meant to be one way communication; speeches are not.

I train many "professional speakers"—people who are in the business of speaking and make a ton of money doing it. You would be surprised at how often these professionals come to me and say, "Something isn't clicking anymore, and I'm not receiving the ratings I used to get."

Once I had a "professional speaker" tell me I wasn't a professional speaker; he said I was a "facilitator." "Facilitators interact and do exercises; true platform speakers just talk." I giggled. The comment wasn't intended to make me laugh—it was meant to slap me down. Things have changed since then. Platform speaking has lost its audience appeal; professional speakers need to learn to interact if they want to get great ratings and results. I'll bet that smarty aleck professional is a facilitator now too.

Platform speaking is the modern day equivalent of a typewritter manufacturer. It was a sad day for the president and employees when computers took over the word processing industry. Just as it is a sad day for professional speakers who don't want to interact—because they have no choice. It's like the last car leaving the parking lot of that buggy whip manufacturer—get on board or we'll leave you behind.

Yes, interacting is scary. Who the heck knows what the freaking audience is going to do. It isn't scripted, it's unexpected, and this is why professionals don't like it. There's no looking back now.

Think about your workplace. How many times a day do you think the humans there watch YouTube or something similar? Whatever number you come up with, add two to it and double it. At least. Our culture is overflowing with perspective junkies right now—and the trend show no signs of tapering off.

You will learn more when you interact with the audience and it will improve your message.

Interaction is the key to being heard and remembered.

 **EXERCISE:**

IT'S LATER THAN YOU THINK

Sometimes audiences need a defibrillator. In other words, sometimes heads are nodding forward, and it isn't your fault. This is when you say, *Vee have vays of making you talk.*

Tell the audience to take out a pen and a piece of paper. Walk around the room looking people in the eye until they do it. They will.

Have audience members write down three things they like about their organization and ask them to stand up quietly when they are finished. When 75 percent of the room is standing, tell everyone to sit down and ask for examples.

Then ask everyone to look at their papers and circle the one that will create the most positive change in their organization. Have them pass up their answers forward, then have someone in the room sort them and put them up on the board.

In other words, have them do something. Anything. They will enjoy it.

Examples:

- Have them stand up and take out their wallet:
    - Open your wallet.
    - How much money is in there?
    - Imagine this room represents the entire USA population. Then ask, What percentage of this room will sit down when I ask this question, "Do you have more money today than you did a year ago?" This will open up a <u>lively</u> conversation about what? Wealth. Politics. Environment. This action will stimulate debate. You can sprinkle your key points into the conversation.

- Close your eyes. Raise your hand if you noticed something cool on the roof of the building next door.
    - This exercise talks about perspective and your topic.

- Turn to the row behind you. Now ask them…
    - This one is funny…since everyone is looking at someone's back.

These are just some silly examples that can be made relevant to your talk. Come up with some of your own. A great place to start, as you can tell from this book, is elementary school.

Facilitate and interact.

CHAPTER 75:
A RHETORICAL QUESTION IS NOT INTERACTION

In case you were wondering, a rhetorical question is not audience interaction. This is another example of an overdone speaking technique found in books.

This one is supposed to make audiences feel like they are a part of your talk—help you add drama and suspense with rhetorical questions. This is simply not true. My experience has shown me that, unlike communication tricks that worked when they were new, this one never worked. It causes the speaker to appear as a weak, poor listener who isn't as funny and profound as they think they are. Don't use it.

If you're asking the audience a question, ask a great one. Expect an answer. Respond with what you hear back from them. Answers from the audience are the seeds of the best presentations.

Asking "if anyone" has the answer to your question is the same as saying, "I don't mean you. Look around to see if anyone has the answer." Folks are less inclined to interact when you ask an "anyone" question. Instead, ask "who" has the answer.

Here are some examples to illustrate my point:

Does anyone know the quantity of pi?	Audience will look around to see who knows.
Do you know the quantity of pi?	Yes/No questions aren't always the best. Short lived response, not a lot of interaction.
Who knows the quantity of pi?	A stronger likelihood that folks will answer if they know.
What is the quantity of pi?	Folks will blurt out the answer then everyone will know and it may not be as compelling.
If you know the quantity of pi, stand up.	Those who know will stand up.
Everyone take out a piece of paper. WAIT. Write down the quantity of pi. Do not look at anyone else's paper. Next question: What is PI used for? Write that down too.	This type of interaction works if used sparingly. Making the audience interact increases participation. There are some fine tuning details to this that I will go over later in the book.
Write down the quantity of Pi to five significant digits. If you are 100 percent sure you have the right answer go to the South corner of the room (point to it); If you are 85 percent sure, go to the West; 50 percent, East; No idea, South.	Couldn't this little exercise I just made up sitting in a refurbished, posh, school bus in Point Arena (thanks Blake and Chris) open up a discussion about information and/or risk?

Get the room moving and interacting. Let the audience tell you what the exercise has to do with your subject. A facilitated conversation creates more learning than your mouth doing all the moving. And you will learn too!

CHAPTER 76:
QUESTIONS DONE WELL

Asking a lot of questions gets the audiences attention. Done correctly, this method gets the audience involved and thinking. If done rhetorically, it bores them silly. Ask great questions instead.

Speakers also have a tendency to parrot the answers given by the audience. Such repetition is only necessary if people didn't hear the answer. I suggest you avoid doing this. Parrots belong in North Beach, and parroting a question only works if the room has more than twenty people in it. Parroting gets real old, real quick, and the audience will feel you are speaking down to them.

Let me share an example of ineffective parroting. In Los Angeles, when I was speaking to a group of professors (who, from the beginning, made it very clear they didn't want me there in the first place), I asked:

"What would you say to a reporter who put a microphone in your face and began asking questions about a student caught cheating in your school?"

"I'd let them know I couldn't discuss specifics based on privacy," answered the head of instruction.

"So you'd say no comment," I said.

The next professor responded, "I'd Say I can't comment."

I said, "No comment."

This went on a few more times, and when I listened to this class on tape it sounded like I was playing some sort of Marco Polo game with the room. It was just darn embarrassing.

The reason we parrot? We believe we are acknowledging the responder and letting them know we are listening. This is another worn-out technique that was fashionable in the 70's. It was called "active listening" and it doesn't work anymore because everyone's in on the secret.

Sometimes people parrot in order to stall for time. They are using the space to figure out what to say next—since the last thing a speaker wants to do is stand in front of a room and not talk. Actually, silence is a powerful speaking technique (See Public Speaking Chapter 87, Silence Is A Terrible Thing To Waste, on page 203). Ask the question and be quiet. Wait and make eye contact. Give people a minute to come up with their responses.

If no one responds, I say "Ahem. In case you hadn't noticed, this is the participation portion of the evening." And ask the question again. If I still don't get a response I pair them up to talk about it and then have them tell me what they heard.

Thirty percent of the intellectual property you are reading about right now was created standing in front of an audience. I risked opening up the discussion to the room and those darn brilliant humans out there gave me some really good, creative ideas. They'd say something that would resonate with my perspective, and my very own IP (intellectual property) was born.

Ask a question…then wait for the answer. Let the room be a part of building perspective. The audience has something to teach you.

CHAPTER 77:
TO ASK A QUESTION IS POWERFUL, TO ACTUALLY LISTEN TO THE ANSWER, DIVINE

As you know by now, the best public speakers are the folks who are comfortable being themselves in front of a roomful of people they don't know.

This is partly because the average American audience member starts creating his or her response about four words into the speech. In order to make this rapid judgment possible, they must lower how intently they listen to the speaker's words and instead watch the speaker. People who are comfortable with themselves and their situation are easier to watch. Ever notice how you can like a speaker who you disagree with and dislike one you agree with. It is the same thing.

By asking the audience questions—probing deeper into their ears—we take the focus off us and what we already know and engage the audience's perspective. This puts everyone in a better position to pay attention and truly understand.

Perspective is reciprocal. If speakers make it their goal to gain more perspective with every speech they give, their public speaking will improve. I have amassed a wealth of valuable teaching material from the naysayers in the audience. It doesn't matter if their words or intentions are right or wrong, I become better at what I do by integrating their input.

Asking the audience real questions and interacting with them improves the experience for everyone. So what do you do if the questioner decides to ask a ten-minute question and steals all the oxygen out of the room?

We've all seen it happen, and it frustrates everyone except the blowhard asking the question. Now Christina! That isn't nice. Moderator training isn't taught in school. Most folks do not know how to moderate a panel or questions from an audience. Avoiding such Q&A nightmares is most possible with a level of control and transparency. We have all been taught to sugarcoat and not really say it, things like:

Looks like I have ten-minutes for questions from the group, who has the first question?

If an asker starts pontificating anyway, how do you stop her? It is difficult because to do so, you must interrupt that person—which is tough for most speakers to do out of courtesy to the audience. So here is a better way to open up the room for questions.

Looks like I only have ten-minutes for questions, raise your hand if you have one?

This way, if only one person raises a hand, he can go on and on with impunity. You don't have a big queue of opinions waiting to be expressed, so just sit back and listen. If there is more than one hand up, say something like:

> *Goody, lots of questions! Please keep your question brief so we can get to everyone.*

This way the audience will help police anyone who decides to steal the show. You can also wrap up a longwinded question by saying "brief" into the microphone, lightly and with a smile. This should be enough to give them the hint. If they need a sledgehammer, chances are one of the folks waiting to ask another question will step in and do it before you have to. Let's just hope the person doesn't shout "Get on with it already!"

Also, be careful nodding while receiving the question. Folks running for office need to be trained out of approbation to all questions. "Clearly you do not care about the environment or you wouldn't have voted for SB15." A politician nodding her head while this dagger is being unsheathed is visually agreeing she doesn't care about the environment. Not good.

Get the audience asking questions.

CHAPTER 78:
DON'T CHANGE THE QUESTION, REFRAME IT

Be warned. There are questions out there meant to mess you up. Sometimes the intent is nefarious; sometimes it is an accident. There are those audience members who want to attack us and make us look small, attract attention to themselves or take over the talk. There are ways to shift these message detractors into champions.

Whatever the asker's motivation, stay calm and don't get huffy when taking such questions. No matter how mean or ill-intended, inane or inconsiderate, figure out a way to <u>educate</u> the person asking the question.

This needs to be repeated. Educate the audience—the questioners and the listeners. This is the goal of taking questions. When we put ourselves in the role of educator, it changes our tone and the way we deal with annoying questions.

When you get a tough question, don't grab the hot potato. Instead, watch it roll on by. Pick it up after you've taken some time to think about the real question at hand. This way you can reframe the question and respond to the part that warrants an answer.

Reframing the question is a hot topic right now. In the 80's, speakers were taught to ignore difficult questions and instead answer the questions they wanted to answer. Like the other tricks, this one no longer works. Reframing does. It is an art, and one that takes practice to do gracefully.

One way to reframe a poorly crafted or sneaky question is to call a flag on it. Barack Obama did this very well at a debate during the 2008 presidential campaign.

> BLITZER: *I want you to raise your hand if you believe English should be the official language of the United States.*

> OBAMA: *This is the kind of question that is designed precisely to divide us. You know, you're right. Everybody is going to learn to speak English if they live in this country. The issue is not whether or not future generations of immigrants are going to learn English. The question is: How can we come up with both a legal and a sensible immigration policy? And when we get distracted by those kinds of questions, we do a disservice to the American people.*[6]

Here are some other reframing examples:

"How do you sleep at night voting the way you did on this bill?"
- What you don't want to answer is "I sleep fine." Instead, you must decipher what the person's really saying— *"What keeps me up at night is the cold hard fact that children in our State do not have proper access to healthcare.*

I supported AB 123 as it will provide healthcare to 300,000 children in the State of California. I have never meet a taxpayer who is unconcerned with the needs of our children. Not one."

- You can also turn the tables on them— *"What part of this bill causes you so much vehemence?"*

"You clearly do not care about the police officers who put their life on the line every day. If you did care you would never devote this much time to harassing men and women in uniform as the chair of this commission. Why aren't you focusing your efforts on making our streets safe?"

- *"I heard a few questions in there, let me answer one of them. My dad was a cop. He faced life and death every day. The uniform represents a longstanding tradition of integrity to "protect and serve." Our role is to work with the police department to make the department and the streets safe. It is often uncomfortable. At times, we investigate our own. We will continue to do this for you, for the community and for the police officers we serve."*

"This is a bunch of crap. It will never work in reality."

- *"I'm used to that response. This reminds me of Ayn Rand's theory that the guy who created fire was likely burned at the stake with it. Let's test the idea here and now. Who'd like to volunteer?"*

"I completely disagree with you."

- *"Good. If you agree with everything I have said, one of us has a problem. Either you are drinking the Kool-Aid or I am not risking offending you by saying what I really think…"*

"You are a white girl from the suburbs. What right do you have to question a long-standing yoga tradition created in India?"

- *"There comes a time in every student's life when they must question their mentor. This yoga tradition is deep enough, strong enough to handle my questions. Such questioning will create better understanding."*

"I don't believe a word you say."

- *"Disillusionment is rampant in our world today. We have good reason for it, and most of us refuse to take things at face value anymore. Here is what I know: Evidence wins in this situation. Ask your local school for a tour of their facility, you will find "No Child Left Behind" has resulted in three things…"*

"You are wrong."

- *"Galileo was wrong too. He bucked conventional wisdom, and at the time he was thought to be insane. The world isn't flat and our children are not better off just because their educational scores are higher. We are creating Generation XXL if we do not include more outdoor play in their lives…"*

"If you cheated on your wife you will cheat on the taxpayers."

- *"I do not have a good answer for this one because I agree with it."*

"All you politicians are the same. You talk out of both sides of your mouth."

- *"Ouch. Please give me a specific example of when I have done such an insulting thing. Seriously, I would like a specific example from you."*

"Last year you said 'no new taxes' and this year you voted for Sb 19"

- *"When presented with facts and evidence, prudent politicians must change their minds if new information proves their stance isn't what's best for the voters. My job is to assess ALL the information and do what is best for you…"*

"You clearly do not know what you are doing leading this association."

- *"Ouch. I suppose that is the fear of most people—that we are not good enough or do not know enough to stay involved. As I look at the membership of this association, we have the same people on the board for the past 20 years. While I have been on the board, for one-year, I continually hear the board bemoaning lack of participation from the members. Your honest comment just may be the reason we lack new leadership. Now we must make the opportunity to cultivate and encourage leaders rather than attack them for the exact thing we want them to be— fresh, new and with perspective."*

Answer difficult questions on your terms. Invite them.

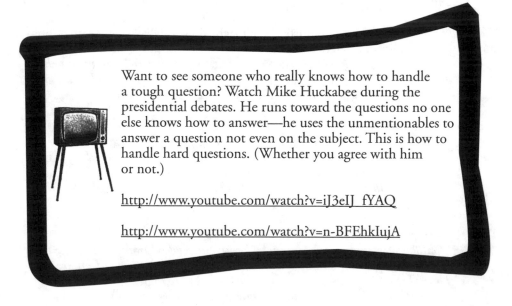

Want to see someone who really knows how to handle a tough question? Watch Mike Huckabee during the presidential debates. He runs toward the questions no one else knows how to answer—he uses the unmentionables to answer a question not even on the subject. This is how to handle hard questions. (Whether you agree with him or not.)

http://www.youtube.com/watch?v=iJ3eIJ_fYAQ

http://www.youtube.com/watch?v=n-BFEhkIujA

CHAPTER 79:
INTERACT WITH ME
OR LOSE ME

Audiences want to be a part of the process in public speaking. You must figure out ways to interact with the audience if you hope to keep everyone engaged.

Maybe you do not care if the audience enjoys your speech. I have seen plenty of speakers who just want to get through their talk rather than figure out a way to communicate to be heard. If this is the case, stop reading; this book just isn't for you.

Talking is boring. Interacting is interesting. It's an easy equation.

Audience members are not all the same. Interacting with an audience member does not mean making them talk or do something: It means communicating to them in the way they want to be communicated with.

Professionals and control freaks avoid interaction. We fear it.

- What is the audience member going to say?
- What if they make me look like a fool?
- What if they ask a question I do not know?
- What if I lose my train of thought?
- What if they bring up something I don't want to talk about?
- What if my message gets lost in their message?
- What if they go on too long and I can't get the conversation back?
- What if they suck all the oxygen out of the room and we all die?!!!

Sit down my kiddies and let me tell you something. I've never had anything happen when I am standing in front of a room full of people that didn't make the event better. As long as I <u>went with</u> what happened and stayed in the moment.

Here's an example to help you believe me:

I am training a group of new instructors. My schedule is insane, and it has been difficult for me to prepare. I created this cool little manifesto that indicates the ways our instructors must be in the world from this moment on. I read the page to the group. Midway through I realized how boring it was and stopped and did something else.

Later that evening, I used my foible as an example of how we do not communicate to be heard. It was a great lesson for the team—on what <u>**not**</u> to do.

If I drop my microphone, show up wearing a dress that has no place to clip the lapel mic or the projector stops working in the middle of my talk—I simply USE it to prove a point.

YOUR PROFESSIONALISM IS KILLING YOU..

Audience interaction is the key to communicating to be heard. There are key facilitation rules that can be implemented to help maintain "control" of the room. I will tell you those in the chapters coming up. You don't get a list this time. You gotta read the whole thing.

Oh, one more thing: Do the exercises. I don't care how hokey they seem—do them. They make a big difference in your understanding and retention.

Speaking of exercises, here's one for you now. As soon as you finish reading this paragraph, write your biggest fear in audience interaction in the white space below. What is it? I know you have one. We all do. Even if you are a great public speaker you still have a fear. My fear is offending someone. What's yours? Write it in the space below:

Whatever happens in the room is a gift to you when you embrace it. Mistakes are future intellectual property.

When possible, interact with the audience. Come up with creative ways to get them involved.

CHAPTER 80:
FILL-UP THE CELLAR,
JUST DON'T LIVE THERE

If you're worried you don't think so well on your feet, prepare for all of the hard questions you might get in advance. I actually like coming up with new and interesting ways to respond to them.

For example, I volunteer for a woman's organization dedicated to getting more women in office. The board is entirely female, and we all work really hard to make training and recruiting events happen.

I decided to present a four minute talk about the woman's organization to a group of CEOs. I thought it might help us get some more donors for our non-profit cause. Before the talk, I sat down and thought of all the hard questions I could get—knowing I likely wouldn't get any.

I practiced:
- Why train just Democratic women?
- Are women better than men in politics?
- What in your background makes you qualified?

While I didn't get any of these difficult questions, my prep work changed the way I talk about this woman's group. In fact, it made me wonder: Are women better than men in politics?

In the end, I decided no—women are not better than men. So why am I training women? Only 14 percent of our politicians are women, while 51 percent of our population is female. If the numbers were reversed, I'd be training men. Laws are created by perspective, and we need equal representation at the table to have a clean perspective.

That answer to a question I did not receive, has changed the way I have the conversation about the organization—changed it for the better.

Ask yourself difficult questions and prepare to expand your vista of perspective.

CHAPTER 81:
INTERACT WITH 'EM

I have a story that involves a cricket. The experience happened when I was twenty-two, and whenever I tell it, I ask the audience to make a chirping sound every eight seconds. Obviously, this makes the story incredibly vivid, loud, and fun. It also illustrates how hard it is for the audience to pay attention while chirping and how hard it is for me to stay on track as everyone chirps at me.

Sometimes it really works. Other times, we have great fun, while the story kind of becomes secondary. Always it works one hundred times better than a boring lecture does. What I lack in perfection and polish I make up in keeping folks interested.

What does it really mean to be entertained? Is that all audiences want? I don't think so. Too many speakers today are so hyper focused on entertaining that they fall short on perspective. I am bored to distraction by fake entertaining. Teach me something.

What do I mean by that? I mean I have a visceral reaction to hyperactive team building. I hate team building for the sake of team building. I think, Oh no! Not another trust-fall exercise.* And what? You are going to make me do it and you aren't even going to bother aligning it with some profound perspective or learning. Please help me figure out how your exercise applies to me and my life.

I was at a meeting recently where a board member put "relationship-building" on the agenda. I have enough friends. Don't relationship build me. If it needs to be on the agenda, thanks for letting me know ahead of time. I'll show up after the team building part is finished. Team building is a needle under the fingernail.

I don't want campfire s'mores bonding. Yuck. Am I ranting again? You betcha. Let me settle down and reiterate the point to remember.

Yes, we want to entertain and entertaining is not the goal. This is not a Zen koan. It is simple fact. Audiences want to be interacted with so they can <u>integrate</u> what we are presenting. Games are a waste of time unless they are steeped in some genuinely higher purpose of learning: Perspective. Help your audience bend their perspective.

Audience participation is not a sing a long.

*Thank you Dhaya for this phrase!

CHAPTER 82:
GET 'EM TO SEE
EACH OTHER

I haven't said it enough. The human relationship is the true currency. People want to interact. Audiences like to interact with the speaker, and groups need to interact with each other.

I get a lot of push back on this. People tell me, "If I am in a room to listen to Bill Gates, I want to hear from Bill Gates, not Joe Schmoe sitting beside me."

Maybe. Though if the speaker isn't a megastar, genuine audience interaction actually makes the speaker more effective. Typically, the speaker is the outsider in the crowd, while the people listening belong to each other in some way. They may be in the same company, in the same field, in the same political party. A speaker who figures out a way to deepen the existing relationships of the audience is automatically heralded as a great communicator.

Think of a political event for a moment. Let's say one hundred volunteers show up to help get a candidate elected. What is the likelihood first time volunteers will come back if no one pays any attention to them? Right. What is the likelihood first time volunteers will come back if they make a personal connection with someone? See how easy that is?

At a meeting for a presidential campaign, I noticed most of the volunteers were standing all by themselves. Nobody was making an effort to bring them into the fold. So I stood up and said, "We are the ambassadors in this room, from this moment on no one stands alone. It is our job to seek out every solo person here and introduce them to others. Help them fit in. It makes a difference." No one stands alone.

Here I go again—I'm about to drive my human currency agenda. Figuring out how to get the audience to participate and interact with each other will strengthen the relationships and lead to greater organizational adhesion. Paaah. "Paaah" is the sound of me spitting all those words out of my mouth. Too complex. Let me say it simpler:

Get people talking to each other. How?

- **Partner work**—Have audience members get up and find a partner and practice something relevant to their purpose for being there.

- **Role-Play**—I hate this term. Role-play implies we are playing a "role." Playing a role is acting. We aren't good at acting. So let's call this "road testing." Teach a concept and have the audience members try it out. Integration is another term for this.

- **Pushback**—This one is fun. I put people in small groups and tell them to "work together to disprove the theory I just presented you with." When they are finished, I bring everyone back together and we talk about the holes they discovered.

- **Group discussion**—Direct audience members into groups and have them discuss a topic or solve a problem. Most people love giving advice, so this is a fun exercise for most.

- **Group Contest**—Group folks up and have them compete against each other. This works especially well with CEO's or any leader. For example, get folks building a structure out of a myriad of materials. Apply this to your subject—only if you can find the application.

My friend Bill used to say, "The mind cannot absorb what the seat cannot endure." If the audience has been sitting in their chairs for an hour, ask them to get up and do one of the exercise suggestions listed above. Have small groups work for three to five minutes, then call the room back together. Ask for a few teams to give a report on their discussions. Your audience will be happier for it.

If you are Bill Gates, don't worry. You can just lecture to folks, and they will like it (though they still might not like you). Everyone else—be creative.

Figure out creative ways to get people interacting with each other in a relevant way.

CHAPTER 83:
USE WHAT'S IN
THE ROOM

Another interactive way to grab the attention of the room is to use something in it. It is organic, not forced, and highly effective. When you use this technique, audience members turn up their attentiveness volume and start anticipating what else you might use.

Humans are curious—they want to know what's coming. The will sit and subconsciously try to figure it out. Luckily, they have to listen to you as they do this, otherwise they will miss your interaction with the next "thing."

Here are some fun ways to use what is in the room to engage the room:

- **Shock Act**—Walk out on stage and pour a glass of water over your head. Then say something like, "I've been so worried I'd do something stupid in front of you today, I thought I'd just get it over with." When I did this, the audience couldn't stop laughing. I followed-up with, "How many in this room are 100 percent confident in public speaking?" The talk continued from there and was very well received.

- **Science Experiment**—Ask participants to bend a metal spoon. There is a trick to this. Someone in the audience likely knows what it is. Imagine you were presenting on an impossible sales goal. Bending a metal spoon felt impossible until we knew the process behind it. Let's break down our goal into a process. First…

- **Touch Experiment**—Ask participants to put their hands in a box of feathers with their eyes closed. Have them describe what they are experiencing. This can apply to any topic about trust and concern, "Who was worried there was wet spaghetti in there?"

- **"Volunteer" Set-up**—A few years ago I was leading a meeting for an association involved with raising money for charity. The folks present were repeatedly asked to "give till it hurt." At the end of the luncheon I asked people to look underneath their coffee cups for a blue dot. After the clatter of plates reduced to a low din, I announced that anyone without a blue dot was hereby volunteered to serve on the fundraising committee. Of course there were no blue dots, and after the laughter died down, I seriously asked for anyone interested in serving on the committee this year to stand so we could acknowledge them. Five people stood.

- **The Last Person Standing**—This only works one time per group, so use it sparingly. For example, when a group was trying to raise money for a Junior Achievement Scholarship, I watched a speaker say, "If you are willing to give $10 for Junior Achievement fund to please stand up. Remain standing if you are willing to contribute $20. Everybody, please give a huge applause to those standing." When the roar died down, he said, "Remain standing if you are willing to give $50." It kept going like this until two guys were left, each vying to be the last man standing. In the end, they both gave $1000, and a total of $2300 was raised that night thanks to this clever method. Be prepared—some folks do get upset when you do something different. Read the conflict section—it is all good.

- **Tell stories that apply directly to the audience**—When you tell stories, use references and information relevant to the people in the room. Humor helps. For example:
    - On the way to a Rotary Club meeting, I was running through the quick speech I was going to give. Each week a Rotarian, (there were about ten of us that volunteered to do this), delivers the current local news to a couple hundred people in attendance. I like to make mine funny, so I stressed a little bit to make sure I hit the bar—and that day, I was having a hard time finding my humor. At the intersection of Powell and Post, I saw two drivers in a bit of a tussle. One guy was leaning on his horn and the other driver had her hand out the window in a one-fingered salute. Ironically, the saluting driver had a Jesus fish sticker on her bumper, while noisy one had a Sunshine Daydream Grateful Dead sticker on his. I kept walking. When I delivered my news speech, I wove this story in after my bit on transportation. Then I made it relevant to Rotary members by saying, "Speaking of transportation, how many of us drove to this meeting today? The entire goal of Rotary is community service. And true community is what we do when no one is watching. Next time we are in our vehicles and in a rush, let's make sure we wave with all five fingers on our hand!"

Involve the room in your speech with words or action.

CHAPTER 84:
USE YOUR BANANA

One year ago, I did a daylong training for a group comprised of twenty male foresters. These men would rather be in the forest than in a conference room listening to a weird chick with red hair. The class was about communication and creating a strong team culture capable of positive conflict. We had a very tall order to deliver: We had to make sure everyone understood and practiced the Sixteen Pillars of Platinum Relationship. (See the next book for these!)

The entire day was interactive and filled with games, metaphor, analogy—even a few poems. To keep the attention of this group I had to jump through some hoops (including the hula hoops I brought with me). By the end of the day, we were all smiling. I learned a ton from the twenty men in that room.

I went to see them again recently, and I asked the group to refresh my memory on what we talked about in our first training. They were silent for a moment, and I was worried until a hand finally came up—Hey, we did that potato thing and that was all about clarity and focus on message. Another hand—We did that rope trick that reminded us to question and listen more. Another hand came up, and another. You get the picture.

Had I stood in front of that room and lectured for the entire day, my question would have garnered a roomful of blank stares. Being heard and remembered is the result of interactivity, stories, exercises—and the boom and the pow! (Don't worry, I'll explain more about the boom and the pow later.)

Objects are great for this, and I have created many interesting ways to incorporate them and get audiences interacting. You can too. To inspire your creative process, here are some examples of objects I use and a few of the exercises and analogies that go with them. (I can use these to teach almost anything by the way—also, be aware there are many "learning examples" though I am only offering a few.)

Orange
- Have participants bite into an orange.
    - Some folks will peel it first. Ask them to bite through the peel. Why won't they? Some will.
        - ✳ Learning example: Where did we learn to peel it first? What does this example have to do with organizational innovation?

- Light an orange peel.
    - Make sure you do not have sprinklers in the room. If you have never lit an orange peel, do this at home first. Be careful. It can be a little explosive.

✴ <u>Learning example</u>: Who knew the orange peel would do this? What does this have to do with employee motivation? Everyone has a spark. Everyone. The better we know people, the greater chance we can ignite their passion.

● Ask the audience to draw an orange.
  ◌ Let them draw for a moment and then ask them to draw it better. Stop them and ask them to draw an even better one. Then interrupt their drawing and teach them how to shade and shadow when drawing. Now you have "taught" them how to draw a better orange.
    ✴ <u>Learning example</u>: Coaching is required for successful teams. In most organizations we simply tell people to be better; we do not teach them how.

● Peel in one peel.
  ◌ Ask the audience to peel the orange in one peel. Give folks their own orange. Ask them what this has to do with the topic presented today (your subject). Folks will come up with what it means. Really.
    ✴ <u>Learning example</u>: Have you ever peeled an orange this way? Why not? Would you do it again? Why or why not? We have some things that keep repeating in our organization that we do not like. How do we change this? How do we get everyone peeling the orange in ways that work for the organization?

Apple
● Give everyone an apple and hand out 3x5 cards.
  ◌ Each card has a different message on it, though don't tell participants there are different messages. Tell them to act out the instructions on the card and that they MUST work alone and keep the words on the card a secret.
  ◌ The 3 x 5 cards say things like:
      There is a worm in the apple.
      There is a gold coin in the middle of this apple.
      This is the only thing you will get to eat today.
      This apple was ripened on the tree; it is the yummiest apple you have ever had.
      Take a bite, Snow White. C'mon.
  ◌ Film this if possible. The reactions and interactions with the apples are very interesting and instructive.
    ✴ <u>Learning example</u>: It's incredible to see all the different ways folks interact with the apple. This is what perspective does to our organization. We have our perspective, it is true for us and that is all that matters. It really was the same apple, the card was lying. Sometimes our perspective is lying.

Banana

- Ask an audience member to show the room how to peel a banana. Then show a video clip of wild chimps peeling a banana.
  - ✱ <u>Learning example:</u> When people stop laughing, walk the audience through the team-building communication steps to make sure there is never a squished incorporative peel when they peel proverbial bananas.

Potato

- Teach the room how to put a straw through a potato. If you have never attempted this, be careful. You can accidentally put the straw through your hand. Creating a whistle that way is quite painful. (wink) Do not try this at home. You could hurt yourself. Mr. Coke taught me this one, and Bill Koefoed perfected it!
  - Get a LONG potato.
  - Hold it as low as possible.
  - Aim the straw at the top portion—the furthest from your hand.
  - Jam the straw through the potato.
  - If it didn't work—lick your thumb and place it over the end of the straw (hold it like a knife with your thumb on top of the potato). This seals off the air and will make it more likely to go through. If this doesn't work, here is the trick. Do not think about the straw.
  - Try to get your hand (the part of your hand under your pinky finger) to hit the potato. Stop thinking about the straw.
    - ✱ <u>**Learning example:**</u> This example can teach focus, communication or sales. Most talks can fit in this exercise.

Hula Hoop

- Hula hoops can be used in a million different ways.
  - As building supplies—with masking tape and paper.
  - Have the group stand in a circle holding the hula hoop. Tell them they are in a boat and it has a leak. They are in the middle of a lake and there are alligators. Tell them they must think and act fast to save themselves. Ask them to pantomime what they will do. It is actually quite fun to watch. Every time I have done this, some other learning comes up. Folks are smart—they come up with all sorts of things this means. I created it to show that folks rarely patch the boat. They paddle; they row and some jump out and try to swim. Few bother to patch the boat. When working together, even if part of the group patches and part of the group bails and part of the group rows—they will make it. Often groups forget to work as a team to solve the situation. Could this teach your subject? I bet it could.
    - ✱ <u>**Learning example:**</u> I have used the hula hoop in about 72 different ways. I suppose I can write a book on "How to use a hula hoop to prove your point."

Use objects to make your point—get folks doing something.

CHAPTER 85:
AN APPLE IS NOT
A FRUIT

Trying to come up with the cover image for this book, I asked my son what he thought I should do, and he said "An apple, mama." The perfect metaphor. We envisioned this gorgeous red apple with a bite taken out of it; we eventually settled on an apple core due to a certain litigious, computer company. Plus we were hungry at the photoshoot! (wink)

Take a moment and look again at the cover of this book. The power of metaphor is dependent upon how quickly a person can get a sense of our message—less time, zero words, big meaning. Remember, words matter least.

A simple image. An apple. It means so many things.

What does an apple mean to you?

- Sir Issac Newton—An ah-ha moment, innovation, science
- Snow White—Careful who you trust, death, sleep, fairytale
- Adam and Eve—Miscommunication, strife, fear
- An apple a day keeps the doctor away—Do what is good for you
- Apple of my eye—Love, happiness
- Johnny Appleseed—Spread the message
- Teacher Apple—Learning, education
- Adams Apple—The differences between men and women
- American as Apple Pie—Slogans, messaging, what we like about who we are
- The Big Apple—New York, city life, change
- Worm In the Apple—Something spoiled, intrusion, organic

An apple can mean whatever we want it to. It is an image that evokes instant recognition, and many metaphors come to mind—the list above is just those off the top of my head. I use it on the cover to cement the message of your professionalism killing the real you. It symbolizes the death of what is so precious and perfect about you—when you act differently than you do when you are with your closest friends. It is that distance from the weirdness you show your household that is lessening your great communication style.

An apple is beautiful in its simplicity. It is perfect the way it is. So are you. Avoid taking bites out of the real you!

CHAPTER 86:
LOOK PEOPLE IN THE EYE
(NOT IN THE UNDERWEAR)

Do not picture people in their underwear unless you work for Victoria's Secret or you are sitting home and looking at your spouse. Do not look above audience heads either. Nor should you scan the room rapidly like a visual sprinkler.

These are tricks, and tricks don't work. Even if a book or a speaking coach told you imagining the audience in dog outfits will calm your nerves, don't do it. It puts you in a perception trap, because you don't experience what is actually going on in the room. New information cannot reach you. You are in actor mode. The audience loses interest.

Speaking is a conversation; public speaking is a conversation with an audience. So make it one. Look people in the eye, linger here and there, and let the words flow naturally. Just like when you are having a conversation. (If you do not normally look people in the eye in conversation, start doing so. It is good practice.) Eye contact is for YOU not the audience. Your brain will work better and you will be having a conversation rather than a speech.

If the audience is hostile, address it. Challenge it. Go with it. Do not imagine it away. (Later in this section, in "Liver Symposiums" on page 293, I'll share an example of struggling with tough audience in London that illustrates this point.)

I have a rule, if I notice something hostile or suspicious about a person or an audience, I have two options: Ask if it is true, or let it go.

Most of us are relationship people; so by looking someone in the eye we feel less like presenters and more like conversationalists. This is an excellent way to let go of your nerves and relax the room. There is a caveat though—if someone is grumpy and causing you to stumble when you look at them, look at someone else. Eye contact with happy people helps keep your energy up.

If I have an evil eye in the audience or someone who is not giving me attention I do not avoid them. I interact with them where possible. I also imagine in my head that they are constipated—poor things. Their intestines are very uncomfortable and that is the reason for the painful face. Poor things. This is not acting. This is projecting...there is a difference!

Looking the engaged audience members in the eye will make your speech feel like a conversation.

EXERCISE:
YOU WILL HATE THIS EXERCISE

This exercise comes in three parts. For it to work, you must do the steps in the order I present them, and do not read ahead until I say you can. I know I say this all the time. I am a control freak. Even in book form. Mine isn't arbitrary control: I am a control freak with a purpose—to experience the gestalt of this exercise (and all the others I asked you not to read ahead on).

You will need to tear this page out of your book and bring it with you to a cocktail party, restaurant, or business reception. This exercise will also work on public transportation or at a coffee shop and is best done in a room of people you have some connection with—even if it is simply eating food at the same restaurant.

Exercise One:
Arrive at your destination. Have <u>nothing</u> in your hands. Hide your bag or purse under a table or between your feet. If you have been served a drink, put it down. You smokers out there, imagine me with a wagging finger telling you no. Then, when socially possible and polite, disentangle yourself from conversation and step toward a wall.

Stand there and look at people. Try to look people across the room in the eye. You may feel uncomfortable doing this. Do this with ten people. Then continue to stand there and look around the room.

Be prepared. People may come over to talk to you. Some might think, who is the weird guy staring at me? Why is that odd chick standing there smiling and not talking to anyone?

Why am I asking you to do this? Your public speaking will improve by practicing the steps above. This exercise helps with eye contact, smiling, pausing and presence. To this day, I still make myself do this—I still hate it. I wish for art on the walls or anything to look at to distract from the fact I am there alone doing nothing—only looking!

While practicing this, feel what is happening with your mouth. Try to enjoy yourself or at least enjoy that you are improving. For most of us, our jaw is clinched, so make sure you breathe in and out so it can relax. Look around. It is only people.

Stop reading, and do this on your own. Five minutes is enough for your first time.

Did you do all the steps in exercise one? If not, you cannot pass go nor collect two hundred dollars. Go do exercise one and come back when you are finished.

I will hold your place for you.

Wasn't that interesting? Make notes on your experience. Okay, now, we can go to exercise two.

Exercise Two:
This time, when looking around the room, instead of looking at people and worrying about yourself, watch for what you like. I am not suggesting you do this in a scary stalker way. Just notice the things you like about the people you see. Watch for detail. Perhaps others are not noticing the things you see. Maybe the way the server keeps smiling at a patron's well-behaved daughter. The great grandmother who dotes on her elderly son. You get the picture. Watch for what you like. Don't just watch one person—watch many.

Now, go do this exercise. When you finish, I will tell you a story about my experience practicing these exercises. I'll hold your place for you.

Are you done? It is a trip isn't it? I just did it with you…

I left my hotel room and went downstairs to the restaurant in the lobby. I hate these exercises; they are uncomfortable. I did both sets of instructions at the same time (for those of you who read ahead anyway, you can do this too). On the second set—this always happens—someone approached me to chat.

Moments before she came over I was noticing how sweet she was to her father. She cut up his meat for him, then asked the server for more water. I smiled sweetly remembering doing the same for my dad. A tinge of melancholy washed over me. I missed my dad and wished I could sit down and eat with him again. Then I shifted my attention to "notice" something else.

She came over to me on her way to the restroom. She smiled and complimented me on my sweater. We talked about her dad: A World War II vet who had a stroke last year. He was stationed in Hawaii like my father-in-law. Then my food came, and she left. I wondered if they knew each other. If we had more time, I imagine we would have discovered they did. It was a feeling.

Why did this woman come to talk to me when I simply looked around the room watching for what I liked? I don't really know. Though I have a few ideas. Namely, people can feel our good energy when we are watching them. Before I deliver a speech I look around the room and find what I like about the room. It sets the audience in a mood to see me liking them the way I do. Yes, I even do this when I speak to a room full of cigar smoking, right wing Republicans. Many of them are my friends.

This exercise does many things:

1)   People listen more to those they like.

2)   We emulate what we focus on.

3)   Getting out of our head before we orate will make us more likely to

communicate to be heard.

4)   Our surroundings are rich with perspective and stories that will move the audience.

5)   Your eye contact will be improved by practicing this exercise.

6)   People know what we are thinking more than we want them to.

Practice looking without speaking; it will greatly improve your presentation ability.

CHAPTER 87:
SILENCE IS A TERRIBLE
THING TO WASTE

The pause is one of the most misunderstood presentation tools.

Ever since grade school, we've been told staring is rude. So why do public speakers hope and pray the audience will stare at them, while ironically, experiencing discomfort on a visceral level when their prayers and hopes are answered? It is a quagmire. We associate staring with judgment (as well as attention), so as the audience stares at us, we know we're being judged—all the time! It is a double edged blade.

This staring dichotomy messes with our natural ability to pause in front of the audience. This hurts us, as quietly looking at the folks in the room is one of the most powerful things we can do as a public speaker.

When we pause, some members of the audience will imagine we've forgotten what we were going to say and feel bad for it. Some will secretly enjoy it. Some will look up from their Blackberry to figure out what's going on.

In reality, we only lose control of the room if we freak out or become nervous in our silence. Silence creates more silence if done in a facilitated way. Silence is just a fancy way to say pausing, and there is a trick to it—eye contact. Find the eyes in the room and look at them. Take time to give the audience a little space to catch up with you. Breathe. Actually stop talking and take a big breath in front of the audience.

"I am going to stop talking now so you can think about what I just said."

Silence is golden and effective.

CHAPTER 88:
THE UM INFECTION

Who decided "um" was such a bad word? It wasn't me. When I coach speakers I do not worry too much about um, though other professional speech coaches often cringe at its utterance. I am unclear why that is. Who cares?

Since we aren't living in my reality, I must spend a moment discussing the um infection. As an audience member, stop judging people by ums, hands in the pockets and all the stuff public speaking professionals have told you not to do. Professionals have learned to listen for um and when they hear it they have permission to project all sorts of opinions and prejudices onto the person using it. Thus most of my clients want to be coached away from the um word, and their careers depend on it. I end up coaching people not to say um primarily because it helps restore confidence.

Of course, um, if overused, is highly distracting and can make the speaker appear indecisive and unfocused. In this case, pausing is an effective and powerful technique to supplant the um. It will be easier if you first forgive yourself and admit um is not your fault. Imagine you came home from vacation with a terrible cold. The guy on the plane who sneezed into your food gave you the cold. It isn't your fault.

Um is the same, so be absolved from the um sin. Think of um as a low grade communication infection. We all get it from time to time. Big deal. Chances are, someone around you is using um a lot, and you are mimicking them. You silly monkey. Humans do this. Don't worry about it.

We pick up other words too:
- Like
- You know
- I mean
- So

"Like", "you know" and "I mean" are usually placeholders in the conversation—a way to keep the verbal ball in our court. They also serve to confirm that the other person is listening. When used too much, these words make us sound like a valley girl. Avoid doing so unless you really like shopping and like live in the valley, like you know what I mean?

If you spend a lot of time with people who use um, like, and so on, try telling them your plight. Say something like, "hey humans are mimics, and I'm really trying hard to remove unnecessary speech habits from my vocabulary." Ask if you can work on it together, and agree on a method to coach each other to breathe instead of using these words.

Then STOP LISTENING FOR it. It is your focus on um that is making you say it more.

Pausing (breathing) is a strong asset for a public speaker. I often stop talking and look at the audience—in the eye. I pan around and say nothing. Audiences shift around when I do this. They think I have forgotten what I was going to say (or they wonder if I am having a seizure). Often I make note of the silence and ask folks to discuss their feelings about it.

Try staring at people without talking. Breathe.

Pausing is better than an infectious word.

CHAPTER 89:
IF THE AUDIENCE APPLAUDS STOP TALKING

Sometimes people laugh at things we didn't intend to be funny. Such as when Hillary Clinton made her "What do I know about Evil men?" statement. She might not have been fully prepared for the hysterical response from the audience.

If the audience starts laughing, <u>stop talking</u>. This is a time when your silence is absolutely necessary. So many presenters talk over this critical moment in the relationship with the audience. This stunts their rapport.

Let me break it down for ya on a frame by frame level:

- You say something funny.
- Audience starts laughing.
- You talk over their laughing.
- Audience knows what you say is important because you just made them laugh.
- So they cut their laughing short to listen some more.
- Laughter is a physical act; physical responses to a speaker increase listening and retention.
- The audience's laughter was creating rapport and relationship building.
- By cutting it short, you are cutting short their capacity to remember you.
- By continuing to talk you are interrupting their experience.
- People do not like to be interrupted.

Train your ear to hear your audience's laughter. Teach yourself to stop talking the moment you hear the roar building. Give everyone a moment to physically react to what you just said. Those who didn't hear it will also have time to ask—what did she just say??

Let the audience have their laugh.

CHAPTER 90:
GIVE 'EM THE GOOSE BUMPS

All talks can be inspirational, or at least bend in that direction. Our job as public speakers is to boldly go where people have not gone before. Otherwise, why bother to speak at all.

Inspiration rarely comes from words. Sure, some words can really inspire; they are rare. Inspiration mostly springs from discovery, emotion and experience—with others, with nature, with self. When you walk in the briar brush of being an emotional, alive human, you open yourself to the spectrum of discovery. When you translate these discoveries for your audiences, you inspire them to go out and gather their own inspiring experiences.

Experience is inspiration, so by creating experiences for your audience, you have a better chance of inspiring them—which means they will remember your message. In previous chapters I have discussed using objects, stories, and exercises to involve the body as well as the brain, and thus get your message to stick. Inspiration is sticky.

There is also the message beneath your message—You! Inspirational speaking has the fabulous fringe benefit of a "you" subtext, for you exist within the substrata of your message. Sometimes audiences are inspired in ways you could not have foreseen. Generally, this means you are being true to yourself and to the room. Remember, if audiences remember you, they are more likely to remember your message.

I work at my son's preschool once a week. On my first day, I was a little nervous. I was told, if a child hurts another child—go to the hurt child and give him/her attention and only discipline children who are with our preschool. Our play park is a public facility, and thus we are warned not to discipline children who are not in the preschool.

About five minutes into my shift in the playground, I watch Paulo throw sand at a little girl. I run to the little girl and get down on my knees to make sure she is okay. She is crying. Her grandmother comes running over to her and pushes me out of the way. "Stay away from bad boys Helen. He is a bad boy. She beings to scream at Paulo, "You are a bad boy. A BAD BOY." I watch Paulo start to tear up and, instead, jut his chin out. I suddenly watched this sweet boy become what she was saying; he stopped crying and became bad.

I fell to my knees in front of him and grabbed his shoulders. "You are NOT a bad boy Paulo. You are a good boy. I have watched you. You are a good boy. What you did was bad behavior, and you and I will work together so that doesn't happen again. You are a good boy."

The grandmother yelled at me that I didn't know how to raise kids. Paulo's lip quivered, and then he hugged me for about two minutes. Now he looks at me out of the corner of his eye right before he throws a wooden block at a kid—and reconsiders his behavior. I am inspired by Paulo.

Audiences are inspired when you give them a belief in the future. Making a person feel bad about themselves reduces their listening; using fear and negativity to motivate won't produce lasting results. So, if you're talking about the dire conditions of global warming, guide people to learn how they can work together toward a solution. End on a positive note. Embrace human resiliency. Lead them on the path of your message.

I am not suggesting "rah rah" inspiration. Usually we inspire people by telling the story that we don't want to tell.

Risk inspiration.

CHAPTER 91:
EARS RESPOND
TO STORIES

The human relationship is the true currency and stories are the transactional medium of relationship in our culture.

What do you do when you are with your closest friends? Think about it. You sit with your favorite beverage and swap stories.

Stories are cool for several reasons. We get to relive the storyteller's adventure. We get to vicariously have a new experience. We get to hear another's perspective.

Similar to our friends, audiences like stories in our communication mix; it makes them more interested. Furthermore, stories make our points sticky—easier to remember because it is something engaging enough to add to their own memory banks.

Stories make them remember us which makes them remember our points.

Stories are also cool because they take us out of nervousness. Everyone gets nervous when they pretend to be something they aren't, such as a factoid-spewing-lectern prop. In our daily lives we are not professional and stiff. We relate to people and gesture naturally as we tell the story of the bus driving by splashing water all over our new shoes.

The key is to translate our natural storytelling ability into public speaking, thus giving us the opportunity to share ourselves fully with the audience:

> *About eight seconds into our bus splashing story, we will stop acting and start being the person we are with our closest friends. This naturalness will engage endorphins in our body and cause our synapses to fire. Our brain will work better. The clouds of doubt will part, audience members will smile, and we will be brilliant.*

Show your personality, give insight into your perspective, help us to see you as a real person rather than a head with a mouth. Risk exposure and experiential intimacy. Overcome the professionalism virus. People like stories, and unlike the popular slang saying, it really is "all about YOU."

A story happens every day. Start watching for them.

CHAPTER 92:
RELIVE THEM

Uh oh, here comes the bad news. Are you ready? Telling a story isn't enough. You must relive the story. Make it real. Offer such realistic detail you make our heads swim with the experience. (Don't worry, this part isn't so hard either; in a little while, I'll give you an exercise to practice what I'm talking about.)

Your experience—i.e, your story—is the only thing that matters. Not your bio, not your CV, not your recent promotion—your unique life perspective makes you the interesting person you are. This is because <u>why</u> is vastly more important than <u>what</u>. Let me say it again. Why you feel the way you do about a subject means more to people than what you think. Your perspective is critical and relevant in any conversation.

Be proud of your perspective and experience, even if it's unconventional or isn't packaged with a PhD. There are countless examples of self-taught people who do great things. They are known as autodidacts, and they don't need fancy degrees or papers to back them up. Their great work speaks for itself. Remember, the earlier story about the microwave inventor Percy Spencer (see Chapter 8, page 27). He was self-taught. So was writer Mark Twain, Zen philosopher Alan Watts, and musician Eddie Van Halen—to name a great few. In other words, your experience and conviction goes much further to back up what you say than any CV ever could.

I'll say this again: Telling stories is just a gimmick unless you relive your story in great detail with real emotion. Reliving an event also makes you more comfortable and natural. I will repeat this like a mantra in the coming chapters—it is vital to public speaking because people only listen to people when they experience a connection to them.

A connection will not occur if you are merely telling your story. Telling a story, as opposed to reliving it, is a rote expression; the story is a repeat performance of the way the story has been told in the past. The story becomes perfunctory and lacks sparkle and nerve. There is no passion because our connection to the actual experience is buried under the weight of memorized words.

By contrast, when we relive a story, we animate the words with every cell of our body—we truly come alive. We bring the past into the present, and our audience travels into the experience with us.

Relive your stories as you tell them. The audience will respond to your unique personality and communication style.

 **EXERCISE:**

You will need about fifteen uninterrupted minutes to complete this exercise. Please do yourself a favor and do not read ahead until you are ready to do the entire exercise.

Ready?

Start by turning off your phone and your computer. Close your door. Shut off the TV and stereo. Take out a pen. On the next page you will find some empty columns, and soon you will be writing in them.

Take a few moments and think about life events that occurred before you were twenty-five. Any event that pops immediately into your head?

These moments could be times you learned a lesson, they could be your favorite funny stories, they could be moments that helped define who you are, they could be happy days or sad days, and so on. They could be things that have happened to you, or things you have seen happen to someone else. These can be pivotal moments in your life or just ones that you tell all the time (or used to tell). If you are under twenty-five, this will be much easier for you. In any event, these stories pop up quickly, so you need simply to allow them to flow into your awareness. Give yourself the green light here—no stopping and thinking about what you wrote.

Time yourself. This is a contest. You are competing with every other person reading this book. And to win, you cannot judge your memories. Write them down as they come without censorship. If you do this right, you will be writing quickly. Don't worry about other people reading this, they can't read your writing anyway.

Set a timer for fifteen minutes. Go ahead, I'll wait. Timer ready? Don't worry, I'll type faster from now on—I want you to win! I hope you can read as fast as I can type.

Don't think too much. Just write the twenty-five events down as they pop up in your mind. No editorializing. Avoid the "I can't write that one down!" trap. Just write it in the table provided on the next page. For example:

The day my cat got rabies.	The day my sister cut off all my hair and hid me in a closet.
The day I put Nair in my brother's shampoo bottle.	Spraying Jean Nate Perfume all over my older brother's entire wardrobe.
The time my brother got me back.	The day my brother Sean died.
My prom date got busted for drugs.	My niece being born on my birthday.
My sister walking on the ceiling.	The day I saved my father's life.
My first time surfing.	My brother Gary's funeral.

Learning how to dance the cabbage patch.	Mini-bike trail in our front yard.
Creating the "Yard of the Decade" sign in our front yard.	Ulcer medicine in 1st grade.
Our dog Poocho being hit by a car.	My mother's boyfriend Emory.
Barrel of Monkeys.	Fleas in the den.
Peeing on my sister.	Going to Monterey with my dad.
Dropping the Mayonnaise jar right before the social workers got to the house.	My mom teaching me piano.
Aunt Rosemary getting stuck in the mud and cream of celery soup in a Thermos.	Uncle Jim and the swimming pool.
The day Nikki was born.	The day Raquel was born.

I just gave you more than twenty-five and it took me two minutes. You can certainly do it. It's easy (and fun too). Go.

Did you do it? If you're answering no, stop where you are and go back and do it. The rest of this chapter won't work if you don't do it sequentially. Skimming will not grant you the benefits of this exercise. The results of all the time you are giving up to read this book are hinging on you doing these exercises in the order you got them. If you read on—you will forever be barred from some magic.

This is because if you know what is going to happen with your twenty-five memory results, your aha experience will be ruined. Had the person holding the back of the bicycle when you learned to ride told you they were letting go, you would've fallen.

Think of me as the person running alongside your bike as you try to ride it. I'm holding on (at least you think I am) and telling you: Go back and do the exercise. I'll wait at the beginning of the next chapter. If you didn't do the first one in this section, do that too.

 ## EXERCISE:
CONTEST TWO: IN IT—NOT ABOUT IT
(IF YOU DIDN'T DO CONTEST ONE, DON'T DO CONTEST TWO)

Hi. Okay. Thanks for doing the exercise. Let's look at your list. Hmmm. Yes. There are definitely some compelling titles. Pretty amazing so much stuff happened before you were twenty-three huh?

Now circle your favorite story—the one you most **like** to tell.

Got it?

We are about to have what a friend of mine (thank you Susie Buell) calls a "Northern California Moment." In twenty seconds I will ask you to close your eyes. Really close them tight and picture the event you circled in all its detail.

What were you wearing? What time of year was it? Who was there? What were their names? What did your hair look like? What shoes were you wearing? Where did you get the shoes? What kind of car did you drive or did your parents drive back then? What did the upholstery look like? Did it have a wink-mirror? What did the carpet look like? The grass? (Not what you were smoking, what you were standing on!) The couch? The sun? What were you doing? What weird thing stuck out? Detail, detail, detail!

Now, close your eyes and relive the details of this event. When you're finished, get a separate piece of paper and write down as much detail as you can remember. The more detail the better you can relive your story as you tell it. MORE detail than you think important or interesting. Do not write out the talk, simply write down detail and notes.

Get a tape recorder if you have one. If not, you can use **www.jott.com** or your voicemail.

Really. Record this as well.

Turn on the recorder and stand up and tell the story with all its detail and flourish.

The key to this is don't give us any expository essay preamble. Instead start IN it not ABOUT it.

Tell it like you would for your closest friends. Emote. Laugh. Cry, pause, question, reveal—all that fun stuff.

When you get to the end of your story, pause the recorder and go to the next chapter.

Oh yeah, don't forget to have fun! Move around. Let your energy flow.

Are you Ready? Go!

Relive the moment in more detail than you have ever remembered.

 EXERCISE:
IF YOU DIDN'T DO CONTEST ONE & TWO DO NOT CONTINUE READING

Go back to the first chapter in the Public Speaking Section (page 143). Remember the topic you wrote down? Write it down again here:

Now, turn the recorder on and start talking. Wait a minute Christina! What do you want me to talk about?? End the story you just told as if you were giving a talk on the topic you wrote in the space above.

Don't over analyze or think, just try to make a segue between the two. Just let go and do it. Trust me. I have been teaching this stuff for years, and 100 percent of the time participants figure out how to use the story they circled to end the talk topic they wrote down.

100 percent of the time! That's pretty good. It just takes some practice. Try it!

Good. Now rewind the tape recorder and listen to what you did. Amazing isn't it? See how well it works? I am not saying you should go out and use this story in your next talk, and you might. Chances are it will need some fine tuning. The point of this exercise is to show how easily you can craft a speech that uses an interesting personal story that folks will listen to.

Your story could open a talk on any concept in this book. It could.

There is not a story on the planet that does not relate in some way to the topic of your speech.

CHAPTER 93:
LIKE SANDS OF
AN HOUR GLASS

Ten years ago I did the previous exercises with a group of twenty women under the age of twenty-five who were interested in San Francisco politics. The room was crowded and uncharacteristically muggy, and we were all tired from a day of training. The women told their stories in a small group exercise.

After the exercise, one woman came rushing toward me; she was clearly angered by the exercise. In a rather loud voice she exclaimed, "I can't believe you just made me do that exercise! I just told a story about stealing hubcaps. I am mortified, embarrassed, and I am leaving!" I held my hand out and asked, "Before you leave will you just tell me what you do for a living?" She spat, "I run a non-profit that keeps troubled kids off the street." The entire room inhaled. The look of shock on her face was incredible. She smiled. "Wow. I never realized the person I was saving was me." There were tears in her eyes, my eyes, and in about half of the eyes in the room.

A stream of congruence runs through our lives. It is there whether we allow it or not, and when we give ourselves permission to see it, it opens all sorts of authentic possibilities. Look for this congruence in your life. Be mindful of how everything in your life ties together. Pay attention to who you are now and what you care about and see how it relates to who you were in the past and what being that person meant.

I have to tell you about where this exercise came from. Once I wanted to be an actress. (Go ahead and laugh. I don't mind. I laugh about it too.) I signed up for a class, and after the first few sessions, I realized I didn't have what it takes. This became glaringly obvious when the teacher asked me to write down a page of details from the saddest time of my life. I thought of my brother's death and cried as I wrote down the details. She then asked me to stand before the group and tell my sad story. I cried, I emoted, I relived the experience. When I was finished, the class gave me a standing ovation. They said it was the best acting they had ever seen. To which the teacher replied, she wasn't acting, she was **referencing**. Rather than an actor, I was an authentic communicator. Referencing. I got it.

Luckily I walked away from acting class with the permission to reveal my personal stories. I tried out my new awareness in my speech class. I knew it was a risk, as my speech teacher was pretty tough on us and really liked agendas and serious talks. Even so, I opened by telling the story of my brother, added some important referential information, and closed with gun safety. I got another standing ovation.

I realized that I lost my nervousness when I relived a story. I became so focused, I forgot my own fear. I quickly came to realize that starting with a genuine story helped keep my nerves at bay. And in my early days of public speaking, I needed all the help I could get!

I was hesitant to include storytelling in here because so many speech people teach it. The difference here is to acknowledge that your stories and experiences (all of them) are relevant to your talk. The key is for you to remember more detail about them than you have ever done before. Reliving stories reveals our perspective; it doesn't just make us great speakers. It isn't a trick to charm the audience with.

Make you and your talks come alive by reliving in great details the stories of your life.

*Authors Note: If the stories of others are truly not interesting to you, you may struggle in the new relationship economy. Stories are the transactional medium of relationship in our culture; great communicators are interested in the perspective of others.

CHAPTER 94:
24-HOUR RULE

I have a book of about three hundred moments from my life. I add to it every day. As things happen to me I write them down; it helps me refer to them later.

I call it the "24-hour rule". Every night I imagine I have to prepare a talk that includes a story that happened in the past twenty-four hours. Then I write it down in my 24-hour rule book. It is a great practice and it works.

Twenty-four hours ago here is what I wrote down:

> *Sebastian doesn't want to stop nursing. I have been trying to figure out all these ways to make it easier to wean him from "Momma's milk" and they aren't working. Finally, I sat him down and explained in a very adult way, "Sebastian, we won't be able to give you a sibling if you don't give up Momma's milk. You need to stop nursing so we can have a sibling." He looked at me. Grabbed both of my hands and said, "Momma. NO sibling." He then ran all over the house saying "No Sibling". This morning, he grabbed my face and said, "No Sibbling."*

If I had to give a talk on your topic, would my 24-hour rule story work? Let's find out. First, I'll search the internet for a topic by randomly typing a few letters and choosing what comes up on Google. Now I'm typing four keys in a row with my left hand—asdf.

Okay. I am cracking up right now. I typed randomly and got the url:

http://www.asdf.com/whatisasdf.html

And guess what. This site focuses on what people should type in a subject line when they have no subject. I am not kidding. Who knew? It also talks about Scrabble. Interesting. Thanks to Google synchronicity, my talk is going to be about talking about not knowing what my subject is.

So I open with a talk about asdf.com and the subject of no subject. Then I segue into my 24-hour rule story:

> *I want my son to hear "no more nursing" and he hears and repeats "No Sibling." This is exactly what my subconscious is doing about picking a subject for this speech today. You are wanting a subject—I am giving a story. What the audience wants depends on the individual sitting in the chair.*

Let's try again, just to prove my point. I will type "quisd" in the Google search box and see what happens. Hmmm. I just got "Home Equity Loans 5.25 percent." So if my topic is Home Equity Lines I could tie my 24-hour rule story in like this:

I want my son to stop nursing not just for me, for his own benefit. I also want my clients to stop interest rate shopping. Instead of listening they run around my office yelling, "No points.. no points" when really they should be yelling, "Select a loan that best serves my needs."

Pretty neat huh? Okay, one more. I just took a break from my writing and got an email from someone asking if I had any how-to tips on introductions. So let's imagine I am giving a talk on proper introduction etiquette. I could work in my 24-hour rule story this way:

Clearly my strategy to help my son move into a new stage in his life isn't working. I want the sibling—he doesn't. Often we think the best strategy for introducing a person is to read their bio so we don't forget anything. When we do this, the audience forgets everything. It isn't memorable. It doesn't fluff the speaker. It is drab.

Keep in mind, these story segues are off the top of my head. I did not go back and make them sexier for you. Imagine what you could do if you actually selected personal stories that correlated to your subject? What you quickly did with your own topic and story is prove to yourself that stories work to elucidate points.

People like stories. Write your stories down so you can remember them for later.

 **EXAMPLE:**

THE ANGEL IS IN THE DETAILS

What makes a story interesting? Hopefully you can guess by now. Got it? Yes, you are right! The details!

When telling a story, use detail in order to make your experience come alive. By detail, I mean you must give many more specifics than you think are possible. The only way to do this is to relive the story. Go back in your mind. Who was there? What time was it? What were you wearing? These finer points jog your memory and call up the actual event.

Becoming a great storyteller is a skill anyone can master. The example below outlines a practice that will improve your storytelling immediately.

Start by noticing everything. Remove any shutters that may be on your peripheral vision. Look around the room you are in right now. Notice something you haven't seen before. Keep looking until you find it.

I have been in the same hotel room for a few days finishing this book. I've leaned my head back at least fifty times to stretch my aching muscles. This time when I do I notice a sprinkler head in the ceiling. I'd noticed the sprinkler head before—I had not noticed the head is rusted. Seems a little odd, as rust signals water and I see no drip.

I get up and feel the floor beneath the sprinkler. It is dry—no clear evidence of a leak. Though as I walk away from the spot I can clearly see the former water damage. This is something I hadn't noticed either. I scan the ceiling again and notice five more sprinkler heads I also hadn't seen. These are not rusted.

The smoke alarm is bright yellow with a light that says FIRE beneath it. I missed it too. Looking around again, I realize there are more sprinklers in this hotel room than most. Perhaps it's because every room has a fireplace and to get the permits for the backwoods luxury, they had to do an overkill on the sprinkler system. Or maybe they were just being careful to prevent fire.

Oh my gosh. There is another smoke alarm plugged in at the base of the coat rack. How weird. Two smoke alarms seem like a lot for such a small room. Then I look closer at the one on the floor and realize it's a carbon monoxide detector.

So what is my point? If I had to, I could turn this experience into a talk. About what? About environmental pollutions and our repeated exposure to it; about lunch with William S. Burroughs; about disaster prevention, fire safety laws, ways to distract myself from writing—the list is endless. I'll bet I could also tie it into the topic you wrote down at the beginning of the Public Speaking Section. Could you? Try it.

Great storytelling is something we practice everyday. In the shower, in the car, at the kitchen table, on a walk, at lunch, at work—anywhere. Start paying attention to everything that happens to you and in great detail. I suggest you keep your own version of my 24-hour rule book. Call it your book of experiences. It is like a journal only better since there is no need to edit or editorialize; instead simply write down experiences and their details.

Let me repeat myself here because it is relevant. Storytelling is not editorializing. Editorializing is lecture. Humans do not like lectures. They like an interesting yarn. They want to know your perspective, to understand what it means to be you with your unique insights and experiences. Your story is like a flashlight on the path, and the guiding angel is in the details.

Stories come alive in the details. They are an illumination, not editorialized commentary. Relive the moments of your life that led to your perspective.

CHAPTER 95:
DIARIES ARE NOT JUST FOR 16-YEAR-OLD LOVE SICK GIRLS

Most of us cannot remember what we had for breakfast, while our lives are teeming with potential fodder for audiences. Every time we speak in public, we innovate a new way of saying things. This is why it is important to write these things down. I strongly urge you to keep a journal—like my 24-hour-rule book (remember, you can call it what you want).

1) Write down successes you have in meetings and how you handled tough communication situations.

2) Add an entry after every presentation. Write down the contact information of the person who hired you, the audience type and size, as well as specific anecdotes and honest self-evaluation. A well-documented history of your public talks will keep you from repeating yourself if the same group invites you back.

3) Make a list of hard questions and ways to respond to them. Do not write out verbatim responses, just a general idea of how you will answer.

4) Note the things you notice and participate in—remember, they are story fodder. Here's another example of tying a simple experience into a talk subject. Yesterday in Vancouver, I stayed at the Terminal City Club. The gentleman who checked me in was quite friendly and helpful. I chuckled to myself as he told me to look to the right when I got in the elevator for the buttons to my floor. Talk about an over-communicator—he made me look silent! A few hours later, after my event, I stepped into the same elevator and realized the numbers were different on each side. The numbers on the left only went up to floor seven; the numbers on the right went from floor eight to fourteen. Thus the over-communicating front desk guy was really helping me out. This tiny example can be used in a talk about over-communication, faulty perspective or vertigo. Like me, you will most likely forget the story and its wonderful details if you don't write them down.

5) Your journal is a place to learn, learn, learn! If ya choke, write about it. It will help you understand it better and help you to avoid it in the future.

Journals help you remember and learn.

FELONY GUY

Debt collection. Why would anyone want to be in such a tough industry? I didn't. I was only there because I was a teenager going to junior college. I had to figure out a way to pay my tuition as well as offer financial help to my terminally ill father. Wendy's wasn't cutting it because I needed a job that paid more than the $3.35 minimum wage—I also didn't like smelling bad after my work shift.

I got there by answering an ad in the newspaper for a collector. When I sent in my resume, I remember thinking, "Wow. Those antique collectors make a lot of money. I can't wait to learn more about furniture."

On the morning of my first day I met the nicest humans on the planet in the employee break room. I had never heard of the collections industry and had no idea what these people did for their money. Somehow the many jokes about bill collectors had never crossed my path. All I knew was that I was dressed up and ready to go to work in the clerical department for $4.04 an hour.

I stood nervously in the middle of the collector floor wanting to appear older than I was as the collectors manned their stations and started dialing for dollars. My first task was to file a stack of papers in the date file, which was within earshot of the busily dialing employees.

I was in shock. The nice people I had met in the break room suddenly took on new personas. They were rude and passive aggressive. I heard threats of wage garnishments and liens on properties. I also heard industry jargon I did not recognize though knew wasn't good. I was so focused on what was occurring around me, I lost my train of thought and opened the top drawer of the file cabinet without closing second drawer from the bottom first. The entire cabinet fell over in a loud crash.

That moment was my chance to run away from collections forever, and I didn't take it. While extremely conflict adverse and shy at the time, the entire experience was so overwhelming it paralyzed me from further action—though in hindsight, the real reason I stayed was because a cute boy worked there, and I was exceptionally boy crazy.

Funny enough, I eventually became a supervisor for the support department. Being timid and shy, I developed a persona to mask my insecurities—I became a pushy bitch. In customer service situations, I slogged my way through the mire and barked orders instead of asking for help. I was a teenager, and I knew everything—and I let everyone else know it too—via some pretty nasty communication habits modeled for me by some truly aggressive people. Basically, I emulated what I saw.

One day, I was in the back office trying to figure out how to post payments. The agency was a family owned business and most of the family was vacationing in Hawaii. Normally the eldest son ran the office while his parents were away, only he was sick with the flu so I was in charge that day and was anxiously trying to figure out how to do his job.

I heard weird noises coming from the front office. They were disturbing me, and I was annoyed. I walked through the break room to get to the front and ran into a few collectors in the break room. "He might have a gun," I heard one of them say. "I don't get paid enough for this," replied the other. I kept walking.

Understand that we collected for the phone company, and if someone can't pay their phone bill, they are in dire financial straits. We didn't care about extenuating circumstances and treated everyone the same—we demanded payment and promised credit destruction or litigation if we didn't get it. At times, people threatened to come discuss their debt with us physically, which I assumed was the reason for the office joke: Just remind them to bring their check book.

When I arrived at the front desk, the debtor was already on the receptionist's side of the counter. He was yelling and discussing dismemberment. My dad had always told me to step forward when being rushed. And even though he was referring to dogs, I took dad's advice and stepped toward the guy anyway. Trying to play tough guy.

I can still remember the brown and white Levi Strauss button on his shirt—I was so close I could actually read the words printed in a circle. Though I was only 4' 11" at the time, the man stepped back; though more because he couldn't see me rather than because my psychology worked. He continued to speak very deliberately about causing harm.

Meanwhile, one of the collectors was frantically trying to dial the police. While she fumbled, I said in a very shaky voice:

> "WAIT. WAIT. Everyone please wait a moment. Sir. All you owe is money. Am I worth a felony to you?"

My voice trembled, and I wondered if he even heard what I had said. He stood still for a moment. Then he said, "No, you aren't" and paid the bill and left. I fainted. Then I quit.

I went home and called my dad. I told him there was something weird going on in our culture about money, and I wanted to help change the collections industry. Characteristically, my dad replied, "Yes, Chrissie, good people of the world always choose to go to Greenpeace, when really, the good people of the world need to be in the industries no one wants to be in—to change them. The whales have enough saviors—the American consumer needs you."

My dad taught me the principals of infiltration from a very early age. The best way to change something is not by dressing funny and protesting on the streets. The real way to change something is to infiltrate. Dress like them and change things from the inside. And thus started my new career. (Though sometimes I still dress funny!)

I relive this experience in front of audiences all the time. My 'point' often changes. Customer Service, Conflict, Environmentalism, Medieval Heraldry—doesn't matter. This story has enough detail that it applies to anything I have formed a perspective on.

The sad thing is I didn't make up the felony sentence on the spot. It was a sentence passed around in a passive aggressive "hah hah" way in our industry. I had heard it before. When I said it that day, I felt a shift in my heart. Why were we letting money ruin lives? When I said it to this guy, it was with an open heart—he felt it and responded accordingly. HOW I said it mattered.

That moment transformed an industry. I spent the next twenty years teaching my team to turn a collections call into a sales call. Be nice, warm and helpful. It worked.

Storytelling teaches YOU and the audience.

CHAPTER 96:
DON'T KILL
THE BUTTERFLIES

Butterflies are sweet creatures. They start out as caterpillars with one primary motive: Move slowly and eat as much as possible.

A friend of mine told me caterpillars cannot see butterflies. This is because caterpillars are metabolically unable to see something moving that fast. (I have not looked this up for confirmation because I really like the metaphor. Let's imagine you do not have a biology degree and I have a poetic license.)

If caterpillars cannot see butterflies, it means they don't know what they're going to be. They go about their days thinking their sole purpose is to eat lots of green stuff. Then one day, they get a little tired. They yawn, stretch and decide to hang upside down.

They don't understand what's come over them, and they tell the other caterpillars they're feeling out of sorts these days. Everybody relates. The caterpillars agree it's a tad chilly hanging there, swaying back and forth in the breeze.

So, they start knitting little blankees for themselves. They have never done this before either. All this toil. No green stuff to eat. They feel weird, and amazed at their new skill. Knit, knit, knit. Suddenly everything is dark. Wow. Where'd everybody go?

There's nothing more to knit and the food is all gone, so the caterpillars decide to sleep. They sleep for quite a while. Then one day, they wake up claustrophobic. Their blankees shrunk while they were sleeping, and it is hard to get out of them. So they struggle for a really long time. Struggle. Struggle. Struggle. Struggle. Struggle. Strain. Struggle. Strife. Strain. Struggle. Ugh. Until they emerge with wings and fly away.

The question is: Do they have recollection of their earlier selves? Can butterflies see caterpillars? Do they know they are the same? Can they get in touch with their earlier selves?

I know what you are thinking. *That's a nice story Christina, but what the hell does this have to do with public speaking?* Hey watch the buts! Just stick with me. You'll see.

Someone once told me a story about a little boy watching a butterfly struggle to get out of a cocoon. As the butterfly thrashed and labored, the concerned boy was afraid the butterfly wouldn't make it, so he ran into the house and got a pair of scissors.

He carefully cut the cocoon without cutting the butterfly; the butterfly continued to struggle on the ground. His wings did not work. His body was too big for the rest of him. It looked bulged and weird. The little boy ran and got his dad. His dad explained that sometimes nature isn't perfect and things are deformed. They watched as the butterfly tried to fly and finally died.

Unfortunately, the little boy and his dad didn't realize the butterfly died because it was taken from its struggle too soon. It is the struggle in the cocoon that forces blood to the veins in a butterfly's wings. Without that struggle, the blood stays in the butterfly's body cavity and it becomes like a fat black slug with useless wings. Unable to fly or move, the slug dies.

I did tell you I was raised by hippies right? (Still, this story isn't about what you think it is.)

It is our imperfection—our struggle—that makes us great communicators. We find better ways of being through our failures. We have no choice; and if we try to avoid this inevitable fact, we lose our ability to communicate authentically. It is okay to struggle. Struggling helps us fly.

Speaking of butterflies, when they are flying around in your stomach, sing their praises. Nerves are good. They are part of your struggle. Do something with them. Move with them. Movement transforms panic into endorphins. Movement gets you out of your head and back into your body. Movement helps you stop thinking and start relaxing.

About every five pages of this book I run up nine flights of stairs. Why? Movement.

Opening your talk with a story about an embarrassing struggle or moment can help move exceptionally vigorous butterflies. I once had a client whose hands shook uncontrollably whenever he stood at the lectern. We devised a plan. It included opening his upcoming speech with an embarrassing story about being trapped under a tractor. He loved this story and was very comfortable telling it. It began with him falling to the floor and mimicking himself in the grips of the tractor. He actually did this (it was hilarious!), and he had so much fun with it, his nervousness disappeared. His ensuing talk was fabulous.

Nerves are only bad when we allow ourselves to cycle doom scenarios over and over in our head. I suggest you use your nerves as motivation to get yourself up and practice what you are going to do.

Butterflies are good. Welcome them. It means you spread pollen.

The challenge is you can't see your earlier self. Amazing growth and greatness in communication is happening and you do not see it. Each year I write a note to myself about my fears and challenges that I am facing at the moment. I write down what I am most worried about. Where I feel I have failed the most. When I pack up my Christmas ornaments I put that writing in the box so that next year I open it when I start decorating the tree. It is amazing how much I have grown and didn't notice.

The butterflies, shaking knees, sweaty palms are just somatic requests for movement! MOVE !

This is big—really integrate what I am saying here. Get out of your head. Get into your body. Most communication can become great when we move around. Get the endorphins and the blood, the stuff that feeds the brain, moving.

Nerves are good—use them.

 EXERCISE:

PRACTICE BEING TRAPPED
UNDER A TRACTOR

Stand. Deliver that talk. With all the detail. No preamble. Use your hands. Use your feet. If you are under a tractor, actually lay down on the floor and get under that tractor. Don't worry about what you are going to say at the end. Allow yourself and trust you will arrive there naturally.

Be physically bigger than you could ever imagine yourself. If you are playing basketball in your story, play basketball. Relive the moment rather than retell it. Keep your reliving fresh, finding new ways to tell it every time.

Structure your talks with lots of words in detail and physical description; keep direction and editorializing to a minimum.

A QUARTER SHY
OF A BIRTHDAY

My niece was born on my 18th birthday. I told my sister she could have got me a sweater, she chose to give me the greatest gift. Born three months early in a time when babies this premature didn't usually survive outside the womb, Tara was a tiny little angel. The doctors prepared us for the worst and suggested we brace ourselves for brain damage, physical impairment and almost certain death.

I must tell you my sister is one tough cookie. After seven days of labor and the very same day Tara was born, Leta asked me to go home and get her things. Then, when I returned, I watched as she got up out of her hospital bed and proceeded to paint her nails, curl her hair, and dress herself in a suit and high heel pumps. Just hours before the family had been told Leta might not survive the delivery and here she was dressing up for the prom or something.

The doctors did not want Leta out of bed, and since this meant she could not see Tara the rest of the day, she was adamant—nothing was going to stop her from being there for her daughter. When I begged her to sit in the wheelchair and take care of herself, she said over her shoulder, "This is the first time I get to meet my daughter and I am going to make her proud." As she walked to the ICU neonatal unit, tiny drops of blood trailed behind her. I cry just thinking about how brave my sister is.

My sister spent the next three months sitting vigil beside Tara's incubator. She sat strong through Tara's brain surgery and did not give up when the doctors again told us Tara probably would not make it. One doctor actually said everything they were doing was to advance scientific understanding in order to help future babies. That comment still rings in my ears at the blantant honesty of it. Furthering science of future babies. Ugh.

Despite the hopeless predictions, Tara came home, and my sister proceeded to do an incredible job of raising her to be independent and strong. Tara did come out of the womb with an inner strength that is inspiring. Wheelchair bound with cerebral palsy, Tara herself refused to be special schooled or treated like she had a disability. She was amazingly full of life, vitality and interest in others.

She was (and still is) witty as hell. One time, standing in the middle of my sister's living room floor, I was in full Drama Queen. That morning, I had flown on a small plane and was wildly explaining to my family the fact that it sounds like a lawnmower is attached to the plane instead of an engine and it is SCARY. "Now, I know when it is your turn to go it is your turn to go. And still I was TERRIFIED the entire flight." My six-year-old niece interrupts me and says, "I know why you were nervous Aunt. Maybe it wasn't your time to go, but maybe it was the pilots time to go.

She was strong. On the way to the Ice Capades one year we stopped at McDonald's to get some fries. A mother admonished her son for staring at Tara. I teared up as I watched that little seven-year-old wheel over and gently tell the mother, "I am a kid IN a wheelchair, I am not a wheelchair. Your son can look. It is okay." She was an observant seven-year-old.

At Tara's 8th grade graduation ceremony, I watched her roll in front of the stage when her name was called. Since Tara was the only wheelchair-bound kid in the school, the administration had forgotten to prepare a disability access to the stage. Sitting below the stage, Tara had her head in her lap and her eyes averted. She looked so sad I had a lump in my throat.

I elbowed my sister. "What is making her so sad," I whispered. Usually stuff like this didn't daunt Tara. Leta reminded me how junior high had messed with all of us. "It was awful," she said. It was true. Both my sister and I hated junior high, and for the first time I imagined junior high for Tara.

I hoped it was more than the emotional rollercoaster of puberty that was making the changes in Tara, so I decided to contact the Shriners Hospital for Children. My dear friend Cathy had connections and managed to get Tara an appointment with one of the doctors pretty quickly.

The team of doctors told my sister nothing really could be done. Tara's curling over was physical, which meant she needed to be strapped in. As soon as Tara's wheelchair was fitted with a new strap apparatus, Leta noticed sores forming on Tara's shoulders from the weight of the downward pressure. It was so hard to watch her suffer that we both grew increasingly desperate for a miracle.

During all this, I was running my collections company and very focused on turning a debt collection call into a sales call by being positive focused and nice. One day my sister and I were talking on the phone, and she asked me what I really believed in. I replied that I thought focusing on what was right would make all the difference in the world. Then Leta said (and I will never forget these words as long as I live), "I wonder what that attitude could do for Tara? Imagine if Junior High would have given her that."

It was like a light bulb went off for both of us. After we talked at length about our own misadventures in high school and what could have made a difference for us, Leta and I devised a plan. We would bring Tara to San Francisco for Camp Aunt. She would stay with me for three weeks, and we would practice the positive team model we developed in my business. We would also get her front tooth fixed—for the fourth time! (SuperTara kept chipping her front tooth every time she decided to get up and walk on her own.)

There was one setback: I didn't have a wheelchair accessible house. Not really insurmountable. I got on the telephone and called all the hotels in town. If I could get three or four of them to donate a hotel room for a few days, Camp Aunt would begin. Fortunately, one phone call solved the problem: Harry Reiter and his team at Marines

Memorial Hotel offered to put us up for the entire three weeks at no charge.

The day before Tara was to arrive, I had a strategic meeting with my team.

> *If Tara lifts her head up off her lap for one second, even a centimeter—tell her she has nice eyes. Tell her you can hear her voice. Tell her she is beautiful. Keep finding positive things to say to her. We are not going to tell her to sit up nor are we going to strap her in.*

With the goal of getting her ready for high school, we created a new kind of boot camp—one that used positive commentary and connection as the drills. Our plan was to take her out on the streets of San Francisco and show her a good time. We made her the center of attention in everything we did, and, as the days progressed, we literally watched Tara bloom.

This was one of the most beautiful and difficult three weeks I have ever experienced. I got a glimmer of what my sister and Tara had endured on a daily basis for all of Tara's life, and it certainly made me respect their stamina. Tara is a dream person—her disability is physically taxing. I am embarrassed to write that as my struggles are a grain of sand compared to Tara's. The reality is I came face to face with reality those three weeks: Just how strong and amazing Tara is and just how difficult a disability is.

My best friend Lorianne stepped in and showed me how it is done. She showed Tara a great time while I moved my company. My co-worker Pete (who subjected himself to seventeen matinees of *The Wedding Singer*) delighted in hanging out with Tara. It was a raucous, great time.

Within three days, Tara sat up and stopped putting her head in her lap. In the second week, her entire attitude changed, brightening her and everyone around her. By the third week, she'd made such an impression on those who worked with her, that she still resonates with them to this day—and they still talk about her!

If a young woman with cerebral palsy and all bets against her can transform herself and those around her by being positive, what can you do?

No one learns by negativity. Focus on what you like that you are doing in communication and you will improve. Focus on what you like about what they are doing and you will improve.

CHAPTER 97:
I WAS MY OWN
PUPPET

....

The first twenty-five times I told Tara's story I cried. I had a really hard time getting through it. Then one day, I had a woman tell me she felt the story was canned and didn't believe it. She actually asked me if I made the story up.

I was mad—really mad. I let her know if she wanted to meet Tara, I'd be happy to arrange the date. Afterwards, I ranted to my friend about this woman and her glaringly obvious trust issues. I was so very offended and cross.

The next time I told this story to a group, I paid closer attention and realized the woman was right. I had become an actor in my own movie. I was recalling the first time I told Tara's story instead of reliving the actual events. I had become so afraid of experiencing the emotion that I merely went through the motions without connecting the dots. And this made all the difference.

I was focused on the words and acting instead of reliving it. Every time I tell the story now I come up with a new detail I didn't remember before that further enriches the story. Two weeks ago I actually cried out loud as I told the story. I am no longer presenting a well rehearsed script. As I relived it I said something I had forgotten about that month.

The last day Tara was in San Francisco we asked her where she wanted to go. Anywhere. We told her. She picked Mel's diner. Lorianne, Pete, Michael and I dressed up funky and took her out. She was glowing and a little sad about leaving us. In the middle of dinner, she accidentally knocked her glass off the table. It flew a couple of feet and landed with a loud crash. The entire restaurant stopped talking and looked at her.

I watched three weeks of work going down the tubes. Her lip quivered—she started to cry. She was so embarrassed. Our waiter walked over and dropped the glass he was holding: "Crash!" He made a grand gesture and said something about good luck in Greece—I'm not sure. We all applauded and so did Tara. She beamed, and I gave him a weighty tip. I wish I could find that guy and thank him again—he taught me more about kindness than almost anyone on the planet. I cry thinking about it.

Why is this part of the story in this chapter? I have completely forgotten about him until one day reliving the story to an audience. Could this part of the story relate to the story topic you wrote in the beginning of this section? It could. We have got to start paying attention to what happens to us. It is our perspective, and it teaches more than anything written in a book by someone else.

My relationship to Tara's story has come full circle. Last week, I told it to one hundred CEO's. At the end of the talk, several people came up to the stage to ask questions. One man waited in the background until everyone else left then walked up to me and held both of my hands.

He looked me deep in the eyes and said, "I have a message for your niece Tara. Will you give it to her for me?" I nodded yes, feeling the emotion rising in both of us. "Thank her for me. Tell her my daughter is here today because of all she went through. Tell your niece that my family is so grateful for all the pain she endured. Tell her it mattered. It really mattered. She did further science and helped produce a beautiful eight-year-old girl. Thank her."

His daughter had been born early years after Tara. Her suffering to "further science" had meant something. I squeezed his hands as we stood silently looking at each other with tears streaming down our faces. We had been at the same conference for three days and never met. Suddenly we were making a difference in each other's lives—we were exchanging the true human currency.

Tara today scares me with just how tough she is. She moved out alone—at 18-years of age—and started college.

We are moved by each other when we risk talking about what matters most. Challenge your own paradigm. Thirst for perspective. Be the true human currency.

CHAPTER 98:
THE BACKSTORY BELONGS
IN THE MIDDLE

Before reliving an event from our lives or others, most people feel compelled to offer the context in which the story occurred—from now on referred to as the "back story." The vast majority of public speaking coaches firmly recommend the avoidance of this process. My early public speaking teachers wanted me to reign in my rambling, and they persistently pounded on my head trying to get me to keep things simple and focus on one event only.

As you might imagine, I do not agree with the majority of public speaking coaches. Especially on the point that speakers should be taciturn in detail and back story. I used to tell the story of the elastic coming out of my slip in front of an audience. It wasn't until I started over telling the detail that the TRUE lesson from that story unfolded.

Details are memory. They come at different times, and uncovering them can be a magical process. I remembered Gary asking me to go riding with him as I was telling the helmet story to one of my audiences, and it wasn't until last year that I realized that the slip I was wearing had been my grandmothers.

Now when I relive the helmet story I add the back story. I do it in the middle of the talk; the beginning is too expository essay-ish. I do not keep to the point; instead I weave "allegory"—many of them—through the talk. This is not a laundry list of facts. It is a tapestry of perspective. This is interesting to the audience. Audiences want transparency. They like the human story.

My friend Simon Sinek refers to this as the "**why** behind the what and how." When he talks about it he is referencing branding and a company mission. He calls his brilliant teaching the "Golden Circle." Look him up. www.sinekpartners.com.

I use his theory here (with his permission) to show how it relates to the human relationship model. Audiences want our perspective. Back stories tell the audience **why** we have the perspective to do **what** we do.

If the idea of weaving back story into your talk scares you, sign up for a creative writing class—it will make you better at storytelling. You will learn to describe things rather than editorialize them. Here is an example of dry, editorialized writing:

The cat jumped off the stove because it was hot.

This is more exciting:

The Amana range coil burned bright red as Stella the cat worked her way toward a plate of salmon hors d'oeuvres. As her nose

YOUR PROFESSIONALISM IS KILLING YOU.............................

neared the prize, her tail excitedly twitched and landed right on the red spiral. She screamed like a angry alley cat and did a perfect figure eight backflip off the stove—landing on her feet of course. Her blistered leather-like pads surrounded by fur.

Additional back story might be:

The smell of cat fur almost ruined our appetites; luckily the delicious food smells overpowered the cat tail, so we ate with relish as the cat eyed us and our salmon feast suspiciously. Did they do that to me on purpose?

Be prepared for the looks. I get the "where is this going" looks all the time from audiences. Only when I skimp on detail do I fail in front of an audience. When I rush through it—the audience doesn't get it, and I am not a great communicator. Trust the detail.

Back story is appropriate and belongs in the middle.

CHAPTER 99:
PRACTICE CREATING AN EXPERIENCE YOU WILL TELL YOU GRANDCHILDREN

Noteworthy experiences are real. And contrary to popular belief, you don't have to sit around passively waiting for something important to happen in your day—you can create it.

Imagine you had to give a talk tomorrow at 9am. You are in meeting all day, and tonight you have a board meeting, so you will not have time to prepare anything special. What do you do? Experience something today that will add relevance and heart to the topic you are presenting in the morning. Yes this is a challenge, and it is not impossible.

Try it.

Okay, here's an example to give you an idea of how easy it is to create a meaningful experience. One of my clients, a political candidate, had to give a speech in a neighborhood in San Francisco. She called me to ask for some help. She wanted a winning oration. I asked her what work she had done in that district, and she didn't have anything to offer. I suggested she go to the Community Center and make something real happen. She did. She went to St. Anthony and served food. After serving the food she sat down and shared a meal with a few of the guests, most of whom were homeless. By the end of her lunch, she not only found a story to share, she rediscovered her inspiration for public service.

Engage your surroundings and find the significant experience waiting in every moment of your day.

Maybe you didn't notice that I left you for about twenty minutes. My husband called and asked me to meet him downstairs. You see, I am at a hotel because it is the only place I can write without interruptions. Even though I love him a lot, I was somewhat frustrated by his intrusion. As I walked through the lobby, I realized my brain needed a break. The energy and movement occurring all around me glittered and fascinated me, and I decided to practice what I was writing about.

I walked through the large entry doors and immediately saw my husband standing proudly in front of the three, ten foot Doggie Diner heads he carts around on a flat bed trailer. What am I talking about? I'm talking about San Francisco culinary icons, as the dogheads once graced dinners throughout the SF Bay. (To learn about these dogs and see that I'm not crazy, visit www.doggiediner.com) To put this in proper perspective, these Doggie Diner heads are Daushunds with chef hats and bow ties; people are supposed to touch their noses for good luck. So I rubbed each of their noses and kissed the handsome thoughtful man I married for bringing the doggie boys as a show of support.

As I walked back into the hotel, I realized the entire lobby staff had been standing at the window watching us. They immediately wanted to know what was going on. A few of the older folks were familiar with the diner, though most just thought the dogheads were visually appealing. "How come they're here," asked one of the younger staff. I told them the story of how the dogheads came to represent the cultural underground in San Francisco, who like the old Doggie Diner restaurants, are often overshadowed by the advances of monoculture and "progress." I then explained how the dogheads have a special significance to our marriage. Not only were they at our ceremony, they very much participated in our engagement.

My husband asked me to marry him on the night the Iraq war started, and he shortly thereafter loaded up a bus with nine San Francisco performers, hitched up the flatbed with the dogheads, and drove the whole show across the country. Our purpose: To celebrate what is amazing about America and its citizens by stopping at roadside attractions. To celebrate what was America. We were not a protest, we were a spectacular and fun-filled alternate reality. (See his movie documenting the experirence, *Head Trip*.)

After tickling the staff with my doghead tales, I headed outside and across the street, where I sit now, looking at ducks bobbing about in the water. I had noticed this bench from my hotel room window—with its view of the marina and nice back support—though the wind is stronger than it looked from my room.

As I walked to get to this bench, I noticed there was an unusual amount of dog poop on the lawn. It was everywhere, and with each pile I had to step over, I became more and more disgusted. I silently cursed the discourteous pet owners as I used all of my avoiding skill to make it to the bench without offending my shoes. When I was five feet from the bench, a bumblebee seemed to have flown up my pant leg. Oh my god! I am devastatingly allergic to bees. I began freaking out and jumping up and down to get it to fly out.

I swear to you this really happened. There I was, in clear view of the nice folks I had been talking to in the hotel lobby, and I am screeching and hopping around like a maniac. I didn't care; all I could think about was that bumble bee stinging me and causing my throat to close—right there in a field full of dog poop! Would the paramedic step in some on his way to save me? Would that make him care more about getting it off his shoe than about getting me to the hospital?

A voice of calm interrupted my panic, and I suddenly realized the poops were actually aerations holes dug by the lawn maintenance crew. Not poop—dirt. I started laughing at my folly, and the bee miraculously disappeared. No bee. No dog poop. It is just dirt. I walk the rest of the way to the bench not worrying about anything. And here I am, talking to you again.

I know some of you may find it hard to believe I actually experienced so much life in such a short period of time. It is true. I did not make any of this up. It just happened. This paying-attention-to-the-world-around-you stuff really works when you let it. Interesting things happen to all of us, and the day is full of little nuances that audiences find so darn interesting.

If your arms are crossed right now, that's okay. I hear you. Perhaps you are one of the 11 percent of humans who want to see a comma after my name, as well as charts, graphs and experts to convince you that what I am saying is true. Your desire for facts is valid and should not be ignored. Hopefully you have noticed that other chapters in this book offer relevant histories, studies and graphs to keep you happy.

If your arms are not crossed, I'm glad. You will harness the new relationship economy with ease. Though don't forget you must always remember to offer some hard facts to those who cross their arms. It will make your communications smoother.

There is moss on the bench that is now my office. Yellowish green moss. Carla and Richard were together in 2006 when they carved their names here. I wonder if their relationship has lasted as long as their moss covered poetry. I sit here writing this book and laughing about the doghead surprise, the dog poop turned to dirt, the disappearing bee. A few hours later (I am back in my hotel now), my husband and my son came to take me to dinner. As we walked across the lawn to the restaurant, he explained that the ducks were actually geese and the dirt was actually goose poop. Isn't life funny?

The bee was not in my pant leg. The dog poop turned into dirt and is actually goose poop. The ducks are actually geese. So, even when you pay attention, what you see may not be what you think you're seeing. Though it will still be interesting if you let it. This is a great one for the 24-hour rule book.

Start paying attention to details and stories that happen around you every day. Write them down.

EXERCISE:
MY LIFE IS BORING AND DRAB AND I HAVE NO STORIES

I don't believe you. I have never met a human on the planet who doesn't have interesting stories.

Remember, interesting stories are in the details. So, one way to improve storytelling skill is to practice referencing events in your life. Write them down. Tell your kids, your friends, your spouse. Practice bringing them to the surface.

Here's an opportunity. As you do this exercise write down the incidents that come to mind right away. Try not to skip. Just go down the list and jot down the first thing you think of:

- A time you were surprised
- Most afraid
- When you were absolutely wrong
- A lie you told
- A promise you broke
- An award or achievement
- A story about you you'd want told at your eulogy
- What are you most proud of
- What story gives you goose bumps
- The time you threw a tantrum as a child
- The time you threw a tantrum as an adult
- The story that makes you laugh out loud
- A favorite teacher and one story about him or her
- A funny animal story
- A favorite quote or poem

Select one answer above and put an asterisk next to it. DO not read ahead!

Did you pick one? Next pick a number one through ten, and write it here: ___

In Appendix I on page 363, find the topic for your number. Make a bridge between your asterisked story and the topic you got at random from that page.

This exercise expands your ability to tie things together so that people can listen, understand and remember your points. Don't worry. With the right amount of practice, you encourage your natural creativity. It is in you. You can do it.

Don't just sit there. Get out of your head. Your brain is a dangerous place and no one should stay in there alone for too long! Sometimes telling the story out loud helps unearth the connection between the story and the topic. Just keep talking. In the car, in the shower, at the breakfast table, on the treadmill. See if you can make the connection. This comes easy for some; for others it takes practice. Everybody can do it. Try.

There is a natural bridge between any story and any topic when we look to the higher message of both.

CHAPTER 100:
IMPROV AND
COMEDY CLUBS

Fifteen years ago I enrolled in an improv class, and this six week class taught me more about public speaking than anything I had ever tried.

On the first night of class, the instructor asked me to go to the front of the room and do some sort of speech. He told me I could read something or make it up. So I launched into a soliloquy, and, in the middle of it, he stood beside me and told me to keep speaking and mimic his actions. It was the craziest four minutes I have ever experienced. He had me climbing ladders, swimming, and shoveling snow—WHILE I was speaking. The entire classroom roared. It was so liberating.

Improv wasn't always this easy. This was because, like most beginners, I had the "no disease." In other words, I said <u>no</u> a lot when presented with an unfamiliar situation.

Here's an example:

> *I am standing on stage with a partner. We have no script, and we have to make everything up as we go along. This means we must play off each other. My partner hands me an imaginary orange, and I say, "no, that's an apple." I hand him back a "banana," and he says, "that's not a banana, it is a baseball bat." Our brains are unable to come up with anything more interesting than no, so we go back and forth like this until the audience falls asleep. We leave the stage vowing never to return again.*

No is pretty boring dialogue. It lacks creative spark and takes us nowhere. It is the power-word we first mastered in our twos. A few folks never got past it, though most of us just revert back to it when our brains are stretched to capacity. In the example above, my partner and I were unable to be creative and agree upon a jumping off point; instead, we both kept making a left turn on the other person's "right" idea.

Good improv cannot happen when the players get stuck on no; it happens when they say yes. The same is true for public speaking. Speakers become afraid of audience interaction because they don't have control over what is going to happen. All unscripted interaction gets lumped into the scary conflict category. They lock themselves tightly into disagreement mode and brace themselves for battle.

Obviously, this is not a helpful attitude. Instead, public speakers must <u>say yes</u> to the audience—to any interaction, even with the buttheads. We must trust ourselves and go with it. Oh, and having fun is a good idea too! Remember, if an audience is interacting, they are at least paying attention.

Improve and comedy classes are a great way to practice talking in front of a room. It will make you better at being you—which means a better public speaker. Really? Yes. The more you say yes with other people, the more comfortable you'll feel being yourself in front of a other people. Public speaking is doing something in front of people—so you'll be comfortable there too. It's really easy math.

Saying yes is powerful. If an audience member launches a verbal grenade, Say yes! Be glad that that they are paying attention. If you fly all the way to London to present to a group of CEO's and absolutely fail in the most humiliating way, Say YES! Find the lessons that experience held. If you speak in front of a group of venture capitalists about an organization you are in and forget EVERYTHING you know about public speaking and end up looking like a bumbling idiot, Say YES! To learning how it happened and why. See it as the butterfly sees the cocoon. Say yes! Say yes.

Practice saying yes to creative situations.

CHAPTER 101:
I ALREADY HEARD THAT ONE

Tell <u>your</u> story.

So many speakers look for quotes and stories from other people. While someone's words can be interesting too, they only work if you can repeat them super well.

Let me illustrate. A group of lobbyists I coached had the motto "Leading Leaders." As I read through their scripts, I was shocked to discover every speech started with a quote from someone famous—the swim with the sharks guy, Tony Robbins, Emerson. Quotable quotes for sure; just not what leaders do. Leaders create things.

I asked the group to imagine sitting at a function for their organization. You do it too. Okay, now visualize yourself wolfing down some delectable rubber chicken, zoning in and out, when suddenly you hear the speaker quote YOU. Imagine. Associations should do this. It is far more powerful to quote the memorable words of their members than of those whom they don't know.

I digress again. If you are going to repeat a quote, do it well. Or maybe just start telling your own stories. Great story telling means you get your whole body into it. Your voice. Your face. Give tons of detail and keep the punch line (or point) of the story a secret until the end whenever possible. Relive it. Telling your story should be as powerful for you as it is the audience.

Another reason to tell your own story is some stories are retold so much in our culture that everybody knows them. Even if you are adding a new twist or detail, you risk the audience assuming they know what you are about to say and checking out. Audiences want to believe they have heard it all. Really. All of it. Not just the story.

And when it is your story, the audience is less likely to have heard it already. Besides, people are more likely to listen when they hear something new. At Allegory, we keep detailed notes of the examples and stories we tell clients. This way if we speak to the same group again, we tell new stories. It is essential to have a deep well of personal stories to draw from.

I do have a couple of moments from my life that I like to tell over and over. I love these stories, as they helped define what I believe. I tell them because I have an emotional connection to them. They also help the audience get to know me. When we are transparent and reveal things about ourselves, it is a breath of fresh air for everyone. Stories are just a gimmick if they are not deeply rooted in who we are. I do not know too many people who can tell a made up story super well—so stick to what is true.

It is okay to amalgamate stories—I often take four stories and tell them together for impact. I also change some of the details so I do not embarrass anyone or tell on them.

Of course storytelling is not the only way to get an audience's attention, so try to come up with new ways to engage audiences too.

Rather than look up what other people said, say what you say. Within you are thoughts worthy of <u>quotes.com</u>. Let us hear them.

CHAPTER 102:
THE SQUIGGLY THINGS BENEATH OTHER PEOPLE'S STORIES

For years, I have told a story about a Special Olympics race when a young runner fell to the ground during the 100-yard dash. I report how there wasn't a dry eye in the stadium as the nine other contestants stopped running, went to her, picked her up, brushed her off, and took her to the finish line—so all ten kids crossed together.

I use this as an example of how to use someone else's story; it shows how it is possible if we emotionally connect with the story. I tear up every time I tell it. The audience does too.

Then Patricia came into my life. Patricia is a disabled rights advocate. After my talk, she came to the podium and attacked me for furthering the myth that all disabled people are kind gentle souls. She informed me that the story was an urban legend that never happened.

It was pretty shocking for me. Like I said, I love that story. So that night, I went home and looked it up on snopes.com (http://www.snopes.com/glurge/special.asp). I discovered the incident did happen—in 1976—just not exactly as I was telling it. Only a few of the contestants went back.

It was enough for me, and I still use it in my talks. I have updated the story to tell it correctly: As it happened, with a few, rather than all, contestants turning around and helping. The impact is the same. Sometimes I also mention the Patricia story.

I do not tell the story to further a stereotype about how gentle and kind people with disabilities are. That is not my point. My point is to show people that it is possible to emotionally connect with a story enough to deliver it with meaning. The story is also a testament to true teamwork. It is a story about the beauty of being human.

Once I got past my initial hackles at Patricia I totally agree with what she said. My niece Tara celebrated when South Park started showing a mischievous, imperfect, not angelic disabled kid. I still tell the story. Yesterday I added Tara's opinion on South Park to the story. Every situation builds on communicating to be heard.

Trust me, not everyone will like you or the story you tell, and if you stick to being you, it won't matter.

Only tell someone else's story if you have some emotional connection to it.

CHAPTER 103:
TELL THE STORY WITH PANACHE (EVEN IF IT ISN'T YOUR STORY)

I've talked a lot about reliving the story. Can you tell the difference?

Imagine you are in a sales meeting, and it's your job to rally the support team who sends out all the contracts. Which approach would you choose?

<u>Ho-hum</u>:
> *We have got to support our VP of Sales in getting the big accounts. It is how we eat.*

<u>Better</u>:
> *In basketball, Michael Jordan received standing ovations from capacity crowds for his jump shots. An unsung position, the power forward, made it possible for Jordan to access the hoop and thereby filled the stadium. We must support our star player: Tom Smith, VP of Sales. He is Michael Jordan— WE are the Power Forward.*

<u>Best</u>:
> *It is 1997 and the Chicago Bulls are playing at home against the Detroit Pistons. It's hot and stuffy. The United Center is packed to capacity, and the stands shake as Michael Jordan performs his signature walking-on-air, tongue-out, slam dunk—much to Isiah Thomas's chagrin. The power forward, Charles Oakley quietly creates each opportunity for Michael, and their combined efforts fill the stadium with cheering fans. As the team of support personnel, we are the power forward. It is up to us to set up our team for success.*

<u>Bestest</u>:
> *I'm sitting about fourteen rows from the court at Chicago Stadium. My hands ache from applauding. My voice is hoarse from screaming. The humidity is 100 percent, and every seat in the house is full. I am certain my shirt is sticking to my back with a dark blue racing stripe down my spine.*
>
> *The roar of the crowd is deafening as Michael Jordan once again runs through the air—defying gravity (imagine him with his tongue out)—to SLAM DUNK with a purposeful "uuuuuh!"*
>
> *Isaiah Thomas cracks his neck to his chest and whips an invisible horse with his hands. The Bull's power forward Charles Oakley down lows a hand slap to Jordan, as he is the guy who made that dunk happen. While the fans were all watching Michael, Charles was setting up the shot to win the game. The Power Forwards make it happen.*

This is us. We are the power forwards in our sales team.

This story is even better if you have basketballs hidden under the table and toss them at the group.

Telling a story isn't a chore—delight in it. People will listen.

CHAPTER 104:
THIS BOOK IS LIKE A CONTAINER SHIP GOING UNDER A BRIDGE

I used to say, "Analogies and Metaphors Prove a Point." They can. Sure, I mostly believe that. Now I say, figure out a way to get them to listen and remember—analogies and metaphors do that.

While I'm sure you already know the definition of analogy, simile, and metaphor, I'm going to review them so we can all be on the same page. I might not have these definitions perfectly stated, so don't count on them in an SAT test.

- **Analogy**—A figure of speech in which a word or phrase that ordinarily designates one thing is used to designate another, thus making a comparison, as in "a sea of troubles" or "All the world's a stage" (Shakespeare). Or to put it another way, an analogy is the comparison of two things that are not alike.

- **Simile**— A figure of speech involving a comparison between two unlike entities. This resemblance is indicated by the words "like" or "as." Similes in everyday speech reflect simple comparisons, as in "He eats like a bird" or "She is slow as molasses."

- **Metaphor**—Also a figure of speech involving a comparison between two unlike entities, though with no "like" or "as". "His sales record is an eagle soaring to unprecedented heights."

These three figures of speech are often used interchangeably. They help audiences relate your message to tangible concepts. Good talks have a common theme and maintain its ribbon through the speech.

Can you guess why I named this chapter the way I did? I looked out of my office window and watched a container ship cruise under the Bay Bridge. There was a lot of smoke coming out of the smoke stack—much more than I usually see. I realized the ship was going faster than usual. Since the bridge was packed with rush hour traffic, I wondered if the people in their cars imagined there was a fire somewhere. All this made me start thinking about smoke and the saying "Where there is smoke there is fire." See the way the mind works when it's been caged at a desk for hours?

Then my thoughts drifted to when bees erected a hive in our roof, and we had to call a professional to help get them out. When the bee guy showed up, he used smoke to get the bees out. He then vacuumed them up into a little bee house; only instead of taking them away like I thought he would, he brought the bee house inside our home. This was more than unpleasant for me since I am horribly allergic to bees. After my persistent questioning, he assured me, that even though the bee house isn't a closed container, not one bee will leave as the queen is inside. It was true. The bees stayed inside, fanning the queen. And for the rest of the day, my home smells like sweet honey. I still have a piece of the honey comb in my freezer. Eventually, he took the beehive and the bees with him. I'm sure they are happy somewhere.

The bees leave the hive when they smell smoke because smoke means there is fire; fire means they must save the queen from her certain death. They calmly and collectively exit the hive—their queen in tow. I used to think the smoke intoxicated them in some way. It doesn't. Bees understand consequences. They understand that problems are not things to freak out about.

Public speaking is the same way. We've all been in a room with a speaker who reads to us and doesn't interact. We politely pretend we are listening. Inside our head we are "fanning the queen." We can't collectively leave the room as long as a speaker is talking—as that would be considered rude. So, we sit there tortured, mentally buzzing around. It doesn't smell like honey.

Did you catch my analogy? Metaphor and simile? I wrote the words above to prove a point. Notice how off the top of my head I made the bee analogy tie into my shipping container observation? It is more interesting to the audience to use metaphor or analogy to discuss things. I purposefully did not go back and edit this for you.

Walk around your world and notice details. Find a common theme with seemingly unrelated topics, and bridge these details to each other using analogy, simile and metaphor. Get creative. Discover ways to apply your observations to the next speech you need to give. Make it your own.

YOU can do it! I am not unusually creative, my friends. You can do this too. I promise.

Creative ways of speaking keep the audience's attention and help them remember your points.

 **EXERCISE:**

SHOE FETISH

Take off your shoe. Really. If you are not wearing shoes, please go grab a shoe from your closet. Got it?

I have no idea what kind of shoe you're holding. There are many different styles of shoes out there—shoes for women, for men, for people under 20 and over

70, for fashion divas and comfort seekers. All I know is that you are holding a metaphor or analogy in your hands.

Think back to the topic you selected in the first chapter of this section. How could you use your shoe to expound upon that topic?

Hey. I saw that look. This might be a stretch for you. Just do it! Get it. I just made a funny shoe slogan reference!

Do not read ahead. Right now, write down three ways your shoe is related to the topic (or like, or not like, the topic).

1.

2.

3.

Hold on there Bucko! Go back and do the exercise before reading on.

Here is an example. My upcoming talk is on the relationship economy and how times have changed.

TYPE OF SHOE	ILLUSTRATIVE CONNECTION
Green Champion Tennis Shoes	They look comfortable. They are not. I bought them at Payless, and they do not have an instep. I assumed they were comfortable by the way they looked. The same is true of people. We have no idea what is going on inside the human. We make assumptions…
Red Patent High-Heel Pumps	These are my favorite shoes, and I paid more for them than any other pair in my closet. On my first day wearing these shoes the button cover on the toe button popped off. I have been unable to find it, and I think my baby ate it. I have meant to go back to the store to exchange the shoe every day for the past four months. Now it is too late. I wear the shoes anyway and hope no one notices. I am a little peeved every time I wear them. This is what happens in organizations. You see pretty shoes and have no idea of the sordid history of those shoes. Assumptions are the kiss of death for managers. You really have <u>no idea</u> what is going on with your team members. You really don't. They aren't telling you…

Birkenstocks in need of repair	I have had these shoes since I was sixteen-years-old. Everyone complained about them in the old days, soles would crumble over time, reducing the life of the shoes. I laugh about that now as I look at how antique these shoes are now. They look exactly the same way they did then. Crumbled heel. Comfortable. I have not worn them in over twenty years. (Crap, I just gave away my age. I didn't used to care about that.) A perfect shoe can be destroyed over time by being worn too much. The same is true of your employees. We tend to give the star players a lot of work as we know it will be done well. The star players then get <u>overwhelmed</u> with too much to do and become medium players…
Platform Boots	These are my white platform Go-Go boots. Eight performers and I bought these shoes in bulk to go with matching "Fembot" outfits we wore in a silly, sci-fi dance performance. These shoes are the most uncomfortable shoes I have ever owned. The rest of the Fembots agree: They are awful. The funny thing is we did our dance performance to the song "These boots are made for walking." Every time we performed that routine, we laughed at the irony of wearing those boots while dancing to that song. It became a thing. In fact, we still laugh about it years later. Why am I telling you this? Bad things can become good things. The struggles we have can create camaraderie and become part of our culture. Living through challenges makes us like each other…

For this exercise, use analogies, metaphors, similes—use objects to explain or simplify things. You are not doing it for me. You are doing it for the audience.

Everything has a story. In fact, my stapler has a story. I have had this stapler since the day I started my company. It's plaid. I painted the plaid with WiteOut while on a conference call ten years ago. It also has a sticker of a pig held down with tape on the top. My friend Tanya put it there so I would know which stapler was mine. (This was before the WiteOut plaid.) There is also an address sticker on the metal part of the stapler. I suppose I put the sticker there because I was worried about the stapler getting lost during lunch and not being able to find its way back. I could do a talk about that stapler—talking about how something as simple as a person using my stapler and not returning it can mess with the culture of an organization. A person can get so upset over a lost office item, and it can cause your profit to drop—that one action!

I suppose I should say it here too: I am weird. I know it, and by now you've figured that out. And guess what—you are weird too.

Start noticing things. Make note of what makes you different from others.

Your weirdness makes you interesting. Show it by telling your weird stories. Audiences want to hear them.

CHAPTER 105:
NERDS NEED
STATISTICS

Warm and fuzzy must be backed up with substance. Regardless of how compelling they are, stories are a gimmick if they don't have meat.

Okay, I'll quiz you. What percent of the audience needs statistics and facts or they disregard the presentation? Yes, 11 percent. And did you know 44.9 percent of all statistics are made up right on the spot!

As much as we love a great story, we also benefit from hard data, especially if statistics and facts are presented in an engaging fashion. I talk about Dr. Mehrabian's communication study in this book so that 11 percent of you will pay attention. You want to know Dr. Mehrabian's expert opinion, and the fact that I took time to share it with you makes you trust me more too.

Rapport speaking focuses on creative ways to get folks to listen to real facts—not simply presenting a fluffy, mamby-pamby storytelling exercise.

This circles back to the "why." Statistics and studies help prove <u>why</u> our perspective is relevant. Hard evidence helps prove our perspective and/or our point.

Overusing evidence, or using evidence in sneaky ways, is why the book *Lying with Statistics* is often cited. Be open about the ways your statistics can be used to prove another point; do not present them as gospel. They are there to augment learning.

The audience does not listen the same way you do so make sure you have evidence, statistics and logic in your presentations as well. Hit on all listeners.

Stories are just tricks if other types of data do not back them up.

CHAPTER 106:
PUBLIC SPEAKING
IS NO JOKE

Careful with this one. Joke telling and public speaking don't always go together. In fact, joke telling can be disastrous for a public speaker.

I am a great joke teller, and I often entertain people with this skill at dinner and cocktail parties. It is fun. I don't tell other people's jokes so much when speaking, as I have found it doesn't build upon my relationship with the audience.

If told poorly, a joke undermines your relationship with the audience; if told well, a joke transforms the audience into a room of folks who would rather be entertained than informed.

Entertainment is the rage in the speaking world. Speakers think they need to entertain more to get the big engagements. While true to some extent, this popular belief undermines the essential role of a public speaker—to inform. Entertainment is not the same as sharing perspective. Entertainment for entertainment's sake does not provide substance.

Jokes are often fabricated facts loosely drawn together for human enjoyment. If we sprinkle our talk with made-up jokes, it can call the rest of our theories into question. Of course, if jokes are working for you, please continue to use them. If the quickest way to share your real self with a roomful of strangers is to tell a joke, do it. If you are not a joke teller, don't become one because you think it will make you a better public speaker. Unless you are a natural, it won't.

Years ago professional speech coaches told people to open with a joke. This technique is worn-out and overused. It doesn't work nearly as well as it used to. Speakers are less effective when they use other people's stories and words to show how smart and funny they are.

You are smart and funny. You do not need to quote another person to prove that. You do not need their joke or their quote to prove your point. Your perspective is funnier and deeper than anything Billy Crystal or Schopenhauer wrote. Start writing down the original things you say to make your friends laugh. Use those.

Take a comedy class—you can be funny. You already are.

Humor is very effective, as long as it is your own.

CHAPTER 107:

SAY BOO!

My grandfather, Peter Cummins, was a quiet, intelligent and extremely religious man. When my parents first divorced, my mother moved my sister and I from Georgia to San Diego to live with Grandpa and his dog Prince. It was a major move for us, and we were tenuous and nerve-riddled in the early days.

Grandpa took Prince for a walk every morning after church, so I started tagging along. As it turns out Grandpa was a wise man, and today, I wish I had tape-recorded the many things he taught me on those walks.

At breakfast one morning I overheard my Aunt Rosemary complaining to 'Papa' that life was going by so fast. So on our walk I asked him about it. I couldn't understand why things were speeded up for her and not for me?

He carefully explained how, when you got older, life starts whizzing by because of the many experiences the person has inside them. I still didn't understand it. He tried again, and this time he gave me advice that I still live with today. Here it is:

> Life goes by fast because we get used to everything. To slow it down, to get every tiny morsel out of life every single day, do one thing: Do something that surprises you, terrifies you, scares you, makes you nervous—every day.

Grandpa's advice is among the best I have ever received. I try new things all the time, and while my life still seems to whiz by, I have volumes of great stories to reflect upon and share with others.

What does this have to do with public speaking? Audiences are the same. They like to be surprised (sometimes even scared—my red hair does that). Surprises peak their interest.

Picture yourself walking into a company meeting. It's the same Monday morning meeting you've had for eight years. Taste the just-okay coffee, the same too-sweet donuts and hear your co-workers reliving their weekends. Everybody wishes they were somewhere else.

Only this time you see your boss clad in leathers. He is wearing a motorcycle helmet. He closes the door and casually walks over and opens all the windows. You notice a mini-bike in the middle of the conference table. He climbs up on the table, gets on the bike and starts to rev it. Everyone in the room is in shock. Ms. Guilderbrand has her hand over her nose and mouth, Tom Smith is cheering, Alicia Masters is covering her ears, you are speechless.

Your boss turns off the motor and quickly turns on two fans to get the

YOUR PROFESSIONALISM IS KILLING YOU...

rest of the exhaust out of the room. He asks everyone to sit down. Then he clasps his hands together, sits, and looks around the room—waiting for someone to say something. Tom finally does: "Way to start a meeting Bob!"

Bob smiles. "I was thinking, team. Last year I got my son a mini-bike for his birthday. I have never seen that kind of excitement. This kid was jumping off the walls for days. All over a mini-bike."

"My question for you is simple. How can we inject similar enthusiasm in what we do every day? I'm looking around this room and wondering if we've lost that loving feeling for our product. Your thoughts?"

The meeting is a success: Bob taked about ways to improve the company and life in general. It started with Bob, and he became a new leader from that day forward. He constantly raised the bar with new and glorious ways to open meetings, and the sparkle in his eyes got passed around the room. If someone lost the spark, another simply murmured "mini-bike" and it came back.

From that moment on the entire culture started using a motorcycle revving gesture to spark enthusiasm.

Do something out of the ordinary. Surprise them!

CHAPTER 108:
EVEN WHEN YOU MAKE IT STICKY,
THEY WILL FORGET

We are constantly bombarded with sights, sounds, smells and information. Our attention span is shortening as technology creates more instantaneous communication. We are so used to being interrupted from our train of thought we find directed and focused communication long and dreary.

This technological, media-driven world poses a rising challenge for speakers. Today's communication environment is like being in a batting cage. You barely have enough time to blink before you are hit with a new thought. Let me explain.

Picture a batting cage. It is a bright sunny day, and the chain link fence is closed behind you. You have a roll of quarters, and you just fed the machine as much as it will take. The balls shoot out of the tube every fifteen seconds. This is communication. The balls are shooting out toward you and you must swing at them with the bat. Over time, your arms get tired. Your swings aren't as hearty, your connects decrease. At strike seventeen you drop the bat and leave the cage—quickly.

Words rarely cut through the distraction of day-to-day life. Figuring out how to improve the <u>how</u> of your communication is the test of a great public speaker.

Humans will remember action more than words.

Words are easy to forget; your actions aren't.

CHAPTER 109:
CATERING IS ONLY GOOD
IF THE FOOD IS GOOD

Keep the audience in mind; do not cater to them. When speakers switch from personality type to personality type to suit situations and audiences, people sense incongruence and lose trust and confidence in their words.

I really hate that paragraph. It sounds like my underwear's too tight or something. Here is what I'm really saying:

> *Politicians lose votes when they say one thing to one audience and something else to another.*

Speak to the issues the audience is interested in and do not change your opinion to suit them. Humans actually <u>love</u> when speakers say what they think.

Henry (I'll be informal and use his first name), a legislator in Nevada, is really great at this. At a meeting in Nevada, the entire front row of the large audience was comprised of energy company representatives; they were there because they wanted to create more coal plants.

Henry said (I am paraphrasing here), "Let me be clear. It isn't that I am saying I do not want more plants in Nevada. I am saying there will be NO more coal plants built in Nevada. Prepare for that." He looked right at them. The audience loved it—even the energy guys. It is much better to know where we are than to wonder about it.

Audiences like to hear your truth, even if they don't agree with it.

CHAPTER 110:
THE MORE YOU TALK
THE LESS THEY BELIEVE YOU

This is a review chapter. I'm tying in a number of points and making them relevant to the same rule: Use specific words.

Story telling must be very detailed and real to keep the attention of an audience. In storytelling, the more descriptive words you use, the better. In this case, using lots of words to describe something is highly effective. The opposite is true if you are telling an audience something. In this case, using lots of words isn't as effective.

Remember, use words to paint the audience a picture so they may come to their own conclusion. Do not use words to tell them what to think. Paste this to your bathroom mirror:

Detail is good.
Editorializing is bad.

The same holds true when giving positive feedback. The more you gush incoherently the less the recipient believes you—even when you are saying something good. Always avoid words like "great" and "super" as they don't tell the person anything. Instead, be specific. Say, "I loved the way you used that banana in the team building exercise. I really got it," instead of "Wow, that was super great."

You are doing a great job is not as effective as being specific about what is great.

Specifics trump superlatives every time.

CHAPTER 111:
THE LECTERN IS NOT
A SPACESHIP

When speaking in front of others you are in the spotlight. Welcome the attention. Most of us didn't get enough attention when we were kids, so relish in it now!

This chapter is designed to teach you a thing or two about speaking furniture. No, not furniture that talks—though imagine being upstaged by a chair! (It happens.) Let's make your speaking experience more pleasurable. Are you ready?

Podium:

A podium is a small raised platform that the conductor of an orchestra, a lecturer, or somebody giving a speech can stand on. In this sense, a podium is a small stage, not a lectern (though the American Heritage Dictionary defines a podium as a lectern in the second definition). Podiums can be quite small in order to make the presenter appear taller. In the presidential debates some candidates stand on boxes so they appear as tall as everyone else. I do not agree with this practice—it's like false advertising!

Podium How-Tos:
- Watch for power cords and other low-lying things that will trip up your feet.
- If possible get off the podium and connect with the crowd (even if you are short!).
- Make sure you blow your nose before stepping up onto the podium. The last thing you want is to have a "bat in the cave"—particularly in pictures.
- Yes, I just said "bat in the cave," it sounds better than booger.
- If possible, center the podium in front of the audience, with your multimedia screen to one side. This way you are the center of focus—not the big screen. It's all about you, remember?

Lectern:

A lectern is a stand with a slanted top that supports the book or lecture notes of a speaker. The lectern is not the steering wheel of a car, nor is it on the podium for speakers to have something to hold on to, lean against or ride like a spaceship. The lectern is there because it supports notes and visual props; it also puts something solid between the speaker and the audience—like a buffer from all that attention. Note of caution: A lectern can also make us appear smaller than we really are.

Lectern Tips:
- Stand to the side of the lectern so a portion of your entire body is visible. This is why lecterns are clear now.
- Whenever possible (and only if the microphone allows), step away from the lectern entirely.

- The lectern is a place to put notes and props if you have any. Notes should NEVER be on a stack of 3x5 cards. 3x5 cards are easy to lose. (I share a great story about this in Chapter 122 on page 277.) The water glass should go on the shelf underneath the lectern. Trust me when I say it's far too easy to make a sudden hand gesture and send your water glass crashing and splashing into the front row. (It's also a tad embarrassing.)
- Decorate the lectern. I have many small signs I drape over the lectern, such as:
  - "If you can read this sign you are close enough that I won't pick on you." I allude to this sign in my talk when I tell the audience I don't pick on the front row.
  - "If you can read this sign, watch for flying objects." I allude to this in my anecdotal story about launching a glass into the front row with a hand gesture.
  - "If you are reading this sign, I am boring you already."
  - "The human relationship is the true currency."
  - "Allegory."
  - "The only person who likes a lecture is the person giving it."
- For voice amplification, move the microphone to the side of the lectern and speak from there. (I'll cover more microphone fun facts in the next chapter.)

Road test the furniture before speaking. Arrive early enough so you can get the lay of the room.

Don't let a bad relationship with furniture upstage your speech.

CHAPTER 112:
IS THIS THING ON?
THE BODY MICROPHONE

Voice amplification is done with the diaphragm first. Sometimes it is then channeled through an electronic device. Sometimes it is not. In any case, you must engage your diaphragm if you want to be heard.

What's a diaphragm? Oh, I know you know the answer. I was just trying to get you to think about it for a minute. Now, experience it.

- Lay on the floor. Put your hand on your stomach right above your navel. Watch your stomach as you breathe. Do this for a few moments. Does your stomach rise and fall. If it doesn't, call 911 immediately.

- Pay attention to when it rises. Does it rise when you inhale or exhale? Breathe normally.

- Hey, stop reading ahead and do the damn exercise.

- If it rises when you exhale, you are like a lot of people. You are not breathing into your diaphragm. My singing teacher in 7th grade choir taught us how to make our voices resonate by breathing into the diaphragm. I didn't like my choir teacher much; even so, she is still right about the breathing.

- Try it now. Breathe so that your stomach goes out when you breathe in and in when you exhale.

Practicing this type of breathing will amplify your voice. Even though I am not a doctor or a yogi, I know this works. You can Google it if you want to know exactly why. It is enough for me to know it in my body. It does take a lot of practice to breath this way, so start today!

Here's another interesting thought on breathing. I have taught breathing for years, and it wasn't until Joseph Giove asked me a few short questions that I really understood it. You can live without food for thirty days. Water for seven. How long can you live without air? Did you guess seven minutes?

Ever wonder why people lose their train of thought or can't come up with the right words? My guess is it is because they are oxygen deprived. Not a scientific fact, mind you, just a deduction. It is elementary, my dear Watson.

So, from now on, start breathing. Prior to a speech, practice breathing into your diaphragm. Take deep clear breaths. Your brain will work better.

Focus on breathing before a speech.

CHAPTER 113:
IS THIS THING ON?
THE ELECTRONIC MICROPHONE

Most public speakers use one of three types of microphones: The lapel microphone, the stationary microphone and the handheld microphone. If you have the option, always opt for the lapel microphone or "lavaliere mic" as the pros call it. This will allow you to walk about the room if you wish. Movement will produce endorphins—standing still and fretting will produce cortisol. We want endorphins!

Here's a breakdown of the three types of microphones.

<u>Lapel/Lavaliere Microphone:</u>
Like I said, this is the type of microphone you want every time you speak. It is the best way to communicate with amplification.

- Spread your thumb and pinkie as far away as possible. This is the distance the lapel mic should be from your mouth (assuming your head is in a normal position while you are speaking).

- Try not to move your head back and forth too much, as most lapel microphones are directional. They also pick up the rustle of clothing.

- Remember to TURN OFF the lapel microphone when you are finished speaking. Last month in San Francisco, I kept my microphone on for five minutes before I realized all of my one-on-one conversations were being amplified. Whoops. Someone should do a book, or better yet, a video, on microphone gaffes of politicians and other speakers! GWB are you listening?

- Sound technicians often want to tuck the microphone power pack in your clothing behind your back. Be mindful of this placement if you decide to take your jacket off during the speech. I've heard some powerpacks go clunking!

- Women, if you wear a dress with no belt in the middle there will be nowhere to tuck the battery pack. Thus, when speaking in public, wear clothing that has a place to hang sound equipment. Men, the same is true for you if you wear a dress to your public speaking engagements. One of the reasons I failed so miserably at a speech in London is my fancy dress did not allow for a microphone. I had to carry around a handheld thus making my gesturing limited.

<u>Stationary Microphone:</u>
Stationary microphones are the second best microphone option. Still, they are a far second to lapel microphones, since they stifle gestures and limit spontaneity.

- Avoid playing with the cord unless you are trained in Roger Daltry, rock-n-roll-microphone acrobatics! Even if you are nervous, you should never fiddle with the cord or hold onto the mic stand. Both of these things could potentially cause feedback and throw you off—not to mention the damage it could do to your audience's ears.

- Fidgeting hands are not the best way to engage endorphins. Yes, it is movement—just not the best movement.

- Okay, sometimes it is good to hold the microphone cord. For example, if you are moving the microphone stand around. Otherwise you might do a Chevy Chase. If you do not know that reference, you are too young to be reading this book. Just kidding—though if you really don't know who Chevy Chase is, you should look up "Chevy Chase Saturday Night Live video" on the internet or rent a DVD of early Saturday Night Live episodes. He was really funny—the Buster Keaton of his day. Oh yeah, google Buster Keaton too.

- When telling a story with gestures, avoid knocking the microphone stand over. It is remarkably easy to do. In fact, I've done it. If you do it, do not fret. Roll with it. Some of my best teaching examples came out of stupid things I did in front of a room. Use the gaffe—don't ignore or apologize for it.

- If the stationery microphone is sitting on a lectern, it can be turned so it points to the side of the lectern. That way your whole body directly faces the audience.

Handheld Microphones:

Avoid handheld microphones. They do not let you use your hands to gesture. And we want to use our hands to gesture. If you must use a handheld microphone, see if you can put it on a freestanding mic stand.

- Spitting into a microphone is never a good idea. Every microphone is different in terms of the distance between your mouth and the mesh. Test distances. Generally, the closer the microphone is to your mouth (as long as you aren't sucking on it) the less background noise the audience will hear. If singing, the microphone should be very close, though not close enough to pick up the "P" sounds. They sound like you are spitting.

- Be careful to not thump the microphone unless you are doing so to create an effect. Bill Cosby used to use this technique to great success. Remember: " Na na na na na NAA…Na na na na NAA…and the baby wheel go-carts rocketing down the hill crash into the stop sign at the bottom!! THUMP!" Microphones amplify sounds. Bumping a mic makes a sound. Audiences do not like bumping sounds as much as they like your voice.

A quick word on feedback—when it happens, take note of where you are in the room. AVOID that spot from then on. I have actually worked this into a bit. I asked for masking tape. I taped a big X on the carpet. "Audience, if I go near

that spot during my talk please ROAR to stop me. Let's practice this, ROAR."
Hysterically, the audience would ROAR as I got close to the spot. I played with
it a lot. We laughed. I tied it into communication in an organization—how
the same thing happens over and over and we don't do anything to stop it. As a
culture we can come up with ways to solve these repeating nightmares.

In order to communicate to be heard…um…you want to be HEARD!

CHAPTER 114:
IS THIS THING ON?
MICROPHONE TROUBLESHOOTING

The last thing a speaker needs to worry about is failing equipment. Here are some ideas to make your sound relationship yummy and worry free.

- Do a sound check before anyone arrives. If you are unable to do this don't fret. The audience will let you know visually if the sound isn't working. If the sound isn't working, remain calm. You can also try hand signals or shadow puppets if you feel like it.

- Before speaking find out who your sound person is; buy him or her coffee— maybe give a foot massage. I'm serious, treat your AV people like gods. They are. I always bring a toy to give the sound people.

- Never talk through bad sound. If the microphone goes dead or feeds back, stop speaking and ask for technical assistance. You can keep the audience occupied by saying something like, "In the meantime, let's take some questions from the audience while we wait for the technology gods to deliver visual again. [Turn to the AV person.] Let me know when it is working. [Then turn to the audience.] Who has the first question? [Improvise if nobody raises a hand.] A question I am often asked is…"

- It is okay to take a five-minute break to see if you can fix the problem. Audiences are fine with this if you keep them in the loop as to what is happening.

- Take the opportunity to have fun with the sound problem. Knowing that most people cannot, I'll silently mouth to the audience "Can you hear me now?" This will make folks laugh a bit. I then put my arms out like an antennae and ask more loudly this time, "Can you hear me now?" A few more people laugh. Next, I put my leg up and contort my body in a funny way. "Now?" If the sound person still hasn't got the equipment to work, I bring three people up to the podium and ask them to stand with their arms up—like a human antennae. I tap on them and say to the audience, "Now?" The audience is usually roaring by then.

- If there is no way to fix the problem and the technical difficulties are insurmountable, don't despair and don't lose your cool. Instead, leave the podium/lectern and speak from the middle of the room. Remember your diaphragm and have fun with this new intimacy with your audience.

- In some circumstances, say if the room is much too big for people to hear you without a microphone, I ask the facilitator what he or she wants to do. They often have a backup plan. In any event, don't give up! Make it fun! Don't fret.

Always check your microphone before the audience arrives. If you have trouble, don't give up and don't fret. Make it work for you.

CHAPTER 115:

WALK WITH IT
RATHER THAN ROCK WITH IT

Many items were available in the 70's that are not sold in stores today—nunchaks, eight tracks and a pair of silver balls that hung from a string and clacked with kenetic energy. My brother used to tell me if I watched the metal ball go back and forth I would be hypnotized and bark like a dog on his command.

Some speakers have a tendency to rock back and forth on their heels when they speak to a room. Perhaps somewhere in the recesses of their brain, they are hoping to hypnotize the audience into remembering their message. Usually such rocking is simply energy moving—a sign of nerves working at warp speed.

I have a friend who shakes his leg whenever he sits. At the dinner table, while watching TV, in the movies. He is like that—a tremendously high energy person. I cannot stop him—nor do I want to—though I can ask him to refrain from doing it against the table.

Rocking back and forth behind the lectern is not the most effective way to get folks to listen. It is highly distracting, and it stretches the audience input limits. They are focused on the speakers left foot.

If you are a rocker, you must become aware of your bridled energy and harness it in a conscious way. My advice: Don't rock it, walk it. If you notice you are rocking back and forth in a seated position, stand up. If you are a side-to-side rocker, walk to the left of the room and stop there. Talk for a minute to that side of the room then walk to the other side. Stop again and talk to the other side of the room. The rocking will subside. The walking method also makes a speech feel more like a conversation.

What if you are trapped behind a lectern? Try to move to the side of the lectern, then to the other side—though not too rapidly, as this will make you seem frenetic. If you absolutely cannot move, use gestures. Somehow get that energy out in a way that is not rocking. A focused movement is key here. Use gestures.

You body wants to move. Communication is a body game. MOVE.

Energy is awesome. It produces endorphins and makes you more present. If you have extra energy, walk with it.

CHAPTER 116:
I DO NOT CARE
WHAT YOU DO WITH YOUR HANDS

Many public speaking trainers spend hours helping people figure out what to do with their hands. This is wasted time in the new relationship economy.

I attended a speakers training, and I was told to gesture from the "speakers box." Basically, gestures should come from a square around your stomach and elbows. It is the most unnatural looking gesturing I have ever seen. Please take an axe and destroy the speakers box.

Professional public speaking trainers (I am not one) also say to use little signature gestures to create audience adhesion. Bill Clinton does that cool thumb thing. Nope, I don't agree with that idea.

I have an idea: Gesture like you do when reliving a story to your friends. That is how you gesture.

If you don't normally put your hands behind your back when you speak, it won't look natural when you do it in front of a roomful of people, so don't do it. Though if you do, it won't be the kiss of death, so please do not worry about it. Basically, I'm trying to get you to stop obsessing so much about your hands. Hands are connected to the feet. If you wiggle your toes, your hands relax. Try it.

If you really do not like what you are doing with your hands, the best thing to do with them is use them to describe things. Show the room what big looks like with your hands. Let's assume you are speaking and you say "I have BIG news for you." Go ahead, stand up and try it.

What did your gesture look like? Did you stretch your hands as wide as they go? You know, "This is BIG," with your arms reaching side to side? No. Try it again, and get bigger. It might feel weird to you, because this gesture seems really big if you are in a small room. In a large room, big with your arms spread apart looks a lot better than big described as hands fourteen inches apart.

Now, stand up and show "little" with your hands. Say, "They had a LITTLE problem." Did you use the thumb and forefinger about an inch apart on one hand to show little? Yes, that is little. I scrunch up my right eye and look through a little crack I make between my thumb and forefinger. That is unmistakably little.

Relaxed and unforced hand gesturing can add to the detail of your story and help you connect more easily with the audience. I wrote this chapter because far too many budding speakers tell me they were told not to use their hands. I can see why you wouldn't want to make wild hand gestures if you work for the bomb squad. Public speaking is scary, though not that scary!

We judge people by their hand gestures. We have been taught folks shouldn't have their hands in their pockets. Who really cares about hands in the pockets except maybe my college professor or a police officer?

If you normally keep your hands in your pockets, be aware: By keeping the hands in our pockets we aren't harnessing the endorphins that will make our brain work better. Again, it is really all about you. If you like having your hands in your pockets when you speak, so be it. AND maybe try sprinkling in a gesture or two and see what the endorphins do for you.

Movement makes your brain function better.

Gesture like you do when you are with your friends—not like you do when alone in a car and a person cuts you off!

CHAPTER 117:
USE LILY PADS
INSTEAD OF BULLET POINTS

For obvious reasons, I hate the term bullet points. From now on, we will not use the term again. Instead, we will use what I call "lily pads." (Did you notice the lily pads studded throughout this book?)

The next time you watch The Nature Channel, pay attention to what frogs do. You will notice that frogs use lilly pads as stopovers in a seemingly random journey—still they get to their destination just the same. Traversing from lily pad to lily pad is not a linear method for getting across a pond. Frogs prefer this circuitous technique—for them it is a more comfortable and organic way to go.

Think of creating a talk in the same way. Shooting straight across a series of ideas— bullet point to bullet point—you can miss much along the way and arrive out of breath.

Public speaking does not have to be linear—provided you have a plan for opening and closing your talk. Once this plan is determined, you can then create lily pad points and exercises that you know you want to get to. Shuffle them around, find your way to them organically, let them find you. They will, and this technique will keep your talk fresh and interesting—for you and your audience.

To do this, you must find the "leaps" between lily pads. Let's go back to the frog example. To get from one pad to another the frog simply leaps. He can also choose to leap to a number of nearby lily pads depending on his mood. Think of your transitions from one lily pad point to another as leaps. Such transitions are everything in public speaking, and knowing how to get from one point to the next, without it seeming canned, is a mark of a great speaker.

A natural segue exists between your points, and it is up to you to find it. (It isn't an expositor essay!) Practicing your talk out loud will help you see how things fit together and allow you to come up with more of your own intellectual property. You have knowledge inside you, and people need to know about it. Otherwise, you are just another person with a microphone.

I need to say that again. Brilliant quotes, thoughts and analogies lay waiting in the leaps between lily pads. The audience wants to hear them. You will miss the opportunity to share these amazing parts of yourself if you're chained to a bullet point script. Bullet point scripts will not create the a-ha you are looking for. You will.

That knowledge will come out of you—I promise. Here's an exercise for you. Create an opening and closing of your talk, then construct a series of lily pads to substantiate your topic. Do not order them. Instead, walk around your humble abode and say the opening and leap from lily pad to lily pad as the mood strikes you. Don't worry, no one is listening. You will surprise yourself with your brilliance. Try it.

Transitions do not have to be literal. I often just simply stop. Look around. Move to the next topic.

Transitions are not details of the next segment or justification on why you just did what you did. Transitions are a natural move to the next point. Sometimes with no segue at all.

Lily Pads are major components of the speech; they are not a rigid map.

 **EXERCISE**

LILY PAD FUN

To do this exercise, I need a topic. I will use my trusty web search technique to come up with the topic. Oh, wait—the radio just started playing Joan of Arc by OMD. Thanks radio. (This example has not been edited—you are reading it just as it happened.)

According to Wikipedia:
> *Joan of Arc, or Jeanne d'Arc in French, (1412-1431) is a Fifteenth Century national heroine of France. She was tried and executed for heresy when she was only nineteen-years-old. The judgment was overturned by the Pope and she was declared an innocent martyr twenty-four years later. She was beatified in 1909 and canonized as a saint in 1920.*

Let's imagine I was speaking to a college history class about Joan of Arc. Do you think the class is riveted by an expositional opening? Sitting through a dry lecture is not a student's favorite thing to do. Despite the real adventure and romance of Joan's story, most students will only find it compelling if they can connect to her feelings, her beliefs, her time and the various motivations of those around her. If I, as a public speaker, gave a talk designed to get them thinking about her in modern terms—and in their own lives—they will be more likely to remember her story and use this information for good.

Below is an example of a process you can go through to create a speech on any topic. In our case, we will make up a speech about Joan of Arc. (Remember, I am not actually a college professor, I was only pretending. I have never done a talk on Joan of Arc.)

Begin by sketching out a rough list of goals you want to attain. Then outline methods (lily pads) you might use to attain them. You can use this method for any public speech.
- <u>What is the main thing I want the class to leave the room with?</u>—A

clear understanding of the history of Joan of Arc.

- <u>What is one thing I'd like to encourage them to do after hearing me speak about Joan?</u>—Think things through. Act. Be passionate.

- <u>Another goal of the session</u>—Seeing how history resonates with their lives and learning how to incorporate these useful understandings into their knowledge base.

- <u>Potential methods (lily pads)</u>—These include role playing, storytelling, personal ancedotes (both mine and the students) that are related in theme, and getting students to describe which of the characters they relate to and why.

- <u>How will I open?</u>—Find a story that relates to my goals, making sure this story will grab the attention of the room and make me feel like myself when I tell it. Since I have plenty of stories on finding faith for no reason, I must pick one with humor that I can tell in great detail (humor is good for me and the students).

- <u>How will I close?</u>—Encourage students to reflect and comment on how they will live differently based upon this historical reflection. End with this Joan of Arc quote: "One life is all we have, and we live it as we believe in living it…to sacrifice what you are and to live without belief, that is a fate more terrible than dying."

- <u>How can I get the class to interact?</u>—Come up with ways to get students up and teaching the class. Devise interesting exercises and historical role play they can do as a group.

<u>Here are my lily pad points in detail:</u>
This is a rough sketch and not a linear roadmap. It is a list of things we can discuss and do in any order I want. If the conversation takes us in a different direction, I know the targets I want to come back to.

- <u>Maternity story</u>: A personal story about believing in something when there is really no reason to:

  My husband is about to drop me off for a meeting. I am late. It is pouring down rain. The parking lot near Pac Bell Park is flooded. I stop to receive a telephone call before jumping out of the car and playing like Noah. It is our fertility doctor. It appears our new pregnancy, a pregnancy we had been working on for four years, is not a pregnancy after all. Our HCG tests did not come back favorable and it appeared we had a Molar pregnancy. There is no chance a Molar pregnancy will result in a baby. In fact, tissue will grow out of control and into my lungs unless I terminate the Molar. I was in absolute shock. I dropped the phone and lost it. How unfair to get pregnant only to not be pregnant. I called an OB/GYN I know to find out more details and to get a second opinion. Basically, we were told we'd have to do some sort of chemical termination. Soon. There was likely no baby in there at all, just tissue. No heartbeat—nothing.

I looked at my husband and said, "There is something in my body. I feel it. Some sort of spirit." Of course I am sobbing. My husband asks, "What do you want to do?" "There is something here— let's take it to Hawaii. Tomorrow." We called a travel agent and left the next day for Maui. We decided we'd take a week off, swim, bike and enjoy this spirit in my body until it was time for it to leave. Our doctor told us this was a little risky and that we should go to the emergency room when we miscarriage.

Interestingly, our trip coincided with the time when the whales were in Maui birthing their babies and teaching them how to be in the world. Each year whales migrate from Alaska to enjoy the warm water. As we snorkeled, it sounded like the whales were right next to us singing. We saw so many whales surface—so near us. It was absolutely beautiful.

We were holding our breath a little while in Maui as we knew the miscarriage was coming. On the last day our plane was scheduled to leave at 10pm, and I woke up that morning with blood and cramps. It was happening. We went to Kaiser. The nurse rushed around as soon as we told her we were having a miscarriage. They rushed me to an exam room—everyone was running around a little chaotic trying to figure out what was happening. We tried to explain about the Molar pregnancy, and, frankly, we couldn't remember what it was called. The doctor was barking orders to staff and rushing the sonogram pad across my stomach. My husband said, "Hey what is that flashing light?" "That is the heartbeat, shhhhh, let me ..." We didn't hear the rest of what she said—we started crying...stammering...wait, we were told due to our HCG levels we didn't have a baby. The doctor laughed, "Well, someone needs to tell that little baby in your stomach that because you have a baby   see..." My husband laughed, if this baby looks like a whale, you are in trouble! We laughed. We held tight for nine long months of a difficult pregnancy with bed rest and tons of emergency room visits. Our son was born on October 29, 2005. I do not know how I knew to take him on vacation that day—I do know I never lost faith that he would be born.

- Distribute cards: Ask the class questions and have them write their answers down on 3 x 5 cards. What do you believe in? What cause are you passionate about? Ask students to put these aside for later.

- Bridge to Joan: Faith. History is replete with humans who lived and died on faith. Give the statistical data on a slide, including the year she was "martyred, who she was, how old she was, what she did, the background of the time and why this was so unusual. Tell her story. (I won't summarize it here—I suggest you look it up if you don't know it.)

- Joan's vision—ask for three volunteers: Bring them up to the front of the room, figure out who will play Joan and who will be her parents. When it is decided, hand Joan a script.

- ◌ Joan of Arc reads from the script, telling her parents she is going to deliver France from England.
- ◌ The parents respond however the students want to—likely acting like she is crazy.
- ◌ Facilitate a conversation about the scene. Get students to discuss how people responded to Joan; why did they think she was nuts; was she really having visions; were visions common?; what did being a woman and young have to do with the story?

- Yes, Joan of Arc had a vision: It is the Middle Ages, and women are typically not leading soldiers in battle. God gave her a vision and compelled her to fight the invading Englishmen. She believed France and her King Charles were sacred. Briefly discuss Joan's approach to King Charles.

- How did Joan get King Charles to listen—Ask for two volunteers: Hand them both a script. One volunteer will read the part of Joan of Arc meeting King Charles. One will play the part of King Charles. Moderate the scene.
  - ◌ Joan of Arc reads from the script, telling King Charles she must have an army to deliver France from England.
  - ◌ King Charles responds however the student wants—perhaps going along with her entirely?; acting like she is crazy?; somewhere in between?
  - ◌ Facilitate a conversation about the scene. Get students to discuss how Joan convinced King Charles to give her an army.

- Tell the rest of the history (with pictures):
  - ◌ First battle of Orleans—Joan wounded; the army won and continued.
  - ◌ More battles. Victory. England driven north.
  - ◌ Charles crowned King in Rheims.
  - ◌ Joan wants to leave because she doesn't hear the heavens anymore.
  - ◌ Joan stays behind and is captured by the Duke of Burgundy.
  - ◌ The Duke ransoms Joan to the English.
  - ◌ Joan jailed for one year then accused of being a sorceress and burned at the stake; she is nineteen-years-old.
  - ◌ What do you think her last words were? Ask folks to guess. (her last word was "Jesus").

- Who would you rather be, Joan of Arc or the Duke of Burgundy?: Facilitate the conversation.

- What did Joan's gender have to do with this story?: Facilitate the conversation.

- Revisit the 3 x 5 cards from the beginning of the discussion: What were you passionate about? Would you be willing to die for that cause?

- <u>Contemporary parallels:</u> If time allows and it feels appropriate, facilitate conversation about terrorism and suicide bombers. Discuss how they are willing to die for their beliefs as Joan was. Talk about the difference.

- <u>Ending slide:</u> "One life is all we have and we live it as we believe in living it…to sacrifice what you are and to live without belief, that is a fate more terrible than dying." = Joan of Arc

In this example, I simply use lily pads as a means of offering topics and outlining methods for facilitating them. The audience will fill the room with rich conversation on the topic. With a little shepherding, this could lead to more engagement with history, a new way to look at the present world, and, for some, a nudge toward finding their place in it.

While most people have heard about Joan of Arc, many of us have a myth-laden, vague image of who she might have been. Using details from her life, the life of her contemporaries and descriptions of day-to-day life in the 15th century will bring the history even closer to a modern audience. Broad strokes comparing Joan and her beliefs to modern age topics relevant to us now (terrorism, evangelical beliefs, the search for the soul, nation-state military campaigns, woman in non-traditional roles, etc.) can be an effective means of bring Joan's story into contemporary times.

The key to lily pad structure is to create markers that allow for a high-impact learning situation. Students will walk out with an experience because an experience increases memory. Perhaps you noticed I used an example, then discussion, then explanation, then another example, and so on. What is great about this style of facilitation is the facilitator learns things too.

Let the room teach too.

CHAPTER 118:
SWIMMING IN THE SHALLOW END
OF POWER POINT

There's a PowerPoint guru whose entire business focuses on teaching people to master PowerPoint. I am not that guy. In my mind, I look better in a dress than he does, and he has a better sense of fashion. This is my way of letting you know my chapter on PowerPoint is a very shallow swim into the pool of visual presentations.

To make up for the fact that I am barely skinning the surface of this complex subject, I will give you a list of things to consider:

- PowerPoint does not exist as notes for the speaker.
- PowerPoint's main role is to engage visual learners—the people who can't listen to the speaker unless there's something else to look at.
- Use less slides than you want to. I have heard many people expose rules and formulas about slide to minutes of airtime ratio. I have no such rule or formula though I can tell you that PowerPoint should never distract from you, the speaker. Too many slides are distracting.
- NEVER EVER EVER EVER read a slide to the audience. This is really boring, especially since everyone knows how to read. Instead, give them a moment to read it, then add to it with your comments.
- Use quality graphics, not clip art. Clip art is more than a little tired. Use photos AND rather than search for a particular photo, just pick a few and work them in. It will improve how you say things. (I pulled a cool photo of an abacus and changed the way I talked about conflict.) Oh, please avoid the stock photos of business people. They look too professional and their professionalism will kill your presentation.
- Seriously, photos of business people do not create the same response as a photo of a hand catching a baton.
- Slides should look clean and not too busy.
- Print the OUTLINE pages of your PowerPoint presentation. It makes a GREAT lilly pad list for you to stay on track, and also gives you a chance to proof your work in hardcopy form.
- Test your equipment and always have a back-up plan. Trust me, this is a huge one. One of my talks is super reliant on PowerPoint as it contains a ton of visual exercises and group tests. Once, I set up and made sure the image showed up on the screen. Only when it came time to click on the next image, the screen stopped moving. Dead. I hit the B key and moved quickly to something else. Luckily an AV guy was in the room and fixed the problem while I moved forward in the talk.

There are many speakers telling folks not to use PowerPoint or KeyNote anymore. They are absolutely wrong. The visual learners NEED the visual. Just don't over-rely on it.

Power Point is not a crutch; it is an excellent tool when used wisely.

CHAPTER 119:
OVATION PREPAREDNESS CHECKLIST

If you know me you are laughing right now. Christina doesn't like to plan or research anything. I have learned over the years that my inability to properly plan has caused me to miss some great standing ovation opportunities.

To bring up my average, I have created a checklist that my team and I use before I speak. We do this before every speech, and it works. I show up prepared, and with my pre-planning out of the way, it gives me time to connect, relate, emote—basically do all the things that make the speaker and the audience relax.

- What is the primary goal of this audience—why are they present?

- What should I read or review beforehand in order to better relate to the attendees?

- What has not worked in the past for this audience or similar audiences?

- How many people are going to be in the room?

- How much time do I have to speak?

- How long is the Q&A period?

- What are my AV needs?
    - Laptop
    - PowerPoint projector
    - DVD Player

- Is a lapel microphone available? When can I do a sound check?

- How will the room be set up?
    - Whenever possible, I choose theatre style since tables make the room less congenial.

- If on a panel, will I be seated behind a table? What is the set up? Who else is on the panel? What do I need to prepare?

- Go over the agenda and determine the timing of the meal and other speakers.

- Ascertain if I can leave things on the tables. If not, what about on the back table?

- What is the name and cell number of my primary contact that day?

- Make sure I have an address and clear directions.

- If someone is picking me up from the airport, how will I know them? Their number?

- What percentage of the audience has heard me speak before?

Take care of the nagging little gnats of details before you arrive to talk.

CHAPTER 120:
WHEN THE SPEECH STARTS

A speech starts the moment we get in the car to come to the event. So, as you drive (or train or bus or walk), you must connect with the person you are when you're having a great time with your closest friends. Sometimes to get into this mindset, you'll need to run up and down stairs or do something equally engaging.

At a Rotary meeting a few years back, eight San Francisco mayoral candidates presented their campaign pitch to members to encourage our endorsement. Of course, all the candidates did a fine job of fluffing our auras and telling us how amazing we were. Rotarians wear little pins on our lapel, and one candidate even went so far as to say when he saw one of those pins he knew he was dealing with a person of honor and integrity. Cool.

The meeting was on the 11th floor. As usual, I had to leave a little bit early to make another meeting, so during the Q&A I ran down the stairs to the bathroom on the 10th floor. After scrubbing my hands, I went to catch the 10th floor elevator out of the building.

As the doors to the elevator opened, one of the candidates was talking to his aide. It seems he had to rush out early too. I started to say something and stopped myself when I realized they had edged me out with their body language. They must have seen my crayola-red head and decided I was an employee of the hotel instead of a Rotarian. (I wasn't wearing my Rotary pin.)

"This was a waste of time," the candidate hissed. "Rotarians are the most conservative people on the planet. They do not care about real social issues. This is a glorified tip club with the pretense of community service. No one in that room gets their nails dirty."

I gasped. As the elevator hit the ground floor, I addressed the Candidate. I'd like to say that I said something witty. Alas, I did not. I stammered out something like, "I sure wish you had told us that during your speech. I have been in Rotary five years and disagree with your assessment of us."

The Candidate stammered some reply about misunderstanding what he said. He actually tried to pretend he was mimicking another person. It was really uncomfortable, and I walked away.

The moral of the story? The speech also continues after you leave the podium. It starts when you wake up in the morning and before you leave your house. Please remember to be you and watch your judgment of the room you are talking to.

People notice when you're saying to yourself, "Its ShowTime!!" Just be real.

CHAPTER 121:
THE LIVING EULOGY
(INTRODUCTIONS ARE DEAD)

An introduction is a living eulogy, and when handled well, it sets a positive tone for the event. Take the time to craft a thoughtful and moving introduction that causes the speaker to <u>feel</u> honored and important.

Pick out two or three impressive things from the speakers bio and talk about what is amazing about this human. Use this time to help the speaker connect with the audience vicariously through your words.

When being introduced, make sure you speak to your introducer prior to showtime. I generally prepare the person introducing me by giving them three things about me that I want the audience to know about. For example:

- Completely unemployable—she has been an entrepreneur most of her life.
- Proud mom of Sebastian James Law.
- Author of the book, *Your Professionalism is Killing You.*

If you are introducing someone you do not know, never read his or her bio verbatim. It isn't compelling, and it lacks emotional texture. Instead, spend a few moments before the talk asking the speaker interesting, thought-provoking questions. Here are some questions you can ask:

- What was your favorite breakfast cereal as a child?
- What are you most proud of?
- Tell me about one of the best days in your career.
- What is your favorite thing to do outside of work?
- Who was your role model growing up?
- Tell me an embarrassing moment.
- What is your astrological sign?
- What is something people don't know about you?
- What is cool about you that isn't on your bio?
- What are you really good at? (A secret skill.)
- Favorite band when you were in high school.
- Favorite knock knock joke.
- Who are you most interested in meeting (alive or dead)?

Do introductions like the Oscars. For example, I once introduced three men who were new to our group of CEOs. Beforehand, I got them to tell me three things about themselves, including their most embarrassing moment (this fit with our group's goal to create intimacy with each other so we can talk honestly about our lives and business). As I revealed the things the men told me about themselves, I had the audience guess which individual I was talking about. It was fun.

An introduction is truly a living eulogy. The better you know someone the more intimate and heartfelt you should be when introducing. The goal of an introduction of someone you know it to give them a lump in the throat—to build their esteem and make the audience feel your love for them.

Set a positive tone for the speaker with an interesting and intimate introduction.

CHAPTER 122:
DO SOMETHING STUPID
IN FRONT OF THE ROOM

I hadn't planned to write this chapter. While writing the previous chapters on speaking furniture and microphone malfunctions, I realized the suggestions I have are based upon years of embarrassing myself in front of others.

Mishaps occur. For everybody! What doesn't work is when speakers pretend the mistake didn't happen or get really flustered by it. No matter what happens in a room, call attention to it and go with it. Every time. Remember, everybody notices the elephant, and pretending it isn't there will not make it go away.

My motto for potentially embarrassing situations is: "Don't apologize. Integrate." Following are a series of examples from my own files of experience.

Unplanned "Co-Speakers":
- The media will probably note the fact that you ignored the protestors. Don't ignore them—engage and disarm them. Never lose your cool. Never insult or berate hecklers. Own the room, it is yours, after all. During the Democratic Convention Nancy Pelosi was heckled by Code Pink. She ignored and spoke over them. Bad idea. Acknowledge and build them into the talk.

- Could this style of integration go wrong? Yes. It's never good to allow members of the audience to control the dialogue. Keep your focus no matter what goes on. In this new political and economic landscape, the human relationship is the true currency. Audiences and voters LIKE politicians who are not canned and do not ignore embarrassing and other all-too-human exchanges. Remember, the audience is there to see you, not the guy in the chicken suit.

Dropping Something:
- Do not get flustered and apologize when you lose your place, drop something or hiccup. Don't go into that embarrassed middle school mode of "I just got caught lying or I peed my britches." Audiences never like that sort of evasion. Own the gaffe and move on.

- If you drop the microphone (as I have done several times), stop talking. Stand and pause for a moment. Quick movements to pick up the microphone make you appear flustered. Don't be flustered.

- Once when I dropped the microphone, I did a Rocky Balboa victory pose, lifting my arms up over my head and holding them there for a few moments. Then I picked up the microphone and said, "I was worried I would forget to do that so I put it in my notes."

- Another time I asked the audience, "Who heard the sound the microphone made when it hit the ground? I wish I had a similar audible cue to alert me that someone isn't listening. Some of you were thinking about lunch. I had to do something to get your attention."

- You can also stop and look around, then purposefully pick up the microphone as if it were misbehaving. "Well. That didn't go as planned. I was supposed to punt it [make a gesture of kicking toward the audience] after that last down! I'll try it again later. First row—be ready."

- Or, of course, you can simply stop talking and pick it up, then continue your talk.

Hurling Something:

- This has also happened to me. I had a glass of water sitting on top of the lectern, and when I gesticulated, I caused the glass to loft into the front row. Water went all over two people. I paid their dry cleaning bills. I was glad it was not wine.

- What to do? Stop talking. Be truly sorry. Ask the wait staff to bring the unwitting victim a towel (or a bandaid).

- In my water gaffe, I first apologized, insisted on paying for the ladies' dry cleaning and made sure they were taken care of with towels and a warm beverage. I next asked them if it was okay if I continued. They nodded yes. I then asked for another glass of water, and when it arrived, I splashed it in my own face. The audience roared, to which I responded, "Audience, this was not planned. This is not a part of my show. It is life. Life happens in business. Things we don't foresee. Things we wish wouldn't have happened. There is always a choice. We must embrace our mistakes and use them to move the dialogue forward."

- In a similar situation, you can never let an incident destroy the rest of your time with the audience. You must rally your energy and continue.

- In the future, I might let one of the lovely women whose outfit I destroyed pour water on my head. No one would forget that!

- I have used this example in my lessons on distraction, since it was such a powerful experience. In fact, at the time, a few people really thought I had intentionally poured water on the two women.

Shaking Hands or Feet:

- Sometimes my knees shake. I don't know why. It scares me. My father was diagnosed with Parkinson's at thirty-three. Trembling appendages often send a shiver up my spine—maybe I too will get the disease.

- What do I do? I move! If you are in a similar situation, mindfully walk around. Use your body. Trembling limbs are caused by muscles that are tensed up. Un-tense them. Jump up and down—do jumping jacks even.

- Here's a technique I have found very effective. When my leg shaking becomes uncontrollable, I stop talking and ask the audience, "Did you see that? There is something going on up here. Does anyone see it? If you see what is happening to me right now, stand up." Most people in the audience stand up. I ask the audience, "What is it?" then choose people one at a time to answer me. One guy says I lost my place. Another guy thinks my voice cracked. A woman guesses my microphone went out. The wise guy in the back says my slip was showing, and gets a large laugh from the audience because I had told the slip story as an opener. And finally, a woman says, "Your legs were shaking." Bingo!

- I use this as a way to illustrate to the audience that what's going on inside does not always match our outside image. I had not noticed that my voice had cracked. I had not lost my place. I was merely encouraging my uncooperative body to dictate my words. There was no uncomfortable cover up or attempt to redirect attention. The audience and I then talked about nerves and shaking. I asked the question, "If I teach public speaking, why am I nervous?" That was something everyone could relate to, and it transformed an embarrassing shake into one of the best talks on public speaking I have ever given—all because I went with what was happening.

Sirens:
- I like to use this one when I encounter a siren: "What starts with an F and ends in a UCK? Fire truck. Oh my gosh, what were you thinking? Hmmm."

- If there is a loud noise or a fire truck going by, stop talking and let it go by. Yelling over loud sounds is never a good idea.

Fire Alarms:
- In the middle of a public speaking class I was giving, the fire alarm sounded, forcing the entire group to walk down nine flights of stairs. I asked everyone to wait outside with me until we found out whether we could go back inside and continue the class. Eventually it was clear to go in, and just as we were settling in, the smoke alarm went off for the second time. We walked downstairs and finished the class in the courtyard. It was exhilarating to convince twenty-five people to do their speeches in a courtyard.

Clothing:
- Be prepared for clothing mishaps. Carry safety pins, a sewing kit, a suit jacket. Once I accidentally ripped my pants in front of an audience. So I took off my outer sweater and tied it around my waist. Done.

Embarrassing moments can be a gift when you jump on board.

 **EXAMPLE:**

NIKE HAD IT WRONG: JUST GO WITH IT!

It is the U.C. Davis Law School graduation. I am sitting in the stands watching my friend Patty accept her diploma. One of the valedictorians is standing at the lectern with a stack of 3x5 cards. She seems poised and prepared to give a well-worded talk.

The valedictorian opens with a standard round of thank yous to the audience—the dean, the alumni, the students. Then something odd happens. I can't really see, though it appears she has lost her 3x5 cards. There's a flurry on the dais, and the crowd starts murmuring. It isn't going well, and I want to run up and pick her slip off the floor (even though she's wearing pants).

Then she waves her hand and takes back the crowd. She says, "As I leave this institution with the power that comes with being an attorney I ask myself and every graduate in this room to remember one thing…" She pauses, and then she sings a heartfelt Tracy Chapman song (do an online search for "All That You Have Is Your Soul" for the song lyric; she sang the third stanza).

When she finishes, the entire crowd jumps to their feet and erupts in applause. Graduates are crying, parents beaming, even the young folks in the audience are paying attention.

As I reflect back on this episode, I am almost certain the woman did not plan on singing that song. She played what she had left—what the energy in the room was leading her to do. No words on 3x5 cards could have left a stronger impression on that room of lawyers.

I still tear up when I read those words. When I am facing a question of integrity—I sing that song. A friend of mine offered to pay me to teach someone else's material—without compensating them. I was struggling and really needed the cash. I sang that song in my head for about 15-seconds and decided to turn down the job. I thought of that lawyer so many years ago and wonder what she is doing now. Her song stayed with me—her words would have left my head days after the presentation.

Go with what happens in a room. Do not shy away from disasters that can become standing ovations.

CHAPTER 123:
SAY IT, DON'T READ IT

Think of the last time you prepared a speech. If you are like most people, you sat at your desk and typed out all the things you wanted to say to the audience. You thought of lovely words and phrases. You used the trusty thesaurus to find new ways to express yourself. Right there in the comfort of your office or home, you found the exact words needed to describe your thoughts.

Forget that. Remember? Words matter the least. In a live presentation, reading a script is about as effective as telemarketing. If you speak loud enough, you might reach two percent of the audience.

Another review: The more famous a speaker is, the more they can get away with poor speaking skills. Oprah Winfrey could walk out on stage and read the telephone book and still get a standing ovation.

Most of us are not famous nor do we have a bio that impresses people to accept whatever we deliver. So the way we communicate is key to getting them to pay attention to us. Reading a script is not going to make the audience listen, and more importantly, is not going to make them remember what we talked about. We must become our words.

Connect with what you are saying and the audience will too.

CHAPTER 124:
WRITTEN SPEECHES ARE NOT ALWAYS THE KISS OF DEATH

Despite all I've said so far, there is a place in the world for a written speech. Specific technical information, poetic points, quotes can all be read if done with connection and purpose.

Public speaking is <u>not</u> organic chemistry. This means every rule can be bent, broken or disregarded by a great speaker as long as they are confident of their connection with the audience. Public speaking is more like free form jazz or surfing in that regard. Once on a riff or wave, ride it.

> *"It is not the critic who counts; not the man who points out how the strong man stumbles, or where the doer of deeds could have done them better. The credit belongs to the man who is actually in the arena, whose face is marred by dust and sweat and blood, who strives valiantly; who errs and comes short again and again; because there is not effort without error and shortcomings; but who does actually strive to do the deed; who knows the great enthusiasm, the great devotion, who spends himself in a worthy cause, who at the best knows in the end the triumph of high achievement and who at the worst, if he fails, at least he fails while daring greatly. So that his place shall never be with those cold and timid souls who know neither victory nor defeat."*

The speech above is attributed to Theodore Roosevelt. In 1972, my father Robert Harbridge was in New York at a roof top party. As he often did, he recited these words from memory. When he finished, the crowd cheered him for his eloquence and heartfelt rendition of the famous words.

A little later the man who owned the flat asked my father to join him in the study. They went downstairs, and the man reached behind an oil painting and opened a safe. Then, he carefully removed a weathered paper tablet with scribblings and words in every margin and handed it to my father. After a few moments, my father realized what he was looking at. When he looked up, the man said, "My dad was a speechwriter for Roosevelt, and he wrote the speech you just recited on the dining room table in the next room."

My dad nearly fell over. This man's words, his sweat on the paper, as spoken by the grand and inspiring Theodore Roosevelt moved a nation; the speechwriter was unknown. His words live on, though. (I regret that I never asked my dad the man's name? I'd love to write it here: To give him credit for such powerful writing.)

I use this example to illustrate my point. Speeches can be read if they are read well. Mr. Speech Writer may not have had the power and passion to hold the audience's attention while reading that quote; Teddy Roosevelt did.

Martin Luther King's famous "I have a Dream" speech was written out. A truly great speaker, King also extemporized, though the backbone of this famous, life changing speech was written just as a poet would shape a signature ode.

Speakers who aren't as agile as King or Roosevelt, often rely too heavily on what they wrote the other day. Reaching for the inspiration of the past, they stifle their natural ability to improvise and innovate based on what is happening in the room around them. When we rely on a written speech we forego the beauty that can come from an open agenda.

Furthermore, something created alone at our desk may not be relevant to the audience once we've engaged them. A pre-fab speech tells the audience they're not really involved in the mutual creation of the experience. When reading a speech, a speaker often needs to look down and away from the audience. The audience— denied the personal interaction—begins to yawn.

If your written speech is written so poetically, perfectly, that you want to present it verbatim, then practice HOW you deliver it. This means you are passionate, connected, feeling your words. Commit key parts to memory so you can look at the audience when you deliver them. Read with flourish. Read it from the deep recesses of your soul and heart. Feel it. Emote.

If you are saying to yourself, hey Christina, I write out my speeches, and then I don't read them. I paraphrase from memory. I say, be careful, if you are attached to the first writing. Make sure you allow enough room to innovate. If you don't, and you veer off in another direction, you will act as if you made a mistake. The audience will see your little facial tick when you go off script.

Uh oh. I just said the word script. Scripts are for actors. We aren't actors. Instead of writing out the speech, use lily pads. Don't memorize words, set up non-linear reference points.

If you are a natural speaker, practice reading your written speech with flourish. If not, shed the writing and share the moment with the audience.

CHAPTER 125:
FIND A SPEECHWRITER
WHO USES YOUR LANGUAGE

This chapter is primarily for political people. I work with legislators who have insane schedules and hugely diverse constituencies. They demand an incredible bandwidth of information to do their job effectively, and good speechwriters are a critical component to their legislative team.

Because most legislators rarely have time to prepare talks, they must rely on speechwriters to synthesize key information, policy, and constituency concern into clear coherent talks. Speechwriters are the backbone of the legislator's public face, thus the speechwriters style must match the natural voice of the legislator.

There are two basic types of speechwriting: Policy and Poetry.

<u>Policy</u>: Policy writers can be brilliant. A great policy writer has an incredible knack for gathering volumes of information, distilling the important parts and conveying them in concise prose. This fact-driven writer is critical for encouraging the passage of bills.

The challenge for this type of speechwriter is to write this heady material in a way that suits the legislator's speaking style. Most people have seen legislators struggling as they read a speech written in someone else's style; this confuses the electorate and weakens the legislators' position. Matching the tone of the legislator can be an enormous challenge for speechwriters—difficult, though not impossible.

Here are a few suggestions to make the speechwriter "translation" process simpler:

- Continue to write as you do, synthesizing the important information into a speech, though making sure you choose vocabulary and sentence structure that are easy to read and understand. Make sure your words give the legislator (and the audience!) a clear and concise picture of the needed legislation.

- Provide a second page of lily pads. Include the points that <u>must</u> be discussed. This way, the legislator can, if so moved, speak spontaneously in his or her singular style and still provide the relevant data.

- In your speech, always start with <u>why</u> the legislation is important. If you can use an example and/or tie into a specific constituent need this will make the speech more powerful. Stories are the transactional relationship medium for our culture. Give the legislator a true story that humanizes and personalizes the bill. For example a speech for a bill to ban the use of phthalates in pacifiers can be started like this:

A year ago, Jane Smith and her young baby visited my legislative office in Sacramento. Her child had been diagnosed with autism and she wanted my help in finding answers. Her daughter, Candace, was a bright energetic fifteen-month-old and one day, things changed…

○ NEVER make these stories up. Aside from being tacky and dishonest, such a story, in today's political blog universe will almost certainly be challenged. When using personal examples always ask constituents if you can use their names and story as an example for the cause. If you do not have permission to cite a particular story, no matter how choice, find another one: there are a million stories in the world!

○ Keep a written log of every voter who contacts your office. Note their demographics, personal contact data and why they contacted your office. This provides an incredible reference library when stories are required in order to illustrate the need for specific legislation.

● Sometimes, instead of using a story, the speechwriter can just explain in plain language why an issue is important:

San Francisco residents depend on Muni to get to work. We have laws in place to make sure our transit system runs efficiently. One piece of legislation provided the diamond lane. This diamond lane ensures that in times of high traffic, Muni can stay on schedule and get our taxpayers to work. Unfortunately, cars are abusing this system, and non-carpooling drivers are abusing this lane. Installing a camera in the diamond lane deters…

● Analogies are an excellent speechwriting tool. They provide verbal hooks; they give folks an image to hold on to, thus helping them remember the proposed legislation. If an analogy comes to mind, it is wise to fact check and road test it before giving it to the legislator. For example:

While lead paint was finally banned in 1977, other dangerous industrial chemicals still threaten our children, and these are like modern day lead paints. For example, using phthalates in pacifiers is just like dipping that pacifier in lead paint. As a legislative body we must step in and do something about this. We must protect our children—today!

○ Analogies can be tricky, as sometimes they don't translate to the audience. We all have our perspective, and we want to be careful not to offend by an imprudent analogy. (Think of Senator Biden's silly-clean-guy comment.) Listen first for how comments can be misconstrued, and, if there is question, come up with a different analogy.

● Whenever possible, take the <u>why</u> to a higher level—such as why the legislation is important to the entire State of California and each person in the room. By doing this you create a powerful position that will move legislation forward.

<u>Poetry Writers:</u> These writers can be very good at writing commanding emotional speeches that connect with the audience; people tend to listen intently to genuinely felt emotion. This type of writer is a strong asset for getting a candidate elected and pushing legislation through by connecting the legislators with their hearts, which in turn, will connect them with their constituents. A heartfelt speech, properly presented, can engage a typically cynical media and consequently inspire the electorate.

Here are some tips for poetic speechwriters:

- To make a lasting impact, emotional writing only works when it includes very clear statistics and facts. Remember, 11 percent of us need proof. The media does too. Make sure the speech is peppered with facts and figures.

- Why is more important than how and what. Most listeners will get behind a person and their legislation, if the <u>why</u> is clearly and passionately stated.

- Why does not work on its own. A clearly stated <u>what we need to do</u> and <u>how we need to do it</u> must follow. Be careful not to simply rely on emotion to present an argument.

- Avoid too much emotional texture. Policymakers will roll their eyes if every speech is imbued with human drama.

- Vary the type of emotion used in the speeches. Some examples:
  - Humor
  - Fear
  - Indignation
  - Inspiration
  - Sorrow
  - Joy

Make sure the speech is written for the speaker, so the speaker can deliver it with emotion and passion.

CHAPTER 126:
OUT DAMN HEAD!

When preparing a speech, most of us focus 75 percent of our time on the words we are going to say—when in reality, our words matter least. To gain real benefit from our efforts, our true practice and consideration must be in the way we say things. (Yes, I have said this before.)

Generally, once we get the words down, we spend the rest of the time practicing in our head. Be careful—as I have also said, the head is a dangerous place and we should be very careful when hanging out in there too long (especially before speaking publicly.)

Public talks should not be practiced in the mind. The best way to practice a speech is to verbalize it out loud, from beginning to end without stopping! By practicing out loud you can spend time creating interesting ways to present the material. Allow yourself to be innovative with your message. Vary your voice. Try things on. Have fun. I suggest you keep a pen handy when you practice and jot down presentation notes to help you remember.

__One Caveat:__ Do not practice too much, because this causes you to fixate on a "right way" to give the talk. There are countless right ways to deliver a single talk. You might have ten to choose from, and the version you choose could change three times between breakfast and the moment you step on to the podium. A "right way" puts you in acting mode, which weakens your ability to connect with and relate to the audience.

__Caveat Two:__ Do not practice within two hours of the speaking event; instead engage in physical exercise or casual conversation. This keeps you from running a destructive tape loop of the talk. If there is a break before your talk, socialize with the individual audience members. This will help relax you and establish an early connection between you and your audience.

Practice your talks <u>out loud</u>—only a few times.

CHAPTER 127:
WHY DO THEY CARE?

Communicating to be heard is much easier if the audience can be convinced they care about your subject. This is _not_ pandering. Have you ever been to a luncheon with a politician and heard her speak to the group as if she belonged to it? Good speakers focus their talk on the audience and perhaps even change history momentarily, painting themselves into the group they are addressing.

Conversely, I have watched the Mayor of a city tell the Hotel Council one thing at an afternoon luncheon, only to tell the Tenant's Union the opposite later that evening. This kind of pandering double speak is never okay, and it is what gives politicians a bad rap.

Audiences don't necessarily have to agree with you to care about what you're saying. Pragmatic discussions about diverse ideas and points of departure can be very effective in bridging the gap between ideas and platforms.

If I am training a room of lobbyists for a Latino organization, I will certainly figure out how to communicate to be heard. If I am training a room of lobbyists for an executive healthcare organization, I will certainly figure out how to communicate to be heard. I _do not_ change what I believe to match either room. I talk about what is relevant to them and adapt my accompanying stories to best engage the ears of those present:

- *The Latino organization must learn how to use pragmatic reasoning. This will help them convey why their bill for immigrants is good for the entire community, not just for people from Mexico. They must keep their culture; and still communicate so everyone will listen.*

- *The Executive healthcare organization must teach their home teams to integrate diagnosis and caring—in everything the medical organization does. The key to making this happen is learning to communicate _internally_ the same way they do _externally_.*

These are not two separate messages. They are nuances focused on the needs of two diverse groups.

When you look closely, both of these messages are about _us_ and _them_. Lobbyists lose traction when they focus too much on turning us into them. Healthcare organizations lose traction when they focus too much on trying to make things great for their patients (them) when it isn't good for staff (us).

Telling an audience why they care should not be done as an expository essay. Instead, the speaker must integrate the audience cares and concerns into their topic or perspective.

If you cannot think of why the audience should care about the topic: Do not give the speech.

CHAPTER 128:
DIDN'T SHE ALREADY
SAY THAT?

Hopefully by now, you've noticed I repeat myself in this book. It is a tactic to help you remember. I explain things in different ways hoping to get your attention and give you a fuller idea of what I'm talking about. This is how to cement learning.

Speakers often want to cram everything they know about their subject into a ten-minute talk. You can't. Audiences can only handle so much material. Have self-discipline in choosing the right amount. You will not get to tell them everything you might like to, so pick the most important stuff and make it memorable.

My editor made me lop off 50 percent of this book and still there is too much information in here. Luckily, this book isn't a single speech. It is hundreds of them!

Decide on a maximum of three key points you want the audience to remember. Then craft creative ways to express them. Use exercises, interaction, stories, metaphors, music, objects and hands-on-practice to help the audience remember those three key points. I learned to do this integrated technique in college. It is truly one thing folks will remember—if you are lucky.

Imagine you are blowing bubbles from the lectern. The bubbles are the messages you want people to remember. The bubbles bounce off the heads of everyone in the room. Every once in a while a bubble will stick on someone's head for a moment before the bubble pops. Creative speaking causes the bubble to be absorbed into the audience's head. Once absorbed it increases the possibility the bubble will come out of their mouth later.

When we start editorializing it reduces listening. The more we tell people what they are supposed to think, the less they will think what we want them to think. People like to arrive at things on their own. Do not cram them. Instead, simplify your message into three palpable points and guide the audience toward them. Let your audiences do the editorializing.

In keeping with the message of this chapter, I will end here.

Simplify your talks.

CHAPTER 129:
YOU'RE NOT
DR. MARTIN LUTHER KING JR

The Moscone Center in San Francisco features a fountain sculpture that incorporates the inspirational words of Dr. Martin Luther King, Jr. The fountain is designed to encourage viewers to follow the water around a surrounding walkway, part of which is set into the hill, so it feels cave-like. Dr. King's words guide the journey.

As I walked the fountain path, I was profoundly struck by the fact that he wasn't even forty-years-old when he spoke such profound words. Wow. So young and so important—such shoes for a public speaker to fill.

Guess what? You don't have to fit into his shoes. It's okay if you do not communicate as inspirationally as he did. In fact, unless it comes naturally, you should skip trying to become a proselytizer.

Too often I see folks stretching way outside their comfort zones. They want to be bigger, more exciting—like Dr. King. This makes them different than who they really are. And it doesn't work. There was one him. There is also only one You.

Yes, you must raise your energy level when you speak. Yes, you must be excited about your topic. Just do not overdo it. There is a fine line between acting and communicating to improve the way people listen. If you are being inauthentically excited, audiences will know you are acting and get the ick.

It is impossible to be your best when you pretend. Pretending means a part of your body and mind are pre-occupied on being something you aren't. Thus your output and strength are reduced. Be yourself when you speak, and the audience will feel you.

I do not care what the audience thinks about me if I am being my true self. I am not for everyone. Some of you aren't even reading this sentence because you put down my book and decided it sucked. This book isn't for everyone. You are not for everyone. You are you.

Everyone didn't like Dr. Martin Luther King, Jr. either—he wasn't for everyone. He was really great at being him. Our world misses him. No one has been able to fill his space.

Don't try to speak like him or anyone else. Be you.

Raise your energy level to the excitement you feel on your best day—not on someone else's day.

CHAPTER 130:
SUBDUE THE EDITOR

I have seen the real you. The one who is open, loving and carefree.

I often see you when I go to the bar. After knockin' back a cocktail or two, you love talking to people. You are laughing and just brilliant.

This is why corporate America uses liver symposiums to facilitate team building. People 'bond' and connect in ways they just "can't" do at the office. I personally dislike liver symposiums, mostly because they tend to create false confidence and weird consequences (see page 293). Don't get me wrong, I participate in them too. They're fun, and it's nice to unwind with folks.

Alcohol subdues the internal editor, so it's a liquid communication elixir. Have you met your internal editor? Chances are he's sporting a green visor, and he's working his mojo on you right now. He's kind of pissy, and he makes it his job to carefully critique every little thing you did wrong in your last speech and throw it back at you right before you speak again.

Let me tell you—your internal editor is no good and must die.

I know what you are thinking. I'm thinking it too. It's hard to kill the editor. The editor keeps us from completely blowing it. The world is full of examples of people who ruined their career over stupid, unedited words.

Since I referenced it earlier, let's look at the stalled presidential campaign of Senator Joe Biden. Senator Biden, referring to his African American opponent in the 2008 presidential race, says, "I mean, you got the first mainstream, African-American who is articulate and bright and clean and a nice-looking guy. I mean, that's a storybook, man."

If you do not know the story it must be 2071, and you are reading this book long after I have passed on. Is Google still around?

That comment was made especially abhorrent because Biden ran against Jesse Jackson in an earlier presidential nomination race—so clearly Barack Obama was not the first mainstream, African-American to be an "articulate and bright and clean and a nice-looking guy."

Clearly, Biden stepped in it, and that comment destroyed Biden's presidential run. I am willing to bet the Senator had said similarly silly things to his team. Why didn't anyone tell him how potentially offensive and deal breaking they were? Those closest to him neglected to point out the verbal spinach in his teeth.

Remember, I use the Senator Biden example to point out why people are afraid of saying the wrong thing. Some of us demand scripts to avoid situations like his. Yes, I have said really dumb things in the past. Partly because I live in a culture that sometimes puts wrong ideas in my head. Partly because I was being lazy and not bothering to fact check my thoughts. I am not perfect, you are not perfect, we are not perfect. Everyone is prejudiced about something or someone. We just are.

Walking through these prejudices and emerging with a better understanding on the other side (even with egg on our face) is much more impressive than pretending we aren't prejudiced at all (or holding a script like a pacifier). I took a prejudice test on line and was alarmed to find I was an ageist: I had negative connotations of people over the age of sixty.

This discovery bothered me, and after serious soul searching, I did some inner work around it. I discovered almost everyone over the age of fifty in my family had some sort of ailment. Because of this, I attached age to illness. Only through acknowledging my prejudice could I let go of it. As part of my anti-ageist therapy I began befriending people outside my generation and hired people over fifty. Perception can change.

Saying one wrong or improper thing will not ruin your entire life. If it does, then you chose for it to. When we blunder, we must be transparent. Transparency— admitting you were off base—will quell the negative wave. Denial brings it on.

I firmly believe if Biden hadn't tried to cover up his mistake with a general apology, people would have cut him some slack. He could have said what everyone was thinking something like:

> *"That comment made it sound like I was ignoring the amazing work of candidate Jesse Jackson in 1988. I certainly didn't mean to slight him or Shirley Chisholm, Carol Moseley Braun, or Al Sharpton…"*

I actually can't write what he should have said as I do not know what he really meant. Though I do know that he faltered in a moment of politics. Had he immediately acknowledged Jesse Jackson and explained his comment, audiences would have more respect for him. Like us, he's not perfect. Had he been transparent he would have had a better chance at the candidacy.

Ask your closest friends to tell you if there's verbal spinach in your teeth before it gets stuck there forever. Don't let them over-spinach you though—it will mess with your confidence. Be CAREFUL who your critics are—they could also be wrong.

 **EXAMPLE:**

LIVER SYMPOSIUMS

Hopefully, this goes without saying, though I will say it anyway. Never, ever engage your liver before speaking.

A little liquid courage might seem like a good idea at the time. Alcohol dulls the senses and impedes our ability to gauge how effectively we are communicating. Booze gives us a false sense of bravado—duh!

A bad case of nerves can be your friend, and most public speaking trainings miss this important fact, instead focusing on eliminating nerves. This is a problem. Nerves are not bad. When harnessed properly, nervous energy can offer brilliant sparks of wit and unique moments of connection with your audience.

True, research shows that people are more relaxed after having alcohol. Research also shows we are more relaxed after having sex, though this doesn't mean we should shag the introducer behind the curtain right before we go up to speak. The same can be said of using beta blockers or any chemical other means to calm you down. Once a crutch is used, you will always wonder if it is you or the crutch speaking. To be a truly great communicator, you must trust yourself and go for it—without the crutch.

Here are some other things you can do to relax:

- Flirt with the introducer—Sex can rumple your clothes and put off the audience, so flirting is much better. Okay, I'm kidding! Somewhat. Though I do believe it is very effective to talk with others before your talk. It gets you out of your head, and helps you stop obsessing about what you are going to say. You have your notes and you have practiced the talk three times out loud. Trust yourself and relax a little right before going on. Your talk will be better because of it.

- Exercise—Right before teaching a class I often stand in the back of the room and do jumping jacks. I am serious. I usually explain my behavior to my students and suggest that they try it to. Those who join me are amazed at how well jumping jacks turn cortisol into endorphins. Since jumping jacks aren't always prudent in front of a large audience of strangers, I stand in the back of the room whenever possible. This way I must walk up the aisle, which means I am moving before I have to turn around and face the audience. If the speech is on a riser or elevated podium, I also do a little jog up the stairs. Of course there are other things you can do if you are limited in your ambulatory ability. You can stretch, move your hands, your neck, your mouth. Whatever part of you allows movement—move it. A mini-workout will help align your energy and make your muscles and your nerves work for you, not against you.

- **Get out of your head**—I am repeating myself. It's important. Get out of your head. Movement, conversation, and mediation (if it means no thinking!) are all great tools. Can you think of any others?

- **Stop editing**—Avoid rewriting a speech moments before giving it. I can't emphasize this point strong enough. Exerting tight control over the minutia of your delivery can actually sabotage a clear presentation of the larger picture. Don't get caught up in the minor details. The bigger picture is already in view—take a breath and keep it there.

Here is a story to illustrate what can happen when you don't heed the suggestions above.

In the late spring, I traveled to London to deliver a speech to a group of British CEO's. It was my first long trip away from my eighteen-month-old son, and since I was nursing at the time, I figured it would be the beginning of the end of my son's nursing. I was a wreck. I worried that I was a horrible mother choosing business over my son. I cried the entire plane ride. In this precarious emotional state (which weakened my immune system) whamo—I caught the cold from hell while on the plane.

Upon arrival, I had two hours before my first presentation. It went okay. Not great—passable (a B minus I would say). I was exhausted. The next morning I woke up very sick, in a different time zone, with a looming case of jet-lag.

Taking my own advice, I decided to exercise to get my nerves aligned with my visit's purpose. Many people had warned me that my particular style of communication may not do as well in London. They speak ENGLISH there. And they're witty! I was worried. So, I spent the entire day walking around London.

Mind you, I was sick as a dog. Through it all, I kept telling myself positive things, convincing myself that I would be able to push through and deliver a great speech that evening. All well and good, until my mind concocted a plan to take cold medicine just before I left the hotel for the speaking engagement. I convinced myself that it would give me the energy boost I needed to do a great job. Mistake number one.

As I got dressed for the fancy dress event ("fancy dress" in England means costume), I wondered if the room would understand my fancy dress: I was wearing a Martha Washington style dress and devil horns—the evil American. I certainly felt like the evil sick person, somewhat relevant. As I put on my makeup, I started feeling sicker and sicker and took my cold medicine early. Then, just before the cab arrived to pick me up, I popped another cold tablet. Mistake numbers two and three.

When I arrived at the event, I was impressed to see that the room was set up in such a decadent, formal and beautiful way. Stunning. Clearly, I couldn't put my normal fun stuff on the table—it just didn't go with the room—so I decided to skip it. Mistake number four.

I accidentally neglected one of my own rules and wore a dress that didn't allow for a lavaliere mic, which meant I would have to carry around a microphone. Mistake number five. I checked the mic to make sure it was working properly, and left the room to join the pre-party in the lobby.

I drank bubble water the entire time except for a half glass of wine. My hands would not stop shaking (from the cold medicine), and I thought it might help. Mistake number six. As the clock ticked on, it became clear we were behind schedule.

At 9:15pm, I started my speech. Unfortunately, this was before a very late dinner, which meant I was standing between seventy people and their gnawing stomachs. I cut my forty-five minute interactive talk to twenty-five minutes; and I was AWFUL!

I forgot all my own teaching and broke many of my own rules. Besides the mistakes I pointed out above, I also watered down my message and tried to fit in. A friend of mine had warned me that the British hate Americans because we take credit for everything. He warned me not to have a lot of bravado. I listened and watered down the details of my story and my part in them. Mistake number seven.

Later some kind folks told me that they really loved it. This helped, as it showed me, despite how awful I felt and how dismal it all seemed at the time, some of my technique and pizzazz got through. This was the WORST talk of my life—I know that I failed in a big way.

I drank four glasses of wine on the flight home—spilled the last one all over me and wept. I beat myself up for days and even considered quitting the speaking business over this.

It wasn't until days later I realized the moral of the story. I am a good mom. I do not like to leave my son and without question I turned down many opportunities after that gig. The next time I spoke I told the story to the group. It made me human—I created a new lesson out of it to teach people. How to recover.

There are so many lessons in this story:
- Rest before a big talk if you are not feeling well.
- Never take cold medicine before a talk if you are a light weight.
- Never stand between hungry people and dinner.
- Wine is always a no-no, especially if you are medicated and exhausted to start with.
- Kill the critic who reminds you of your failures. Failures are intellectual property in the making. Don't worry.
- Most important—know what kind of speaker you are. I'm not an evening event speaker; I'm a teacher.

Using a chemical to change your body will dull your speech and weaken your message. Decide what kind of speaker you are. If you are interactive like I am, drinking alcohol before a speech is especially debilitating.

CHAPTER 131:
THE LOUDEST CRITIC IS USUALLY YOU

How many times have you sat down after a talk and gone over all the things you forgot to say, wished you didn't say, wished you said differently? And then beat yourself up for it. Well, stop it. It doesn't help!

Instead, notice three things you liked about your presentation after every public speaking engagement. Write them down. This will help you formulate a plan for improvement that is based on your experience—and not negatively generated. Do not focus on the bad; focus on what worked, learn from what didn't. This will help you improve and embolden you for the next talk.

I need to repeat myself. If you truly want to be a better communicator, focusing on what you didn't like, beating yourself up, getting out the wet noodle and giving yourself one hundred lashes is not how you do it. Put away the wet noodle and encourage the great communicator in you by celebrating what works and gently improving what doesn't.

It is the incessant internal monologue that destroys great communicators. STOP it. There is always another chance. There is always a great reason why you needed to blow it at that moment—you just don't know what it is at the moment.

Stop beating yourself up. It will only make you repeat it.

The loudest critic is actually you. Tell yourself to shut up!

CHAPTER 132:
CHOOSE YOUR CRITICS
WISELY

I am going to risk offending half the speaking world. Are you ready? Toastmasters teaches through negativity, and therefore I do not agree with their process. People should not pick apart each other's speaking styles. The person picking may be wrong.

It is **silly** for them to critique you as they are just cementing in their brain to mimic what they are watching for. They will start doing what they notice—if they notice the bad—they will do it too.

The human brain is funny. If someone blurts out that your little hop at the podium annoys them (especially when you combine it with that funny inhale), this habit is going to be negatively cemented in your consciousness from then on. You might start doing it more without even realizing it. Or you might start thinking so much about not doing it that it takes you out of the moment while you speak.

Last time I checked, we are individuals, and each of us has our own style. Public speakers do not need to be pelted with negativity. There is enough of it in the world. Letting people pick apart your attempts at oration is not a good idea—especially when you are learning (which we always are!).

Whether you are in Toastmasters or not, people will want to offer advice on what you can do differently in the future. You have a couple of choices when this happens. Stop them or listen politely. When you stop them, tell them you are very deliberate about whom you allow to critique your talks. When you listen, refrain from saying anything snide or rude. Simply let them have their soap box and move on. I often thank such people for taking the time to give me their feedback—sometimes they are right about what they say and more than often they are wrong.

On the first day of my seminar teaching a group of CEO's about relationship and rapport, I purposely did not introduce myself to the group. One of the segments of the session looks at judgment and how we harm relationships and rapport by the pre-evaluations we do in our head. It took me a grueling ninety minutes to get the group to lighten up and start connecting with each other. The survey results were extremely positive.

A young man approached me after the session and chided me for not introducing myself at the start. "Had you told us you were also a CEO the room would have paid more attention to what you said. Because you made the mistake of not introducing yourself, you lost credibility." Um…that was my point.

I must admit his remark chafed me. I felt inwardly vindicated the next day as I watched him do his presentation for the group. He hadn't harnessed his rapport speaking ability, so he just didn't resonate with the room. I felt for him. After his talk I approached him to give him feedback. I watched as he braced himself. I let him know one thing that I really liked that he did and walked away. Later that day, he asked if he could hire me as a coach.

You know what. When I put my head on my pillow that night, I realized he did have a point. An introduction is an important piece of the presentation puzzle. And, as you know from previous chapters, I purposely do not fluff my bio before a talk. If my background impresses the audience, I don't have to try as hard. I like to try hard. It makes me a better public speaker. In fact, I improve with the uphill climb that comes without a bio. When I trust this process, the audience experiences the "ah ha" when the information eventually comes—just like the CEO I mentioned above.

Since feedback is important, you must mindfully choose those you allow to criticize or advise you. Hand select two or three people you trust. Make sure they are folks who have your best interests at heart. They must want you to improve. Ask them to come to your talks, to listen to your practices, give you feedback. This way you aren't adversely impacted by a negative comment hurled by a stranger and instead have the headspace to grow and improve.

When they give advice—let it marinate for a while. Please do not let anyone take away the part of you that is weird and wonderful. Please do not fit in.

Be careful about who you let critique you. They may be petty and absolutely wrong.

CHAPTER 133:
CRITICS ARE TOAST

Sorry everyone. I'm going to take one more swipe at Toastmasters. The last thing we need is <u>someone unlike us</u> to tell us they do not like that part of us that is really us. You get that? We want to keep the part of us most people will connect to, the part of us that makes us unique public speakers, the part of us that audiences want to see most.

Think of it like learning how to ride a bicycle for the first time. It is a hot sunny day, and you've got a red popsicle ring around your mouth. You cool off the purple glitter banana seat bicycle (now you know how old I am) with a spray bottle and straddle the Huffy Rocket. You are nervous. It's your first time trying to ride a two wheel.

What would happen if the person holding the bike said, "Well, your feet are a little small. You are too short. You aren't holding the handlebars right. Those shorts are an embarrassment. The humidity is a little too high to be riding today. I'm just not happy with your peddling performance. Hey, who am I to stop you. Give it a go." A lot of would be cyclists wouldn't bother, and Critical Mass (w<u>ww.critical-mass.org</u>) wouldn't have so many riders if this was how kids learned bicycling.

Public speaking is the same way. If you want to be better at it, which should you do, find someone to pick you apart or find someone to encourage you?

Good public speaking coaches (and friends) look for what you are doing well and build upon that. Now hold on there partner, I'm not saying they should only feed you sugarcoated truth. We all know this doesn't help a bit. No, I'm saying their main concern should be to help you be as great as you can be. And this is done best through positive encouragement and embodied feedback.

Build on each success. Turn the voice behind the bicycle off. Grading yourself doesn't work. Nor does comparing yourself to others. Turn off the critic. Be done with it.

John Yokoyama, founder of Pikes Place Fish Company in Seattle, says this wonderfully. During a speech to a group of entrepreneurs, he asked us to stop listening to the voice in our head. He repeated it a few more times and said, "Okay. Let's do this. I am going to stop talking. I am going to give you thirty seconds to listen to the voice in your head."

When our thirty seconds was up, he said, "I know what you're saying, 'What voice in my head. I don't have a voice in my head." Then he pointed and said, "THAT ONE!" The audience laughed. It was true. We all have it: The internal voice.

And this internal voice also criticizes others. The person who walks up and points out all your mistakes had an internal voice that told them to talk to you. Who gave their internal voice the right to become your critic? Did you? This chapter is for those folks. The ones out there who want to tell us how to improve. Please keep your unsolicited internal voices to yourselves, will ya.

Only listen to the voice that builds on your strengths.

*A note here. One of the toughest things for me to teach a facilitator is how to help people see what is great about what they are doing **and** to not sugarcoat what is not great. When we **only** talk about fluff—folks reduce listening. We need to be real. For example, if I am teaching a class on conflict I often point out to the room what their 'listening' faces look like. Scary. We reduce the other person's listening by the way we listen. The audience is more likely to listen to me if I am honest with them when I see things that truly reduce their effectiveness. There needs to be a balance.

 EXAMPLE:

ATTACK THE CRITIC

Imagine a room full of women running for office. Not just women, incredibly powerful women hell bent on changing the world.

Now picture a woman named Kenya bringing a room to its feet with a very powerful story illustrating how young people are the answer to the world's problems. She was moved to tears, and most of us were covered in goose bumps when she was through. We stood and applauded wildly as she made it back to her chair.

"I am such a cry baby," she said as she started to sit down.

A panther leapt out of me, and I ran toward her and said to her in a very strong, loud voice:

> *"HOW DARE YOU TALK TO MY FRIEND THAT WAY. The entire room just watched a woman move mountains, and you dare call her a name. I will not allow you do ever treat her that way. She didn't deserve it so you must apologize to her right now."*

The entire room burst into thunderous applause. Without trying or expecting it, I embodied the essence of the panther spirit. I have been asking women to be good to themselves, and on that day I <u>demanded</u> it.

Later in the afternoon, I asked all the women present to take an oath. We swore we would bring out the panther to help friends who talk to themselves in a negative, self-abasing way. We will no longer allow it. We will say, as your friend, I will not allow you to talk to yourself in a way that marginalizes the great person you are.

Later in the day, a woman made a disparaging remark about her own voice, so the woman next to her launched:

> *"NO! You do not get to do that. I am your friend and I just heard a powerful woman's voice. You do not get to treat her that way while I am around."*

The group got it on a deep level. Actually, I got it. Be nice to yourself, or I will hunt you down and demand an apology. It is not okay to bring your internal critic to every meal.

Every time I attack someone for blatent self-deprecation, someone in the room tears up. They 'feel' it on a level that is difficult to describe. I have found in some instances we must **demand** rather than soothe.

Celebrate every small success in communication and stop calling yourself names. It is no longer allowed.

CHAPTER 134:
MAKE THE RECORD SCRATCH ON GOOD SHIP LOLLYPOP

Few happy people wake up singing "we'll never make it" or "go away sunny day." What goes on in our head affects our ability to communicate. Positive thoughts in, positive thoughts out.

Here is my dilemma. I have a two-year-old son, and I hate to leave him. I get a lot of requests to travel internationally to speak. The choice before me is agonizing—saying yes is good for my business and bad for my family, saying no is bad for my business and good for my family. I wish I could do both. The torture is beginning to wear on me.

As I mentioned before, accepting the London speaking engagement meant being away from my son. Weeks before the trip, I began agonizing about being away. I questioned my choice, I fantasized about ways to get out of it, and when my departure day finally came, I was a mess.

As you remember, the trip was a disaster. I got horrifically sick and flubbed my speech. In hindsight, I realize I didn't perform to my usual ability because of the chatter that dominated my head leading into the event. I had a mantra of negative thoughts:

- I shouldn't be here.
- I miss my son.
- I am a bad mom.
- I wonder if what I am teaching will translate for a British audience.
- Did the guy really mean it when he said I likely wouldn't go over well in London?

And so on. These negative statements were loud and persistent. They depleted my confidence. I forgot how important confidence is to public speaking, and I failed because I left my confidence at home with my son. I'm human. It was a hard lesson. I'm glad I learned it.

What was going on in my head **made** me fail. It also proved to me that I am a good mom.

Speaking is a confidence game. Command only positive thoughts in your head before a speech. Make it so.

WHAT HAPPENS WHEN YOU CHOKE DURING THE OLYMPICS?

I am great at what I do. I kick ass. When I returned home from London, I was relieved that I had gotten stumbling out of the way. Cool. I won't choke again, and I can be a better coach with that experience in my journal. Whew.

Then I did it again. This time the stakes where higher so it meant more. I stalked the king of the VCs (venture capitalists) and convinced him to let me present to his partners. It took seven months for him to say yes, and as I prepared for my talk, I wasn't even a little bit worried. I knew I would make them like me; I always do (except that one time in London). People cheer and applaud by the time I'm finished.

When I walked into the room on the scheduled day, I entered the coldest room I have ever been in—full of 'seen it all' types. Just before I went on, an organizer told me to shorten my talk and hurry up; the day was behind schedule, and it was obvious he didn't think I should be there in the first place. He was rude, and the entire room mirrored his attitude.

I tried to introduce myself. Nobody was interested. In fact, many of the team members didn't even look up as I spoke. I decided to do what the organizer wanted. So I skipped all the great things I teach and just presented the data. I opened with a story and kept out all the time-consuming details that make it cool. In a rush, I tried to talk about "why" I was there. My mouth didn't work. My words wouldn't come out. I sucked. Really.

I ended up giving them the "what" and the "how" instead of an experience.

I left the presentation feeling pretty badly. The VC later called and said they weren't going to hire me to talk to their two hundred CEOs after all; all he could offer was to give the CEOs information about my organization. That was nice of him. He's a really great guy.

Why did I choke? I am still working that out. Though the conditions were harsh, I cannot blame the humans in the room. I have presented to plenty of tough audiences, and I always open them up with the magic I teach. I stay true to myself, and people respond.

Only this time I didn't honor my unique self. I put down my sparkle to meet their deadline. Looking back, I realize I should have told a three minute story, led a ninety second exercise and finished with a thirty second wrap up on why I was there.

Why did I forget everything I believe in? That is a good question, and I am still trying to figure it out. Perhaps it was professional self-sabotage. Human emotions are funny, and maybe the mom in me didn't really want more business. She wants more time with her son. Even if she didn't want to come right out and say it, she was afraid if I gave a talk to two hundred CEOs, my business would take me away even more. My inner struggle manifested as the reality in that room. It's amazing how this stuff works.

I believe my other obstacle was that I tried to be something I'm not— disinterested. As I sat in the waiting room, I downplayed how great it was to be there. I watched entrepreneurs walk in and out of that room begging for investment funds, and I silently commended myself that I didn't care about all their creative power and influence. It wasn't that important to me.

Now I realize it was. Reputation is everything, and now the people in that room still don't know my talent and communication prowess. What can I do about it? Dwell on it and weaken my confidence? Or spin that day into a successful learning opportunity? The answer is obvious: I am still great at what I do—even if twice I wasn't. The me doesn't change just because a moment went sour.

Of course, I will also work to make sure the situation doesn't repeat itself. I must befriend my very important inner mom and make sure she gets her needs met too. That way we can peacefully exist in the same body.

Had I hit it out of the park I would have earned the opportunity to speak before 200 of their CEOs—imagine the business I could have garnered from that! Of course, on the flipside, the increased work load would have stalled this book and taken me away from my son during his most impressionable years. As the Dali Lama says, "You never know when you are getting good luck." Missing that green light may be what saved you from getting hit by a semi-truck around the corner. Your failures are a part of the road to success. Remember that.

Just so you know, this hasn't been easy chapter for me to write, as I am still struggling with that day. I haven't FULLY integrated it. I still have to slap my face if I find myself getting into a rut over it. Let it go!!

If you have a bad day in your head, get it out! Redirect your inner voice and focus on the times you succeed, and you will be a great communicator.

CHAPTER 135:
IF THE BRIDGE IS OUT
TURN BACK

The fairy of great public speaking is testing me. For years I have experienced perfect presentations, standing ovations, and delighted audiences. In the past three months (as I've been finishing up this book), I've had three less than perfect public speaking experiences. I stumbled in London, I hiccupped in Vancouver, then I choked in Menlo Park.

Hmm. Now something is really going on. It is forcing me to look even closer at myself. It isn't always pretty, though it makes my story interesting.

I was in a hurry. My computer froze. I tried to explain something visually without the visual assistance of PowerPoint or a flip chart. It didn't work. Instead of refocusing and trying another way, I hammered on, trying to get them to understand the missing visual. And then I did it again—became the loud American who speaks SLOWER and LOUDER when talking with someone who speaks several languages and not English.

On my post-presentation surveys, five people suggested I get rid of that exercise. They still gave me high marks—and they also said the directions sucked. And I am a communications specialist.

I am human. You are too. Humans fall in love with our ideas and sometimes refuse to take the 10,000 foot view. Had I stopped for a moment and listened to what I do in this book, I would have succeeded. Did the audience get the exercise? Yes. They also got confused and frustrated as I tried to rebuild a fallen bridge with incorrect tools.

When you are in a moment and it doesn't feel right. STOP. Try something else.

 EXAMPLE:

WHAT IF I REALLY WANT TO FAIL?

It must be said. I will write it and please do not tell anyone. I secretly want to fail in this business. There. I said it. It's between us okay?

Remember when I talked about the mother inside me? Well she is the public speaker too. I am a mother who hates to leave her son for an overnight stay—so much so that I become somewhat of an emotional snot bubble whenever I'm away from him. I have been a tough cookie my entire life. Only when it comes to leaving my son, I'm still looking for my inner power muffin.

My travel schedule is bulging. Secretly, I do not want it to. My straddling of two opposing goals is...um...killing me more than my professionalism.

Why should you care? This could never be you, could it?

Great communication starts with you. To do it, you must be able to look at who you are in the light of who you want to be. We must see both to manifest our dreams and goals. And maybe being who we really are isn't the same as what we really want.

At the end of the road—past discontent, fight, perfection, glorious speaking skills, the right way to do it, acceptance, fitting in, success, a college education for my son, 12 lbs of flab, once weekly tooth flossing, exhaustion and my insatiable desire to be liked—is me. Sitting there. Waiting. Deciding. Rubbing the cuticle of my thumb, looking in the rearview mirror and wishing, so silently even I have trouble hearing it, that I never have to communicate with anyone again.

The other person is there too. I want them to like each other. Exhaustion reduces great communication, so take care of you—however many there are!

You must acknowledge and incorporate your dark side if you wish to truly communicate to be heard.

CHAPTER 136:
DUCK DUCK GOOSE

We've all been there. You're sitting in a meeting, waiting for your turn to speak. Introductions or comments are going in order around the room. And as the wave gets closer, you're only half listening—your other half is figuring out what you're going to say.

The words become a mantra in your head. You swallow. And swallow again. Your nerves tense up, until finally, something witty comes to mind. Thank goodness. Only one more person to go. Then that person steals your punch line. Uh…uh… The great moment passes.

GOOOOOSE!

You say something you hadn't planned on saying. Your voice cracks. You don't have that witty retort. Ugh. You missed the promotion.

Listen, everyone. I am that you. Some days my brain just doesn't work. Everyone expects me to be a great communicator because I teach the stuff. The pressure to be eloquent can be overwhelming when my brain is tired. So I have devised a way to stop playing duck duck goose when I am in a room: I brand myself.

No, not with hot metal—with my company mission and how it relates to the event I'm about to attend. I contemplate what I really care about, so before I walk in the room, I know why I am there. This way if round robin introductions happen, I already have a general idea of what I want to say.

I also give myself a break. Bad brain days are like bad hair days. They happen. Sometimes I am simply unable to be fantastic. I deal with it because I know there is always another opportunity. Always.

There are so many stories in our history of someone having one moment when it all changed. The musician-poet Eminem sings about it in his song *Lose Yourself.* I am going to paraphrase for you, as copyright law won't allow me to put it here. Basically, he says (much more poetically than I do): if you had but one chance, or opportunity to make your wildest dream happen, to get everything you ever wanted, only one moment, would you go for it? Or would you let it pass you by?

This belief kills us. When we believe we only have one moment—this moment—to capture everything we want, it stifles our creativity. There are many moments. Yes, even for Olympiads.

Please take a moment to visit the artist's website for the rest of this song's lyrics:

http://www.azlyrics.com/lyrics/eminem/loseyourself.html

then place the first verse, line by line, next to my comments. I gave you the first two words to make it easy to line up. This one is too good to pass up. Really. Look it up!

His palms...(Sound familiar?)
There's vomit...(I hope that doesn't sound familiar.)
He's nervous...(You look calmer than you think too.)
To drop...(Why writing it down is bad.)
He opens...(A good time to just pause.)
He's chokin...(As long as they aren't pointing, you are okay.)
The clock's...(The rest of his words are pretty clear, don't you agree?)

Whether you like his music or not, the man sure knows how to make a point. My point? There are many moments. We need to lighten up and be easier on ourselves when we speak in public.

You always get a second chance to make another impression. Stop worrying so much.*

(*And maybe don't eat a lot of spaghetti before a speech. Wink.)

CHAPTER 137:
DON'T LAY YOUR NECK
UNDER THE AXE

Don't lay your head under the axe simply means do not allow anyone to cut your head off when you are controlling the room. As the speaker, people are there to see and hear you—not to watch you get your head cut off (and remember, don't let them cut your head off in conflict either).

Here is a story to illustrate my point. Years ago, I found Mush—a kind-hearted frisky little puppy—on the street. She was pretty beat up. Her vagina was hanging outside her body—she clearly had just given birth. There was blood everywhere. She had not eaten much in months, as her skin was hanging from her bones.

I scooped her up and took her to the vet. The vet was furious; he said she looked the way she did because her previous owners had given her hormones so she would be able to have puppies at an early age. You see, people often do this to pit bulls, so they can breed them with their siblings and make their offspring mean. Fortunately, the vet was able to save her, and I took her home and nursed her back to health. I loved taking her to Fort Funston to go for walks, and this is where she got the name Mush—since pulling people up the paths was her favorite thing to do.

One day, I came home from work early, and, when I opened the door, she rushed into the house. Though I thought she was acting funny, I was a bit distracted by my lack of clean clothes to wear that night, so I went downstairs to do laundry. I could hear her racing around upstairs at top speed. Her behavior was weirder than normal, and I kept hearing her nails on the hardwood floor above—running back and forth and back and forth. Then, all of a sudden, I heard her nails come into the laundry room—though I still heard them running around upstairs.

I stopped for a split second and thought I had lost my mind. Then I turned the corner and saw the biggest pit pull I had ever seen standing in my laundry room. Its jaws were the size of a basketball. As soon as it saw me, it growled and leaned back.

Fortunately, I had ridden my motorcycle that day, so I had on my biker boots. On impulse and adrenaline, I charged at him, screaming an obscenity as I side kicked his face as hard as I could. He yelped and jumped over the fence. Mind you, the fence was six feet high. Then I realized why Mush was acting so strange—she'd been in the yard with that damn scary dog all day.

I ran upstairs and found Mush, and sure enough, she was pretty cut up. I took her to the vet again, and the vet told me that the big dog would have attacked me had I not kicked him. Because I didn't hesitate, I caught him in a weak moment and overpowered him. Even though Mush cost me a few pennies, I saved myself a lot of money in hospital bills.

Don't lay your head under an axe means no one is served by you being small and cowering under an attack. While brute strength is rarely a great response to a verbal attack, brute intelligence is. Believe in your ability to ward off attackers.

Don't let the bullies steal the show.

 EXAMPLE:

KISS OR HUG HECKLERS AND PROTESTERS

Imagine being in the audience at a political fundraiser for Hillary Clinton. The ground team has done much leg work to make sure everything goes as planned. Right after Clinton begins her remarks, the protest group Code Pink starts chanting and shouting "END THE WAR." Clinton ignores them for a few minutes and then says, "I agree we should end this war" and continues her talk. The protestors are eventually subdued.

Code Pink did the same thing during the Democratic Convention while Nancy Pelosi spoke. Pelosi completely ignored the chanting.

Both of these women are loud critics of the war. Both say they want to end the war and talk about working to make this happen. And they both missed an opportunity to take what was happening in the moment and use it to encourage a better understanding with all of the voters in the room.

Chances are, both of these politicians protested the Vietnam war. Joining thousands of others, they too may have voiced the sentiment of the times and carried posters and sang antiwar songs—though let's hope neither of them wore tie-dye!

My point is: Integrate. When I am heckled by someone in the crowd, I do my best to work it into my talk. Here is what Clinton and Pelosi could have done when they were interrupted by Code Pink; they could have stopped their respective talks and said:

> *"All of you out there stop for a minute and listen. What you are hearing right now is democracy and freedom of speech. Listen. Our great country allows organizations like Code Pink to exist and to freely state their opinions. I don't believe our goals are so different: End the War now. End the War now. End the War now." [The audience will join the chant.] "Code Pink, please allow me to speak directly to you and this entire room for a moment. I am on the same team as you are. Though I am not wearing pink, I am still a part of the movement to end this war. WE...the people in this room, the people on the hill who agree with this movement, the people at home, at work—we must all join TOGETHER to end this war. When*

we protest our own team or disrupt genuine attempts to find solutions to truly difficult problems, our ability to band together and end the war is weakened."

If Code Pink refuses to stop screaming, Hillary or Nancy could simply respond by noting that she understands their donnybrook is purposefully disruptive and, that in the interest of true free speech, she will continue with her remarks: "I'm going to do my very best to exercise my right to be heard despite AND because of our fellow Americans over there exercising their First Amendment rights!!"

Do not ignore what is going on in the room. Incorporate it into your talk.

CHAPTER 138:
THE ONLY TIME TO APOLOGIZE IS IF YOU STEP ON SOMEONE'S FOOT

Never, ever apologize for your public speaking performance, for not being prepared or for having to lay the ground rules for the audience. Such hollow apologies turn off audiences. They make you seem insecure and make them wonder if they are wasting their time. My rule: Only apologize if you step on someone's foot.

If you feel you must apologize for setting housekeeping rules, let someone else do it—someone who doesn't feel bad about setting appropriate boundaries for the audience. Though I challenge you to figure out how to make "housekeeping" interesting. It is possible you know.

Here's an example.

> *"Before we start today, I have to go over some rules. Please return your name badges at the end of the session. If you are late, we will need to start without you. Please turn your cell phones to silence. I'm sorry, just a couple more ground rules and we'll be finished…."*

Ugh! Or, how about:

> *"Please stand if you care about the environment. Put your right hand over your heart. There you will find your name badge. At the end of the evening, please return it to Susie over there by the registration table. [Susie waves.] Notice where your hand was—you just made an oath to return your badge. Thank you for being so easy.*

> *"Oh. Hold on. Please remain standing. If you want to improve your public speaking skills by the time you leave today, raise your hand. If you have not raised your hand you are wasting your time being here, so go ahead, raise your hand.*

> *"One way to make sure that improvement happens is for you to take that hand—go ahead and look at the hand you have in the air—and use it to turn off your cell phone, blackberry or pda. The next two hours belong to you. These devices are not allowed to interrupt you during your time."*

Housekeeping does not have to be painful: It can be a part of the experience. Perhaps you are saying to yourself, "But Christina that just isn't my style." Okay. I'm with you—even though you said but! My response is: Something is your style. Find it. Don't apologize for it.

Here comes the hammer again. You are communicating to be heard. Way too many speakers are not being heard. In order to change a mind, lead a team or do anything that involves communication, you must first be heard. Only then will you be remembered.

All speakers, including myself, can improve. No more wasting words and time by saying we're sorry. Rather let's use our words to create an experience that will be heard and remembered.

Only talk a lot about the things they want to hear. Usually, I'm sorry (and housekeeping) is not one of them.

CHAPTER 139:
SAYING THANKS

Many speakers start their talks by thanking the audience; they have been taught to start this way by the countless others who have come before them. I have already talked about why this is not a good thing. I will refresh your memory just to make sure you have it firmly in your noggin.

Starting a talk with a thank you will not get you into your groove. It brings the energy of your talk to a standstill. The audience is bored, you are not really thankful and the people you're thanking aren't really listening. And your talk is just beginning!

Start with a robust story and then weave your thanks throughout your talk. Give the person you're thanking something special to remember. To do this, you could tell a story that gives the audience an example of how amazing this person is. You could talk about them as if it was their memorial. You could sing them a song. Whatever you do, make it your personal goal to get them to tear up. That is a thank you.

I'll use a banana to teach you about this. Imagine you have a banana in your hand. Now mimic the way most people would peel that banana. How did we learn to hold the bottom of the banana with one hand, then grab the stem with the other and peel?

Have you ever experienced an uncooperative banana? You know, the kind that has a stem that won't give, so the peel splits in the middle and you end up with smashed banana on your hand.

If we had time, we could go to the jungle and watch monkeys in the wild. A monkey (who's main diet is bananas) does not peel the banana from the stem. He holds the banana by the stem. Then he pinches the bottom of the banana (where the bud was) and starts the peel from that point. Actually, the banana is designed to be peeled this way. When peeled from the bud side, it will automatically peel with less mess or struggle.

So where did humans learn to peel a banana? First graders learn the alphabet song and the pledge of allegiance—while nobody shows them how to peel a banana. So we must have learned by watching others. Since everyone does it that way, we do it that way too.

Starting a talk with a thank you is the same as peeling the banana the wrong way. Sure it will get your talk going—and it won't be as heartfelt or interesting as you want it to be.

Of course, there are always exceptions—my friend Fiona, for example. When running for office, she thanked the person who introduced her by starting with a story reflecting how incredible the introducer was. That works. Fiona didn't thank the audience for coming; she related directly to the person in front of her. That is a thank you.

Spare the audience and weave your thank yous into your talk.

MEANING THANKS

If you absolutely must start your talk with thanking someone, at least be genuinely thankful!

Check out the beginning of this YouTube clip of Senator Clinton questioning General Douglas Lute at his confirmation hearing:

http://www.youtube.com/
watch?v=gjksyR_64tw

Senator Clinton begins her comments by thanking General Lute for his years of service. After watching the clip, do you think she seems thankful? Probably, though it certainly doesn't seem like it in the clip.

Why doesn't she seem thankful? Because she isn't emoting; she's reading the words and not relating to the general as a human. In the new relationship economy, we lower our stock price with people when we speak and do not mean it. In this case, it would be much better not to bother with the thank you at all.

On YouTube you can find many Senate confirmation hearings that begin with equally lackluster thank yous. In one clip, I watched a Senator start his talk by thanking an Admiral for his years of military service; the whole time the Senator looked down at his paperwork and never once made eye contact with the Admiral. This type of thank you is not really a thank you. The Admiral did not feel appreciated, and the Senator did not feel thankful. It seemed more like the Senator had "thank you" on his to do list and wanted to scratch it off.

Imagine if the Senator ignored the paperwork on the desk, leaned forward, looked directly at the Admiral, and said:

> *"Admiral, it is my understanding you have devoted your entire life to service in the military. The choices you have made, to serve in Vietnam, to serve in Korea, in Desert Storm and now in Iraq—to continually answer the call and put yourself in the way of harm. You are the true definition of courage and bravery. I applaud you for keeping our country safe. Thank you."*

Now that's a thank you!

If a thank you sounds like you're just checking something off your to do list, it isn't really a thank you.

CHAPTER 140:
SO, HOW DO WE THANK
THE AUDIENCE?

Since step-by-step thank yous often feel canned, it is wise to experiment with the following elements. Incorporate some, ignore others, change them, combine them—whatever you do, make them your own.

- Give them a great talk to listen to—Honor their presence and avoid egregious fluffing. They won't believe you and you won't be off to an engaging start.

- Make a personal connection—Connect with the audience as humans rather than as an audience.

- Spotlight one person to thank—We tend to be more grateful when we focus on a single individual. If it is not appropriate to spotlight one person, figure out how to thank the team with real human connection.

- Mention one specific thing—What did the person do? Do not go on and on about it. Remember, if you use too many words, folks stop believing what you're saying.

- Tell the audience why the thank you is important—What did the person do? Why is it rare? Beautiful? Why should the audience care?

- Devote less words to the thank you and more words to description—Use one-word acknowledgements. These are powerful lead-ins to the description part of your thank you. For example, "When I think of Susie, I think of the word—Giant." Then explain.

- Weave your thank yous into your talk.

- Make sure you mean it.

When thanking someone, think of why you like this person. What is amazing about them? What did they specifically do to deserve your appreciation? Perhaps you can surprise the room (and the thankee) by sharing something interesting about them that most people don't know.

Which is better:

Thank you for having me today. I appreciate each and every one of you…

Or

When I was seven, I earned the nickname "Sped." Even though I didn't know how I got the nickname and noticed some kids snickering when Hope called me Sped, I kind of liked the attention. After a week of my new name, Gus—my 2nd grade arch nemesis—followed me to my speech therapy class. He used his grubby little hands to show me how I earned the nickname. First he covered the ECIAL with his left and and the the UCATION with his right. SP ED was all that remained.

    It is interesting that Sped, a kid who spent a few years in speech therapy, is standing before a room full of physicians in order to teach them public speaking. Your trust in me means something. And it isn't about me.

    Every single person in this room has dedicated his or her life to children—like the little Sped in me—who are in cognitive speech therapies. You have helped children find the confidence and will to communicate through their verbal challenges...

This seems a little long-winded doesn't it? It's not. When said aloud, this thank you takes about ninety seconds and will mean more to the audience than "thank you for coming."

Rapport is increased when we devote time to a real thank you.

CHAPTER 141:
TURN JAPANESE

A popular song when I was in high school had the lyrics "I think I'm turning Japanese, I really think so." To this day, I still do not know what the hell that song was supposed to be about; fortunately I do know that I've learned a valuable lesson about receiving from the Japanese businessmen who have come to the United States to work with me.

In 1994 (and many years after that), I was visited by groups of Japanese businessmen (no women) who wanted to learn my style of debt collection. During this time, Japan was just beginning to allow private debt collectors, and my style of respect, honor and kindness meshed well with their culture.

Before the first group came, I asked a seminar coordinator to school me on basic Japanese social niceties so I wouldn't mistakenly offend anyone. I was especially impressed by her lessons on business card exchange and how important this ritual was in Japan. To this day, I still accept business cards like the Japanese do. I take a moment and review the card. I turn it over. I make eye contact with the individual who gave it to me and say something about it. I strive to be gracious and treat the business card as I would a fine painting.

The same is true of receiving awards. If you are lucky enough to receive an award, or even a speakers gift, take a moment and admire it in front of the room. Be honored to receive it. Treat it like the honor it is. If the award is wrapped, you can ask the presenter if they'd like you to open it now or later. In Japan absolutely open it right then.

Interestingly, it took many years before I realized my Japanese audience more than got what I was saying. While I had an interpreter, the audience always seemed to laugh at the wrong times, and I was always a bit worried that they weren't catching the point of my words. Then one day, at the end of a presentation, an audience member approached the lectern and presented me with a gift.

I asked the gentleman if I should open it now. The translator translated to the audience. The audience laughed and made physical gestures to indicate "YES! Yes! Open it now." I treated it like a business card and took my time. I admired the wrapping paper and the box (something I still do today), and when I opened it, I discovered a trifold clock. It had cherry blossoms on the first fold, a clock in the middle, and birds on the third fold. It was set to the right time, and it was lovely.

I bowed, thanking them for such a beautiful gift. As the man stood and spoke to me, his eyes were brimming with tears. I felt what he was saying before the translator could repeat it in English, and I said to him, "Time will move slowly until I see you again."

The translator was surprised, "You speak Japanese?"

I had just said the same thing he had said to me. The translator explained what had just happened to the audience. The man and I stood quietly looking at each other in awe and respect as the audience clapped and laughed.

The following year, this man and his group came back to train with me, and just before I was about to speak, he came up to the podium and handed me his business card. I immediately recognized his eyes and smile. I admired his business card and bowed. His assistant said to me in English, he wants you to know the time has gone slowly.

I still tear up when I read that story. If I hadn't taken the time to write down this story in its entirety when it occured, I might have lost much of its wonderful detail and emotion.

Remember to take a moment and receive the human behind the award or the gift. These moments are precious.

CHAPTER 142:
ELEVATOR CLOSING

Your closing is for the audience, so it is important to close with one or two sentences referencing what you want people to remember from your talk. Be very clear and direct with your ending. Avoid trailing off or giving audiences too much to think about.

It is tempting to put a few semi-colons on our end, and keep adding and adding, and and and to our thoughts. Audiences can't remember all that stuff. The moment their hear a semi-colon, they are lost. Shorten up the last thought and give them something clear to go home with. Get them to interact if it doesn't seem too gimmicky.

Which of these endings will most likely be remembered?

> *"For all the reasons I have stated today, we need to work together and save the environment. Right now Prop 11 is in serious need of your vote."*

> Or

> *"It is time for each of us to wear the red cape and save the planet—A vote for the Prop 11 is a vote for our future!"*

> Or

> *"If you brought your calendar with you, please take it out now. I'll give you a moment. Go to November 6th of this year. In the 5pm slot, write VOTE for Prop 11!!! A vote for Prop 11 is a vote for our future!"*

You are right. The latter is more likely to be remembered and acted upon because the audience interacted.

The ending of the talk should be memorable, short and with just one message to remember.

 **EXAMPLE:**

ONE SENTENCE ENDING

One-word or one-sentence endings are very powerful.

Franz spoke to an all CEO crowd in Berlin, Germany. As the final keynote speaker of the conference, the audience was tired, bleary-eyed and had low expectations. And Franz still blew the room away. Why?

He got the audience's attention by doing something different from the beginning of the talk through the end. He introduced himself using PowerPoint, and it was the best introduction I have ever seen. He flipped through the pages very quickly and had humor all throughout.

In the middle of his talk he stated a statistic: Every twenty-two minutes a coal factory opens in China. He set a kitchen timer and laid it on the lectern. Two times during his talk the timer went off. It was an effective way of interrupting his own speech to continue making an earlier point.

At the end, he flipped through multiple slides on innovation. He called back some things he had said earlier, flashing through three minutes of examples of innovation and creative thinking that led to success.

He then said, "There is a ton of opportunity out there…success…I just think it should be…" He stopped talking. And flashed a giant "YOU" up on the screen before the hushed audience.

The crowd loved it. LOVED it. His timing made it work, though it also worked because he mirrored our inner thoughts. All during his talk, it was impossible not to think, "Hey, that could be me!!" A point that he captured so succinctly at the end.

End powerfully and creatively, and your audience will listen and remember.

CHAPTER 143:
TWIST MY ARM:
HERE'S A HOW-TO FOR YOU

Rather than writing out every word, select the three things you want the audience to remember. Then create your talk.

1) **What is the title of the talk?**—It is critical you reference the title during the talk to match the expectations of the audience. Last week I gave a talk to a roomful of executives. My talk was billed "Courageous Speaking" despite the fact that I have never referenced my work this way. During the talk, I paid homage to the title, referencing it a couple of times so the audience felt they got what they came for. This simple technique increases audience rapport and helps the audience feel like they were in the right room.

My friend Andrea and I flew home from Las Vegas on Mother's Day this year. We couldn't wait to get home to our babies, and in our sleep deprived haze we ate breakfast on the wrong side of the security line. When we finished we realized that the line was so long we might miss our flight.

After chewing our nails and straining our neck 3,451 times to see how long the line really was, we made it to the other side. Then we ran to our plane and managed to get on just before take off. Sweaty and relieved, we sat down and buckled up. Imagine our faces when we heard the flight attendant announce, "Welcome to Southwest Airlines serving Seattle." Panic. Fortunately, a moment later she added, "by way of Oakland." Whew.

Audiences are just like the rest of us. We have all experienced the fear of being on the wrong plane, the wrong bus, at the wrong restaurant for a meeting. So, make sure you remind folks that they are not at the wrong talk by mentioning the title now and then. Though do not bore them with it!

2) **Who is the audience?**—Presenters too often skip this step. This is not recommended. Audiences have changed in this new millennium. We want our experiences more individualized than ever before.

My firm uses the on-line survey program (www.surveymonkey.com) to survey participants and find out how they viewed their experience. This shows me what they connected to and what they did not. It helps me define my audiences. When working with an organization, we use the internet to investigate the organizations mission and purpose. This helps me target my talk to benefit their perspective.

A few years ago, a dear friend of mine asked me to step in for him and teach a class on public speaking at Merrill Lynch. The audience was a group of hedge fund folks. I had never heard the term "hedge fund" and thus had to figure out what these folks did. In addition to my internet research, I contacted a few finance people and asked them for their perspective on hedge funds. I also talked with the person organizing the training session. As a result, I was able to sprinkle in what little knowledge I had during my talk, while also being clear that I was no expert in their business. My legwork made the training much more relevant to those in the room.

Humans do not like it when speakers drive personal agendas <u>nor</u> when they offer talks that have no relevance for the room. How I teach public speaking to a group of hedge fund folks is much different than how I teach a room full of environmentalists. They speak different languages. Of course, as you remember from an earlier chapter, I use the same methods with both groups; I simply change the referential wording and analogies to suit the room.

For example, when trying to help environmentalists embrace the tough idea of collaborating with the legislature on bills, I might tell a story of trees watching in horror as the lumberjack wields his wood handled axe—"Oh no, the murderer is one of us!" Alternately, when trying to get hedge funders to work with legislature on bills, I might point out that Walt Disney got turned down for funding more than 300 times before he was successful.

Again, know your audience. Do not pander to them, just know them.

3) **If you can only pick one, what is the main point you want your audience to remember?**—For me, I usually want my audience to remember the power in the positive. This seems broad and it is. I make it less broad by closing with a story or an exercise to elucidate my point.

What about you? To get you thinking about it, take out a piece of paper and write down the one thing you want the audience to remember. Many humans I coach will write down "I want them to vote for me" or "I want them to buy from my company." To this, I say YUCK! Ending a talk with some sort of selling platform is not very memorable.

Humans tune out when they hear advertisements and commercials. If you leave them with a grander focus, this will make them want to buy your company's product. Yes, it is okay to ask the audience for the vote or the order—if you do this in the middle of your talk. Just do not make it your closing statement.

Listen. In order to buy from you, vote for you, save the planet, join your club, etc. they must first HEAR you and then REMEMBER you. You. Not your message. They will remember your message when they remember you.

Closing statements give you the opportunity to lift the audience to a higher spectrum of belief or vision. This feeling will stay with them long after any sales pitch will.

And yes, coming up with a memorable and uplifting closing isn't necessarily easy. The simplest way to figure it out is to think of why you want people to vote for you or buy your product. For instance, Mary is running for office on the platform of children, because she knows when children's lives are improved, the future gets brighter.

Mary also works for a lucrative law firm where she is one of the only female partners. When asked to connect her fancy law firm to her candidacy, she simply could not do it. This is not okay. We must establish congruence between what we are wanting the audience to do and who we are as individuals. Whether we like it or not, what we do for a living makes a difference in how people view us.

What is my point? Until this candidate can make the connection between her job and her candidacy, she will not be able to inspire others.

The connection is obvious to me: She was a high level attorney living *La Vida Loca* and then she had a son. Being a mother made her realize children are the most important asset in our world. Being a lawyer was no longer enough to make a difference in the world; now she wants to improve the lives of children and make all of our lives better.

If you are still confused, refer back to the chapters on story telling. These should help you figure this out. Your ending is what the audience will remember. How do you want them to feel?

Let's have a Northern California moment. When you are done reading this paragraph, close your eyes and imagine you have a magic wand. If that wand could give you <u>one</u> thing that every audience member would do as a result of hearing you speak: What would it be? Take a moment to really see it in your mind. Okay, <u>now</u> close your eyes and do it.

Are you done? If so, get up and move around. Hold onto this book. Stretch with it in your hand. How can you remember the thing your magic wand gave you? Is there a story that elucidates your desire? Expand.

MICROSCOPIC SPOTS

Pick a spot on the wall. Now walk ten steps backward and away from that spot. Hold your hands above your head

- The space between your hands and the wall—is EVERYTHING you know about the topic.

- Take one step forward. The space between your hands and the wall—is EVERYTHING you want to tell the audience about your topic.

- Take one step forward. The space between your hands and the wall—is EVERYTHING you plan to tell the audience about your topic.

- Take one step forward. The space between your hands and the wall—is EVERYTHING you have time to tell the audience about your topic.

- Take one step forward. The space between your hands and the wall—is EVERYTHING you actually say about the topic.

- Take one step forward. The space between your hands and the wall—is EVERYTHING the audience hears you say.

- Take one step forward. The space between your hands and the wall—is EVERYTHING the audience understands.

- Take one step forward. The space between your hands and the wall—is EVERYTHING the audience remembers. So you better make it good!!

Most speakers try to cram too much material into a short speech. Select very few things for the audience to remember and practice delivering it in a way they will recall later.

CHAPTER 144:
REMEMBER A LITTLE MAGIC

In preparing a speech, always add a little MAGIC:

- Metaphor, analogy or Simile;

- Action-oriented exercise;

- Goo—get their hands dirty;

- Interactivity with you or with each other;

- Creativity and Risk.

When speaking, always remember your magic!

CHAPTER 145:
SHOOK-UP CAN TO MY HEAD CHECKLIST

My editor is mean. She says I have to give you a public speaking checklist. I've covered this information in different places throughout the book, and now she says I should put it all in one place. She says it will make it easier for you. All right, I'll do it. Just realize my arms are crossed! Harumpf.

<u>Title:</u> What I call my talk:

- _____

<u>Key points:</u> Three Key Points I want my audience to remember are:

- _____
- _____
- _____

<u>Opening:</u> How can I open my talk so I get into my groove? What stories and experiences do I have that I can tell with detail and animation that will connect to my three key points. If I'm stumped by this, I can think of five stories I have told in my life and jot down a sentence about each one of these five stories:

- _____
- _____
- _____
- _____
- _____
- How can I make a bridge between these stories and my three key points?

<u>Metaphor-Analogy Mania:</u>
Where does my subject matter appear in my every day life and experiences? How can I use clear and interesting concepts to explain my idea? How can I tell these stories and metaphors with color, detail and action? The three metaphors I will use to illustrate my key points are:

- _____

- _____
- _____

How will the talk end?: Using no more than three sentences, this is a summary of what I want the audience to remember:

- _____

_____

_____

_____

Story Example:

I am twelve-years-old and my father is away on a business trip. I am terrified to be home alone and have every light on in the house. I peek around every corner as I enter the downstairs den, certain the hairs standing on the back of my neck are going to get tangled in my pony tail. I rush over to my cat Siddartha to pick him up for comfort; he rears back, lets out the scariest human-devil cry and bites me. He had never bitten me before. I look down and see a rat's tail in his mouth. He looks at me with red devil eyes. I realize, OH MY GOD, he has rabies. I had seen the movie. I know what happens next. They will shoot my cat. And... oh no! I HAVE RABIES!!! They will shoot ME too! I rush over to the linen closet and grab a blanket. I throw it over the cat and stuff him in a box, rat's tail and all. I balance this box on my ten-speed and rush to the Veterinarian's office a few blocks away. I burst in the door "HELP!! I have rabies...my cat has rabies...someone help me!" The vet takes the cat. A nurse dresses my wound. I listen as my cat protests and sounds like Linda Blair. in the movie The Exorcist. A few moments later, as my racking shoulders subside and my sobbing quiets, the vet comes out and puts a hand on my hand. "Sweetheart, I have been a vet for eleven years...and I have never seen a cat...get rabies...from a shoestring."

This is a true story. I write it out for you so you can imagine me telling the story in front of a group. The purpose? This could be my opening talk for almost any topic.

Remember to stay out of your head before the talk. Have fun. Use this checklist to create your next public talk. Let me know how it goes!

PART V

MEDIA SKILLS

CHAPTER 146:
THE TV CAMERA IS
AN AUDIENCE MEMBER

Ten years ago, I taught media training as a discipline completely separate from public speaking. At that time the skill set needed for each seemed to be on opposite ends of the spectrum. This is no longer true. Communication has changed, media has changed and you are in the middle.

Many folks in media training today will disagree with my approach to the media; they might even tell you to use this chapter for kindling and skip to the closing section. I disagree.

In the old days, reporters were the enemy of public speakers; they were tricksters hoping we would slip on a verbal banana peel and improve their ratings. Now I realize reporters are human, so I have amended my thoughts. Likely no more than three percent of them are looking for the "gotcha." The rest want to connect with us and see us succeed. They want an interesting story. They want engaging, 3D individuals. They applaud spectacular personalities and, well, nice people.

So, besides making yourself wonderful, how can you have a successful relationship with the media? I say, the first step is to befriend reporters. I am not suggesting you beg them to go out for beers with you. Instead, remember their goals and help them find the story. Be genuinely friendly. Be a source for them. Respond immediately when they call, stay connected, offer them stories when they ask, and if you aren't the right person, suggest the person who is. This will keep them calling you back when they need your type of expertise. (On second thought, taking them out for beers isn't such a bad idea either.)

In an interview, see reporters as human beings, not a vehicle for your message. Talk to them before and after the interview, ask them questions, get them (and you) to relax. Even though we are repeatedly told "reporters are not our friends" I say reporters can be our friends. They have a desire to get the news out there, and we have the desire to get our message out there. We are the same.

With all of this said, speaking "off the record" poses real risk. Some reporters are not honest. Some people are not honest. Some public speaking trainers are not honest. To lump all reporters into one big deceitful pie is not fair; nor is it wise. Still, it is difficult to discern who is going to keep "off the record" off the record and who is not.

If being interviewed on camera, off the record TRULY doesn't exist. It is forever on film. Before starting the interview get some exercise—run up the stairs—do something to get your endorphins rolling.

When it does come time to sit down with the reporter and the camera—who do you look at?

Reporters want the interview to seem like an interview, so they want you to view the camera as a disinterested third party. Therefore, they prefer that the person being interviewed ignore the camera. They may even specifically ask you not to look at the camera.

So what do you do? Look at reporter during the interview. Every once in a while look into the camera. Ignore the media trainers. In the new relationship economy (which includes the advent of reality television, MySpace.com, YouTube.com, etc.), the camera is an audience member. Glancing at the camera a couple of times will rarely annoy the reporter, and it will give the viewers at home a chance to connect with you.

Look the camera square in the eye a few times.

CHAPTER 147:
HIDING YOUR CARROTS
IN THE JELLY BEANS

My son hates vegetables. He will eat "mac-moni" and cheese, "hippy dogs with dippy sauce" and "beeberries" until he is stuffed silly. In order to get him to eat vegetables I have to hide the vegetables in other food. Hence the chapter title: Hiding the carrots in the Jelly Beans. My son will grow up thinking that peanut butter and jelly sandwiches should have peas in them. He will be a teenager before he realizes that green dogs are really asparagus.

Reporters are the same way. Most reporters do not like vanilla. They are looking for a 'personality' to interview. Be yourself. Be interesting. Be brief (seven to twelve second sound bytes). Do not make it obvious you are hiding carrots in their jelly beans.

Most reporters do not want to voice their own questions on air. If you pay close attention to the news media, you will notice most interviewees answering their "own" questions; those who don't generally end up on the proverbial "editing room floor."

Here's an example (of hiding the "carrots" in the question):
Reporter: *What do you think about Obama going after the woman's vote in this election?*

Response: *Women are 51 percent of the population: Obama is going after the woman's vote because it is a smart thing to do. Women voters are pragmatic and will choose the best person for the job.*

Another tack is to respond directly with a statement reflecting their question:
Reporter: *Is America ready for a female president?*

Response: *America is ready for a female president. I look forward to the day when race or gender of a candidate is no longer news—the day we finally cross these thresholds of diversity. Our national non-profit organization Emerge America is focused on recruiting and training Democratic women to run for and get elected to office. Last year 26 percent of our California class graduates were women of color. Good legislation requires perspective: Our legislature must match the American demographic.*

Reporter: *Why does EmergeAmerica only train women?*

Response: *EmergeAmerica only trains Democratic women who are ready to run for office. Right now, only 14 percent of our national representation is female— while our nation is 51 percent female. This puts America at 90th in the world in terms of gender equality. If our elected government were only 14 percent male, I'd be teaching men.*

Put the question in your answer and answer questions in twelve-second sound bytes.

CHAPTER 148:
IF THERE IS A DEATH
BE UPSET ABOUT IT, REALLY

Match or exceed the reporter's concern for the problem. Too many hospital administrators strap on Mr. Professional guy right after an error in their hospital caused a death.

The hospital made a mistake, the unspeakable happened, and rather than rising to the heart-wrenching emotion of the situation, the hospital representatives flat-lined when faced with the upset family and the media onslaught. No doubt, emotional stress causes poor communication. When we are upset we often move from fear and sadness to blame and anger. It is a human thing. It doesn't make us bad people.

For a healthcare organization, a mistake that results in death is the worst thing that can happen. The executive who answered the media call is often very scripted and cold. He says the hospital was sad about the loss, though he merely <u>says</u> the words—it doesn't seem like he means them. This only adds to their problems. A better approach is to put the nurse who cared for the patient in front of the camera and let the cold executive deal with the insurance lawyers behind the scenes.

Hospital spokespeople are really bad at emotion. They harden themselves to the pain and suffering they witness everyday. Something awful happens in their facility all the time—and most of the time it isn't their fault. When it is, they come on camera clearly watching their words and reciting a script. Even if they are personally upset by the problem or mistake, their "professionalism" makes them seem robotic and uncaring. The hospital's reputation requires they say only the "right" thing.

In today's relationship economy, the public wants to know if we're upset. If they see that we're upset they are less likely to make us upset. Think back to childhood and the infamous parental words: "I'll give you something to cry about." If we <u>do not</u> express genuine concern when faced with a dramatic situation, we will get something to cry about later—bad publicity or a lawsuit. Simply stating real concern and sorrow over a difficult situation is not an admission of culpability nor does it increase liability.

If it is a real problem, match or exceed the media's concern for the problem. Ignoring it will not make it go away.

 **EXAMPLE:**

ANSWERS WRITTEN ON
A KID'S LEG

Imagine a private school in ABC City, USA. It is the educational home to the kids of the stars; parents have high expectations and lots of power. One day a group of kids gets caught cheating, and suddenly the faculty is in a pickle. They must balance the right to privacy of the accused students, satisfy the concerns of other parents who are demanding information, and maintain the reputation of school's academic integrity.

Add more than a dash of hungry media, and, depending on who's in the kitchen, this challenging situation offers a recipe for a perfectly formed message or a sunken catastrophe.

> Reporter's question: *There are reports of students cheating on tests. Who are these students and what are you doing to discipline them?*

The headmaster goes into a long diatribe about how they have systems in place to address this type of situation. He runs on. Blah blah blah. He does not answer the reporters question. He says he cares, though he doesn't even look concerned about the problem. It is clear he is defensive and protecting the school. The media doesn't buy it, and now the school has a PR problem as well as a cheating problem.

The public doesn't care about the school. They care about the kids. What if the headmaster sat down moments after news of the cheating came to his attention and pulled a yearbook off the shelf and started looking at the faces of his students. What if he connected back <u>why</u> the school existed—for the children—and thought about their primary directive: Educate kids and give them the confidence to go out into the world and live a legacy.

Confidence. Wait. Hmmm. Somehow the students lacked the confidence to believe they could succeed without failing. He then schedules a parent meeting and a press conference to discuss the situation.

> Reporter's question: *There are reports of students cheating on tests. Who are these students and what are you doing to discipline them?*

> Headmaster's answer: *Yes, we have discovered a small group of students cheated. Their cheating serves a message to me and the faculty. We are very concerned that ANY student in this school lacks the self-confidence to believe he or she can succeed without cheating. I know these kids—they do not need to cheat. Our administration staff is evaluating this situation right now and a meeting has been scheduled with the parents; we plan to devise an early warning system. We must build their confidence so they don't resort to cheating. The school administration, staff, parents and students are working as a team, and together we can solve this problem.*

Notice how he focuses on creating a positive, affirming experience for students. He also points out that the faculty needs to work on improving confidence and early detection. The school's position is prevention rather than defensiveness.

Since the school instructs the offspring of famous people, the reporter may be unrelenting in his pursuit for the names of the cheating students. In such cases, the headmaster must champion the right of privacy to the individual:

> Headmaster: *In these walls we teach the basic tenants of this country's human rights. Innocent until proven guilty is one of those rights. There is no value in publicly devastating the life of a student.*

Let the media know you have uncovered the cause of the problem and are committed to fixing it.

CHAPTER 149:
DON'T LET THE COMPOUND QUESTIONS GET YOU DOWN

Often reporters will ask several questions in one breath. When this happens stop for a moment and breathe. Decide which question to answer or ask for clarification. For example:

I heard several questions in there. The first question was _____.

Then answer that one. Be clear you know there were several questions. This way you will not look like you are avoiding the questions AND you don't have to try and remember all of them.

When trying to remember all the questions a reporter asks, you can easily get thrown off your message. This style of questioning distracts the interviewee. To avoid this problem, simply focus on the first question and ask the reporter to repeat the others—one at a time!

Take a breath. When launched a multi-level question, answer the question you are ready to answer.

CHAPTER 150:
MAURY WEARS MORE MAKE-UP THAN YOU DO

Much of the media training I have received in the past focused on how I looked. In the new media approach, I believe looks are still important, though for a more complex reason: We want to look nice for ourselves as well as for the audience.

The last thing any great communicator needs is a reduction in confidence due to a hair being out of place. The more famous we are, the more likely we will be picked on for how we look. I can't imagine being a star on the cover of *Us* magazine looking like I look Sunday mornings as a I drag myself out to get a cup of joe at Madhouse Café.

Sure, I'm contradicting myself here. In the first pages of this book, I told you not to worry about how you look. Let me clarify. There is a difference between "not worrying" and "giving attention." Confidence promotes great communication. Anything we can do to increase confidence and reduce distracting thoughts works in our favor.

Obviously, looking our best is something we can do. I don't mean you should look model perfect nor spend hours perfecting pancake makeup. Take the time to feel good about how you look—to yourself! I feel better when I shower, wear something I feel good in, and dab on a little make up. Maybe you feel good when you wear a particular shirt and have oatmeal for breakfast.

Whether we like it or not, we live, work, and play in image conscious times. When facing the media, pay attention to how you look— even if it is a newspaper reporter. Don't stress about it, just take a little time to feel good about the way you look.

Here are a few tips:
- Have a change of clothes ready at the office—just in case.

- Low-cut looks better at bars, unless you're addressing the annual MILF awards.

- Carry a spare jacket with you always; it hides the coffee stain created by the hole in your lip.

- God created safety pins. Have them on hand in case you have a pucker between buttons or some other defenestrating protuberance.

- Spit out your gum. Need I say more?

- If wearing a jacket, be careful of it bunching up around the shoulders. Pull the back of your jacket down to avoid this. If you are seated, you can also sit on the hem of your jacket.

- Light colors add pounds on video. I once wore a lavender suit for a TV interview. I weighed about 110 lbs at the time. When I watched myself later, I was wearing a white suit and weighed about 130 lbs.

- Make-up is essential. I was on the Maury Povich show once. In the makeup room, I laughed about how much makeup Maury had on. It was ridiculously thick, and I wouldn't let the make up guy do that to me. I regretted it. The camera sees things very differently than a human. He looked normal; I looked like a ghost. If you are going on camera, apply powder so <u>at least</u> you don't shine like a disco ball.

- Primp more than you usually do. Yes, I am serious. Take the time to really look the way you want to look. You will feel better for it.

- Before the camera is rolling, ask the reporter if she has any inside tips to help your physical appearance on camera or specific do's and don'ts about how to present yourself on camera. Even if you're an old pro who's seen it all, you might learn something new. Reporters <u>love</u> this and it helps create a relationship.

- Look in the mirror right before going on. Any spinach in your teeth?

- Dress so you have "I'm looking good" music in your head.

Looks may not be everything; they are something to you.

CHAPTER 151:
DON'T MAP OUT EVERYTHING YOU ARE GOING TO SAY

While I covered this point in the public speaking section, it warrants a mention here: Be careful with pre-scripting your interview answers. Scripting sounds scripted. Only the rare human can read a script and sound natural.

As you prepare, definitely jot down ideas and the important points you want to make. Think up pithy sayings—they make people smile and help your ideas stick. I had fun with the chapter headings of this book. I threw a tennis ball around with one of my friends, and we came up with funny things.

"Funny things" is who I am. I make up words and sayings and use them when I speak. It makes my work interesting to me. It also hurts me. When blue chip companies contact me about the trainings I offer, I sometimes lose business because I call it "Rapport Speaking" and they want "Presentation Training." Being weird has its price. It also allows me to be who I really am—I refuse to let my professionalism kill me.

At a recent interview, I used the metaphor "hiding the carrots in the jelly beans." The reporter loved it so much, he stopped the camera so he could laugh unabashedly. I made a note to use that one again.

Instead of working on a script, work on creative ways to deliver your message. Then pay attention to what works and what doesn't. Keep the winners, discard the others. Never give up and always innovate. This book is full of suggestions on how to make your words and ideas interesting to the minds of others. These work for the media too. Think of a reporter as the face of a large audience and answer his questions with variety and interest so everyone will want to listen.

If a reporter calls me for a comment on interest rates in the U.S., I might say, "I know more about the mating habits of the Tsi tsi fly. I do know how fear impacts communication in our culture. If that isn't the angle you are looking for, I know someone you can call…" This approach keeps the reporter engaged and more likely to call you back when covering a story about communication in business.

For practice thinking on your feet, have someone in your family or office practice firing questions at you. Answer each question differently. Have fun. When the interview happens, you'll be a little less stiff and more you.

Let spontaneity and pre-planning guide your interview.

CHAPTER 152:
JULIA CHILD DID NOT COOK THAT MEAL

Avoid using other people's recipes in your mix. Recipes are futile attempts at recreating the work of the masters. The best chefs make up their own recipes. Sure, they borrow ingredients and methods; they also keep them fresh and peppered with their own creative ideas.

My brandy pepper steak never tastes like the yummy, crafted delight at the Brazenhead. I have tried at least twenty-five times to recreate the tossed salad from the House of Prime Rib and can't seem to get it. And I can make amazing Brussels sprouts with shallots, mushrooms and a spicy curry sauce; I came up with that recipe on my own.

We in the training world try too hard to come up with sure-fire recipes—easy to follow steps to help a person recreate magic. Rarely do we tell people that magic is created from within. Tapping into this inner magic is the only fail proof recipe for success.

We fall flat when we try to recreate the magic of others. Sure, we may get some folks to laugh, cry and enjoy us; unfortunately this won't last. We will get tired of being someone else. Others will notice we are missing our unique vibration, our creative individualized spin on things—the stuff that makes us real.

Mining your magic requires a walk through your past. You must search for the stories and experiences that created your perspective. Remember, reporters are looking for the <u>human</u> interest behind the story. They are interested in your perspective and in lively vignettes elucidating your points.

They also want the truth. Twinkies are spray painted with food coloring to look like they are baked. When I discovered this, it changed my attitude toward Twinkies. I could no longer enjoy the spongy yellow cakes knowing they were fake. Stories are the same. Fabricating a human interest story is a bad idea. Period. Borrowing someone else's interesting anecdote and saying it is your own is a bad idea. Period. The actual events of your life are far more interesting—they belong to you.

Of course, you might amalgamate multiple events into one story. This is vastly different from saying something that isn't true. You are not fabricating; you are combining for simplicity and the sake of time.

Avoid borrowing stories and ideas from others; your perspective is what the reporter wants.

CHAPTER 153:
PRACTICE WITH A 150 WATT LIGHT BULB IN YOUR FACE

Get out of your head. Practice does not happen there. Practice happens in <u>real time</u> scenarios when you simulate a real time interview or talk.

A 400 watt light bulb shining in your face makes it extremely difficult to be natural. Imagine trying to keep your cool when a person is attacking you for what you believe in <u>and</u> you are blind and sweaty. It is darn near impossible—at least without experience. And how do you get experience? Practice.

The best way to practice for media interviews is to set up a camera and recruit a friend or coworker to be the reporter. Then have them point the camera at you, press record and start firing questions at you.

This has many benefits. You get to see what you look like on film. Watching a recording of yourself helps you figure out how to best stand, talk and connect with the camera. For example, I no longer let media photographers take my picture from the ground up. I look ghastly that way. It took a magazine cover and three articles to finally understand why I looked so awful. I could have saved myself the pain by doing a practice "media shoot."

You will also improve your ability to think on your feet. Tough questions are like baseballs. You can't learn how to hit a baseball by thinking about it. Have your interviewer ask you difficult and thought-provoking questions; let them surprise you. Perhaps you stutter slightly when stumped or you make distracting gestures with your hands. You will see what works and what doesn't—and make adjustments accordingly.

Put the tape away after you watch it the first time, then play it again a couple of days later. This gives you a different perspective. Some parts will seem better, others worse. Where did you miss hitting it out of the park? (I am staying with the baseball metaphor here!) Did you slide into home plate or decide to saunter through the conversation without a spark of enthusiasm and human interest? Video doesn't lie.

Neither do digital files. Today, I recorded a wav file over the telephone for a client who wanted an audio sample to send to potential attendees of a training session. I love technology, and I was excited. Since you can't see the grimace on my face, I'll tell you I'm being sarcastic. I don't love technology, and I was far from excited. I looked more like Pooh's friend Eeyore. Making that phone call felt like going to the vice principals office to get my mandatory summer school schedule.

Guess what? I sucked on my first take. I sounded like a blow up doll on helium. My team listened to it and agreed. Why? I didn't take my own advice. I forgot to do jumping jacks. I sat down while speaking. I didn't have my mouth three inches from the receiver. I practiced in my head. I told myself it wasn't going to go well. And I certainly didn't have any fun. I did all these things even though I know they hinder great media communication.

Fortunately, I had another chance. This time, I followed my own advice. I told myself I would do well and that it was going to be fun. I walked the stairs in the building and practiced what I was going to say out loud. Then I stood up during the recording, and my second attempt at recording the audio sample was much better.

Good thing I had the opportunity to throw away my first take. Most of the time we aren't always so lucky. It is best to prepare and practice before the real interviewer presses record.

Remember, media interviews are a great opportunity to be heard. Be happy about it. Relax and have fun with the interview. Everybody will notice.

Practice with a bright light in your face, a camera (or voice mail recorder) and a tough questioner.

EXERCISE:
TAKE SWINGS IN THE BATTING CAGE

What is the best way to handle difficult questions? Practice. Think of this as Dodge Ball for interviewees.

Sit at your desk. Ask five of your friends to call you one at a time in ten minute intervals. Email them a schedule and a set of questions. Instruct your friends to spice up the questions and make them even harder when they ask them.

Stay in character when you answer the phone; tell yourself these are not your friends, they are anonymous reporters. Take the questions with the voice mail recorder on. As soon as you're finished with each interview, take a few moments and jot down the additional things you wish you had said. Usually the first few minutes after an interview is when your best ideas pop out.

As you listen to your recordings later, ask yourself the following questions:

- **Did you appear defensive?**—Hopefully not. You never want to appear defensive in an interview. It puts the reporters hackles up, thus hindering your rapport with the audience. A trick to manage defensiveness is to picture the reporters challenging words as baseballs being launched toward you. There is no need to catch them, just let them go by and stick to the positive value of your message. This will help you avoid getting emotionally hooked into the reporter's agenda.

- **Did you hit it out of the park?**—Hitting it out of the park means you stayed on message <u>without</u> manipulating the question (and the audience) into sticking to your message. Crafting a response that does not answer a reporter's question is tricky. People do not like tricky. It worked in the 80s; it doesn't work now.

- **Did you say "um" and "ah" a lot?**—If so, don't fret. There are much bigger things to worry about. For now, focus on what is working well.

- **Did you miss important points?**—Listen to the recording a day later. If you had it to do all over again, what would you eliminate? What would you add? Write these additions down. Not verbatim, just the general idea. Come up with pithy statements and retorts.

- **Did you establish some sort of human connection or rapport with the questioner?**—If you didn't, work on doing so. In our current relationship economy audiences demand a transparency to the individual. We want humans not androids.

CHAPTER 154:
BE WARMED-UP AND READY FOR CRISIS

"The ultimate measure of a man is not where he stands in moments of comfort and convenience, but where he stands at times of challenge and controversy."
—Dr. Martin Luther King, Jr.

The good work we do long before the 'crisis conversation' makes all the difference in the world. People are more likely to give us a pass, or at least give us a listen, if we have a history, a relationship or a good reputation with them.

Even with the best of relationships, crisis can occur. In crisis situations, we are forced to communicate on the spot, and often "pre-practice" and "message crafting" are impossible. Sometimes, an issue is so difficult and/or divisive that our message has zero impact.

In times like these, it is best to remember that bad things happen to good people and good organizations. When you take yourself off the hook, you think more clearly and can come up with a clear response to the challenge. In fact, there are a few things you can do to prepare for communicating clearly when your intentions are questioned and your organization is in crisis.

Crisis PR guru Sandra K. Clawson-Freeo defines a crisis situation as:

> *Any situation that threatens the integrity or reputation of your company, usually brought on by adverse or negative media attention. These situations can be any kind of legal dispute, theft, accident, fire, flood or manmade disaster that could be attributed to your company. It can also be a situation where in the eyes of the media or general public your company did not react to one of the above situations in the appropriate manner.*

Do you notice that the crisis can be caused by natural disasters—not just bad management or a faulty product. Think of Hurricane Katrina and all of the media frenzy over the improper handling of the disaster. Certainly the media was well in its rights to criticize the situation; even so, the crisis occurred separate from the media response.

The media does not need to be involved for the situation to be crisis communication; though often, in crisis, they find their way to you. It is up to you to be ready for their tough and probing questions. Relax, and be transparent. Let your emotions show. Talk to reporters candidly.

To avoid making easily avoidable mistakes, take a look at how crisis communication trends changed through the decades. When tempted to revert to an antiquated response, remind yourself that it's the 21st century.

- 50's—Show your audience a polished utopian view that exaggerates or conceals the truth.
- 60's—Make it about 'us and them.'
- 70's—When backed in a corner give them a 'No comment.'
- 80's—Change the subject. Use the media to divert attention away from the issue.

- 90's—Stay "on message."
- 00's—Be transparent. Be the same you that you already are. Emote as you have the emotion.

To prepare:
- Come up with some likely scenarios for crisis.
- Practice how you would respond if a reporter stuck a mic in your face as you fumbled for the keys to your car.
- Work with your team to improve your responses.

A crisis gives you the opportunity to show the audience how great a communicator you really are.

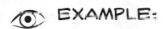 **EXAMPLE:**

CRISIS COMMUNICATION WITHOUT MEDIA

Taylor called Maria and let her know that Sam was going to be fine. While playing with Taylor's son Joey, Sam's finger accidentally got slammed in the door. Taylor told Maria that Sammy's hand was hurt and that an ambulance was taking him to the hospital. Since Maria was out of town on business, she asked Taylor to stay on the phone with her as she drove to meet Sammy at the emergency room.

While on the phone, Taylor let Maria know she shared her concern, and that, as the monitoring adult, she held herself responsible for the accident. She spoke calmly to Maria and kept their interaction going for the entire car ride. Even though Taylor felt awful for what had happened, she did not ask for any support or forgiveness during the car ride, instead she simply focused on Maria's feelings and concerns.

Certainly, Taylor used her CPR training to help keep Maria calm; really, it was the years of friendship and their ongoing relationship that made this critical conversation possible. Maria implicitly trusted Taylor, and, although her maternal instincts made her prone to it, she didn't resort to blaming Taylor for Sammy's injury. In fact, this incident made them even closer, as they realized they could communicate just as beautifully in a crisis.

What did Taylor do?
- She had paved a powerful relationship with Maria before the situation occurred.
- She had, by virtue of their long association, earned Maria's trust.
- She clearly recounted all the facts of the situation with no evasions.
- She showed concern and emotion for Maria's situation.
- She matched or exceeded Maria's concern for the issue.
- She accepted responsibility; she was not defensive nor did she avoid the topic.
- She focused on Maria's needs before addressing any of her own.

Pave relationships with trust and respect, and crisis times are more likely to be met with mutual understanding and a desire to work together toward a solution.

CHAPTER 155:
IT IS BETTER TO KNOW HOW TO USE THE FIRE EXTINGUISHER BEFORE THERE IS A FIRE

It's always a good idea to have stock responses to likely problems.

Any messaging a company does must filter through the value lens of the organization.

All communication must come from the gut of the organization—the brand promise, the core values and the company mission statement. When you respond to a crisis, you want your response to be reflective of these core values. This is work that can be done before the crisis.

All organizations have mission statements. When drafting these statements, many organizations spend days—and sometimes months—debating and deciding upon their core values. All too often this heartfelt and painstakingly crafted philosophy is put into brochures and promptly forgotten.

Dust it off. Look at it. Memorize it. Figure out how to use it in your organizations media statements.

A core value is not a goal nor a PR ruse. Real core values are corporate qualities and ideals—what we are without even thinking about it. Enron is a perfect example of a company that promoted a core value that was really a goal to dupe the unsuspecting public. Enron literature trumpeted "integrity" in their mission statement. Obviously, we California residents learned first hand that integrity wasn't a genuine core value.

To prepare yourself for a crisis, ask yourself and your team the following questions:

- What is the worst thing that can happen?

- How do we feel about this?

- How can we respond?

Decide on your core values and practice communicating them—in good times and bad.

CHAPTER 156:
GET ALL THE FACTS

This seems obvious. And you would be surprised how nutty things can get when a crisis occurs. Remember to breathe. Stay in your body. Make sure you communicate your facts calmly and clearly.

Look back to Chapter 27 (page 76) and re-read the 911-call example. See how easy it is to miscommunicate when excited? Here's another example:

> A team of interior decorators is remodeling the San Francisco office of a high-profile law firm. They won the bid because they agreed to complete the work in a very tight time frame. On the last scheduled day of work in the front waiting area, a stepladder disappeared. This threw everyone into a tizzy, and the receptionist got the brunt of it. She was asked to make an announcement through the company phone intercom system, and without thinking, she said: "Would the person who took the step ladder yesterday please bring it back or further steps will be taken."

This sounds like a silly Internet joke. It is. Though it does illustrate my point. Make sure you get your facts and details straight before answering a question. State your response clearly and coherently. If you don't know something, say you don't know—then find out. Never make stuff up. Somebody will question you and then you are going to have a bigger crisis on your hands.

Always have your facts and thoughts straight when you speak with the media.

CHAPTER 157:
PARKING LOT INTERVIEWS

Often organizations choose a single spokesperson to deal with media situations. While training one person to handle everything media seems like a cost effective approach, it isn't the best idea.

Why? Because everyone on staff needs to have basic media communication skills. The best person to handle internet media may be the web designer. The best person to be the "face" of the company may be the CEO. The best person to deal with print media may be the in house PR person. You get the picture. Media communication is most effective when looked at as a company wide approach.

In any event, the best people to deal with reporters are those who think quickly on their feet, can emote like a human and remain themselves under fire. While such skill and awareness guide the media liaison selection process, training everyone on the team ensures everyone can do their part to make media communications transparent and effective.

Why is this necessary? Well, the parking lot isn't off limits to reporters. By this I mean, reporters often target an employee who is not trained to speak on the subject. Since most reporters know that media liaisons always have a crafty response to the story, they may stake out the company parking lot looking for good copy. All employees need to know how to say "No Comment," without **ever uttering** those words.

For example:
> *A few years ago, the Winston Kidney Transplant Center caused the death of a patient by using a kidney with the wrong blood type. A reporter stopped a nurse walking to her car and asked her what happened. She said, "No comment" and the media played her "no comment" sound byte over and over on the airwaves. Weasel news reported being appalled at how the transplant center could fail to have a comment on such a horrible thing.*

Had the nurse received media training, the incident could have gone like this:
> *A reporter stopped a nurse walking to her car and asked her what happened. The nurse responded, "I am heartbroken by the loss of a patient. And hospital employees are prohibited by federal law from discussing it with you. As a nurse I face life and death every day, and I am personally devastated by every loss— every one. Excuse me."*

Notice how media training taught the nurse to use "and" statements instead of saying "but." This makes it difficult for the reporter to interrupt her in mid-sentence.

Train everyone how to respond to the media.

CHAPTER 158:
ANSWER THE QUESTION
BEFORE IT IS ASKED

In business, being first to market with a product is a major coup. Corporations forget this critical business goal when it comes to media. This is too bad, because breaking a story first, especially a controversial one, takes the wind out of the media's sails.

For example, consider this Barack Obama anecdote:

> A reported asked him about his drug use. Obama had been open about his drug use, so it was already common knowledge. Hoping to fan the flames of the story, the reporter quipped, "Senator Obama, you have admitted to marijuana use. Did you inhale?" To which Obama responded dramatically, "Um...that was the point."

His response made the story go away and resulted in greater voter adhesion due to his honesty. It made him human rather than a villainous drug addict.

The moral of the story? Call a press conference and deal with controversial issues head-on. Face your woes. Break your own story. Scoop the papers. This will give you some control over the way your story is told—at least initially. It also adds to transparency, which makes people want to listen to your version of the story. It might even make the controversy go away sooner.

As you face the media, remember to craft stock answers to questions that will come up— particularly those questions that you do not want to answer.

Be the first to market. Break the story with a press release instead of waiting for Fox to put its own spin on your story.

 EXAMPLE:

SOMETIMES SILENCE
IS RUSTY

Picture this California Assembly race between two opponents: Fiona Ma and Janet Reilly. Both women were progressives with very similar views, and both were adamantly pro-choice.

A story broke. A supposed IRS website hacking revealed that Fiona Ma was listed as the campaign treasurer for a South Dakota governor who is radically anti-choice. Most likely, someone on the Janet Reilly campaign leaked the website to the press and hinted to reporters that Fiona's pro-choice stance was in question.

For anyone desiring to investigate further, it became clear that the story was a hoax. Fiona Ma was listed on the actual website page—though when you clicked to open the PDF of officers, someone else was the treasurer. A thorough reporter figured this out before breaking the story.

As the hoax hit the media, the Reilly campaign had an opportunity to call a press conference and chastise the hoax. Reilly could have said something like, "My opponent is clearly pro-choice, and the IRS website has been hacked. There must be an immediate investigation to determine how the IRS website was tampered with in such an alarming way. If hackers can do something like this, imagine what can they do with our personal financial information? When I become a member of the Assembly, I will focus on protecting your privacy."

Instead, Reilly merely said "We don't know if the document is accurate or not, but we look forward to hearing an explanation from the IRS about why it was posted online in 2002."

Think through responses. Taking the high ground will endear you to the media and the audience in the relationship economy.

Always take the high ground in media.

 **EXAMPLE:**

THE HIGH GROUND HAS GREENER GRASS

Most Americans are sick of politics. Polarization, big money interests and party politics are killing public interest, and as a result, our electoral process is suffering. People are yawning.

For example, as the 2008 presidential campaign ramped into full swing, two of the top ranking Democratic contenders released their fundraising numbers. Hillary Clinton raised $26 million; Barack Obama raised $25 million. Their figures set a new high for presidential fundraising within the same Democratic Party.

When asked, both campaigns offered a typical blah blah in response to the other candidate's figures. Obama's campaign stated that his funds came from twice as many people and thus meant more voters. Hillary's people said she had raised more money than any candidate running for president ever had in the first quarter, and that "she won the first primary—the money primary." Not even mildly interesting.

Keep in mind, these two folks were running against each other to be the nominee in the primary—their overall objective was to get a Democrat into office, or at least we would hope! Primary candidates must compete in a way that ensures a Democrat ends up in the Whitehouse, regardless of which one of them gets put on the presidential ballot. With this in mind, these two could've cooperated and won the hearts of undecided voters.

Imagine they called a press conference together. The purpose: To celebrate the clear indication that the American people want change.

> *Today is a celebration of what is right in our country—that a black man and a woman can be the top fundraisers in America. These numbers prove we are breaking the barriers of gender and race. We celebrate together today and look forward to the best person for the job becoming the President of the United States of America.*

Think about it for a second. This is higher ground. It paves the way for more votes for the democratic candidate and far outrivals the stiff, campaign-speak media responses they gave.

Think about their missed opportunity again. America has never had a black man or a woman as president. No matter what party you are for, what candidate you are for, it is historically and socially relevant that the top fundraisers in the 2008 American Presidential election were a black man and a woman.*

Being noble and inspiring trumps careful and crafted.

*(As a side note, I did offer this as a suggestion to the candidates; they chose to take the professionalism route. Though at a later debate, with just the two of them, they finally got this right.)

CHAPTER 159:
THEY DO SEE YOU BEHIND THE CURTAIN, AND YOUR BUTT LOOKS BIG IN THOSE PANTS

I do not know any human on the planet who likes a phony. Though when I first became a public speaker, I was taught to be phony. I learned (and learned quite well, I must add) to act bigger than life, more excited than I was, more knowledgeable than I was, older than I was, and so on. Subliminally I was told that who I was—the actual person inside—was not enough and was not to be trusted.

It worked. I became a great public speaker, and I also became a pretender. I hid the parts of my life that the audience wouldn't like. I adopted a rah rah, flashy Vegas style of presenting myself. I wore clothes that were too professional, used a semi-permanent haircolor spray to make my orange-dyed hair a nice mousy brown, and rarely told anyone what I really thought. People seemed to love me.

I didn't become a true leader and public speaker until I learned to stop acting. I will never forget the fated "training" session with a group of speakers who awakened my perspective. It was there that I discovered no one likes a phony once they figure out they are dealing with one. Mind you, this was subtle. I started noticing how people were watching more intently when the person wasn't presenting thus reducing listening if the presenter is fake.

My ability to stir an audience took off when I realized I had to reach back into my life and share my true self with others.

For example, what if you are angry, and instead of saying so you put on a fake smile and stiffen up. This is a neon sign. Why not simply say you are pissed (or angry or frustrated or annoyed) and work through the problem? Directly dealing with anger or frustration works much better than processing it in your own head outside the conversation.

The same is true when someone is droning on and on about something that bothers them. Rather than saying "I hear you" just to get the other person to stop complaining, how about saying, "you've been talking about this for a while, and I'm wondering if we can move on to a solution?" or "Hey, you are kind of raining all over my floor here, let's talk about something else."

Such honesty strengthens relationships and makes your words trustworthy. Now, I run like hell from anything phony. It is not okay to teach a public speaker to be fake. Who and how you are makes you interesting.

"The Human Relationship is the True Currency" is a quote I hear others use all over the country. I am proud that I birthed this thought and that it works for personal, business, and non-profit relationships. How did I come up with this saying? It came from my unique life. I am the offspring of master infiltrators. I worked in the collection industry. And I've managed to live through all the death and sadness in my family.

Or was it just luck? Either way, it came from my true experience not the stuff I was pretending to be in order to teach a class.

Quote yourself. The words of others pale in comparison to those swirling around in your mind and body.

CHAPTER 160:
CORPORATE EMOTIONAL TRANSPARENCY

Let's look at crisis communication from a corporate perspective. When an error occurs, the legal team usually rushes in and persuades the company to withhold information or to completely avoid addressing the situation publicly. If cornered, they are counseled to say as little as humanly possible—which is basically defend the company's position and deliver a carefully crafted message that cannot be used against them in a lawsuit.

These excessively protective measures weaken the trust of the community, especially since everybody knows the company is eventually going to have to write a check. Corporations need to focus on their true core values and communicate them to the community. They need to ask themselves "what part of the mistake occurred as a result of our error" and "how can we help those who've been wronged."

Without question, good legal advice is necessary; though upcoming litigation should not be allowed to drive the dialogue. When simple human decency and common sense are disregarded out of fear of reprisal, it generally costs the company more in the long run.

When one bottle of Tylenol was tampered with, the drug company pulled their entire product lines from retail shelves. When they reintroduced the product lines a few weeks later, all had tamper resistant packaging. Enormously expensive to the company, Tylenol took a huge risk in such a competitive business. Their corporate strategy—honesty—paid off brilliantly. Tylenol became one of the top brands, and all drug manufacturers eventually copied Tylenol's tamper-proof packaging to assure no such incident could ever be replicated.

The opposite response occurred when diners got food poisoning from a chicken chain restaurant in California. A few people died, and my dear high school friend and her entire family nearly died. It was devastating. When the organizational spokesperson spoke to the media, he was emotionally flat and unconcerned. All he said was, "we are investigating the situation."

I like to replay the situation like this:

> Company Spokesperson: *I just came from AMD Medical Center where I met with the families of the patients. We are very distressed by the pain and suffering these families are enduring. We will stand at their side and offer whatever help we can in this time of crisis. We have set up a fund for the families at Westfield Bank if any listeners want to help as well.*
>
> Reporter: *How did this happen?*
>
> Company Spokesperson: *We are determining that right now. We have given authorities complete access to our processing facility and restaurants so that a*

thorough investigation can be done. Food safety is the most important goal of any food organization. Once we know what happened, you will know too. In the meantime, we are rallying as a company and a community to support the families.

Could these words be used to hurt them? Sure they could. Had they handled the situation differently, maybe the offending restaurant could have stayed in business after the situation.

Be willing to risk financial loss and be truly sorry for any error or pain caused by the company.

CHAPTER 161:
TALK ABOUT WHAT
IS WRONG

Being under the media microscope gives firms the opportunity to engage and road test their core values. Since I am living a passion rather than "building a business," I have learned to navigate the bumps in the road and keep moving forward. Problems give me the opportunity to re-evaluate my mission and see if my practices are in alignment with my promises.

If you discover your organization isn't fulfilling its stated policies, say so and make a commitment to align. If you are being congruent and are simply getting slammed by fate, note it and move on. Whichever the case, don't get overly caught up in word-smithing and polishing up a pretty apple to present to the community; instead allow the challenge to shed light on your policies and practices and let it guide you back to your original principles.

An honest attempt to rectify a problem—as well as a promise to do better next time—can go a long way toward mending relations with the public. When a negative report came out about a dialysis center the center temporarily shut its doors. The CEO held a press conference and told reporters:

> *This report claims the Nopad Dialysis Center is harming patients. If true, this is not okay. We have closed the center so we may immediately investigate and align this center with Nopad's values of safety and excellent healthcare. Nopad cares about our patients. Patient care is our number one priority and clearly we need to make sure quality care is really happening.*

Do not be defensive. Be open, transparent, community-minded.

CHAPTER 162:
NEVER PICK YOUR NOSE ON CAMERA

Seems simple doesn't it? We all have bad habits. Nose picking, fingernail biting, foot tapping. None of them look good on camera. The only way to avoid doing these things in front of the camera is to stop doing them in our daily lives.

I have a habit of messing with my left ear. I have done it since I was a kid, and people often comment on it. I do not know why I do it. I didn't think much about it until I watched a video of myself at a business meeting. My ear fidgeting was incredibly distracting and made me look like I had hives. It was horrifying.

I vowed to stop this habit. I asked those closest to me to slap my hand when they saw me doing it. I also went to a hypnotist. I no longer tug on my ear. Now I rub the cuticles on my left thumb with my left forefinger. I have seen this on film, and it's not that noticeable so I have decided to let myself continue this one. It is a gift to my inner neurotic.

Everyone has habits, and some of them aren't so visually appealing. If you have one of the latter, it's best to rid yourself of it (or them) before the camera is recording your every move. Otherwise, you must be hyper-vigilant and avoid doing it in front of the camera, or this will distract you from communicating the important things.

Remember, great communication is a mathematical model that includes confidence. Anything you can do to build confidence will increase your ability to communicate. Cuticle chewing does not build confidence.

Trade your bad habits in for camera friendly ones.

CHAPTER 163:
MEDIA RECIPE
(FOR THOSE WHO NEED IT)

- Come up with as many potentially difficult crisis scenarios that you can think of, then prepare appropriate responses. Practice directly addressing the issue as well as crafting a public relations response. It is better to be proactive and to be prepared for any potentially damaging event that might occur. Your organization wants to be talking about the issues and offering potential solutions before the evening news teams—or the internet bloggers!—pick it up.

- Pave a powerful relationship with audiences and the media long before any crisis occurs.

- Practice your presentation out loud before talking with reporters or any other audience.

- Give only relevant facts.

- Show genuine concern or emotion. If your company spokesperson is not empathetic by nature, hire someone who is.

- Match or exceed the concern the public and the media hold for the issue.

- Accept responsibility for you or your company's part in the crisis situation; never be defensive nor duck from direct questions.

- In your initial response, be focused on the needs of any injured parties and the community first. After these issues are addressed, you may discuss corporate concerns, providing they relate to the issues. I advise you to do so only in response to direct questions.

Be vocal about your future plans, and share how you are incorporating the lessons learned by the crisis that just occurred.

PART VI

CLOSING

CHAPTER 164:
YOU ARE THE ONE

"Between stimulus and response is a space. In that space is where we choose our response. It is in those choices we find our happiness."
~Author unknown

Perhaps you are like me. A person who sits through the whole movie credits—waiting to see if a special treat awaits. Remember *Antz*? Everybody cleared the theater, and you got to sit and laugh at all the funny outtakes at the end of the credits. Now you titter quietly to yourself, realizing that no one knows what you're talking about when you mention the little fish from *Nemo* swallowing the big fish with the light bulb on its head.

This paragraph is for you. I like you. Call me.

I am sweating a bit. I'm feeling a little dewy. What can I say here to sum it all up? My ending line. Gulp.

You. All of you. The perfections and imperfections. The parts you share and the parts you hide from the world. The happy memories, the painful ones. The moments when you kicked ass. The moments you fell on your ass. The times when the ribbon tore across your chest. The times when your shirt button burst open. You are the sum total of all these parts. You are these experiences, thoughts and feelings.

All of this makes you the only person who can give your much-needed perspective to the world. You can save us. It is you.

We are counting on you.

PART VII

APPENDIX

APPENDIX I:

TEN RANDOM
STORY TOPICS

1) Global Warming

2) Quality Matters

3) Leadership

4) The Presidential Elections

5) The Civil Rights Movement

6) Soda Vending Machines In Public Schools

7) Human Rights

8) Helmet Laws

9) The Iraq War

10) Our Public School System

Bonus Topic:

11) How To Succeed In Business

APPENDIX II:
NOTES & BIBLIOGRAPHY

1) pg 19: http://findarticles.com/p/articles/mi_m4021/is_2001_Sept_1/ai_78426786

2) pg 27: http://www.gallawa.com/microtech/history.html

3) pg 30: http://en.wikipedia.org/wiki/Enron

4) pg 49: http://www.bizsum.com/articles/art_how-to-win-friends-and-influence-people.php

5) pg 106: http://en.wikipedia.org/wiki/Aikido

6) pg 184: *To Catch a Wolf: How to Stop Conservative Frames in Their Tracks*, by Christina Smith, Rockridge Institute, June 12, 2007.